Six Byzantine
Portraits

Six Byzantine Portraits

BY

DIMITRI OBOLENSKY

CLARENDON PRESS · OXFORD

1988

Oxford University Press, Walton Street, Oxford OX2 6DP
Oxford New York Toronto
Delhi Bombay Calcutta Madras Karachi
Petaling Jaya Singapore Hong Kong Tokyo
Nairobi Dar es Salaam Cape Town
Melbourne Auckland
and associated companies in
Beirut Berlin Ibadan Nicosia

Oxford is a trade mark of Oxford University Press

Published in the United States
by Oxford University Press, New York

© Sir Dimitri Obolensky, 1988

British Library Cataloguing in Publication Data
Obolensky, Dimitri
Six Byzantine portraits.
1. Byzantine Empire—Biography
I. Title
949.5′0092′2   DF506
ISBN 0-19-821951-2

Library of Congress Cataloging in Publication Data
Obolensky, Dimitri, 1918–
Six Byzantine portraits.
Bibliography: p.
Includes index.
Contents: Clement of Ohrid—Theophylact of Ohrid—Vladimir Monomakh—[etc.]
1. Christian saints—Europe, Eastern—Biography. 2. Orthodox Eastern Church—
Biography. 3. Civilization, Slavic—Byzantine influences. 4. Byzantine Empire—
Church history. 6. Slavic countries—Church history. I. Title.
BX393.026 1988 947.0009′92 [B] 87-20255
ISBN 0-19-821951-2

Printed in Great Britain by
the Alden Press, Oxford

TO CHLOE

Acknowledgements

I AM indebted to a number of friends and colleagues for help at various stages during the preparation of this book. Some generously agreed to read and comment on separate chapters in typescript. I am thus beholden to Anne Kindersley, Hugh Lloyd-Jones, Mary MacRobert, Margaret Mullett, Sir Steven Runciman, Ihor Ševčenko, and Jonathan Shepard. Others, notably Glen Bowersock, Slobodan Ćurčić, Philip Sherrard, Anthony Tachiaos, and Nigel Wilson, gave me valuable advice on particular points. John Karayannopulos kindly lent me the proofs of Paul Gautier's edition of the letters of Theophylact of Ohrid. I owe a special debt of gratitude to Patrick Leigh Fermor, who read two of the chapters and suggested many stylistic improvements. I am also much indebted to the vigilance and learning of my copy-editor, Dr Leofranc Holford-Strevens. None of these scholars is, of course, responsible for whatever errors of fact or interpretation may be found in this book.

The Institute for Advanced Study at Princeton, by electing me Andrew W. Mellon Visiting Professor for the academic year 1985/6, enabled me to complete the early drafts of two chapters. I am grateful to its School of Historical Studies for providing me with ideal working conditions and the opportunities to make new friends.

The last two chapters, both originally given as lectures, have appeared before: Ch. 5, in a slightly shorter form, in *Dumbarton Oaks Papers*, xxxii (1978); Ch. 6, as the Raleigh Lecture on History, in the *Proceedings of the British Academy*, lxvii (1981). I am grateful to the editors of these publications for permission to reproduce them here. The first four chapters were written specially for this book.

For permission to reproduce photographs, or for making them available to me, I am grateful to K. Balabanov, Skopje; S. Ćurčić, Princeton; V. J. Djurić, Belgrade; B. Drnkov, Skopje; S. Gabelić, Belgrade; the Institute for Art History, Belgrade; the Institute for the Protection of Monuments, Belgrade; R. K. Kindersley, Oxford; the late V. N. Lazarev, Moscow; S. Petković, Belgrade; the Library of the

Academy of Sciences of the USSR, Leningrad; V. M. and N. V. Teteryatnikov, Washington; and the Yugoslav National Tourist Office, London.

Finally, I should like to say how much I owe to two masters, Father Francis Dvornik and Roman Jakobson, who many years ago introduced me to the absorbing world of Byzantinoslavica.

D.O.

Oxford, December 1986

Note on Proper Names

THE ritual, semi-apologetic, note about the transcription of proper names—Greek and Slavonic—can hardly be avoided here. There is no way known to me of achieving consistency in this thankless task without breaking the rules of common sense or falling into pedantry. I have therefore applied several rather arbitrary rules of thumb. Greek first names, when well known, are given their English form: thus Constantine, John, Michael, Theodore. Latin forms are used when these seem more familiar: e.g. Alexius, Athanasius, Nicephorus, Photius. Less well-known first names, e.g. Maximos, Philotheos, are left in their Greek form. The same guidelines have been applied to less familiar family names, such as Angelos, Bryennios, Chomatianos, Psellos, while better-known ones appear in Latin dress: Comnenus, Cerularius. Slavonic names have been treated similarly, with one important exception: Serbian names are mostly transcribed according to standard Yugoslav practice.

Contents

List of Plates

List of Maps

Abbreviations

Alexiad	Anna Comnena, *Alexiade*, ed. B. Leib, 3 vols. (Paris, 1937–45)
APC	*Acta Patriarchatus Constantinopolitani*, ed. F. Miklosich and I. Müller, 2 vols. (Vienna, 1860–2)
Cherepnin, *Obrazovanie*	L. V. Cherepnin, *Obrazovanie russkogo tsentralizovannogo gosudarstva v XIV–XV vekakh* (Moscow, 1960)
Dmitriev, 'Rol' i znachenie'	L. A. Dmitriev, 'Rol' i znachenie mitropolita Kipriana v istorii drevnerusskoy literatury', *TODRL* xix (1963), 215–54
Dölger, *Regesten*	F. Dölger, *Regesten der Kaiserurkunden des oströmischen Reiches*, v (Munich–Berlin, 1965) .
Domentijan	Domentijan, *Život svetoga Simeuna i svetoga Save*, ed. Dj. Daničić (Belgrade, 1865)
Dvornik, *Byzantine Missions*	F. Dvornik, *Byzantine Missions among the Slavs: SS. Constantine-Cyril and Methodius* (New Brunswick, NJ, 1970)
ET	English translation
G	*Théophylacte d'Achrida: Lettres*, introduction, texte, traduction et notes par Paul Gautier (Thessalonica, 1986)
Grivec–Tomšič	F. Grivec and F. Tomšič, *Constantinus et Methodius Thessalonicenses: Fontes* (Zagreb, 1960)
Historia Martyrii	Theophylact of Ohrid, *Historia Martyrii XV Martyrum*, PG cxxvi, cols. 152–221
Hussey, *Church and Learning*	J. M. Hussey, *Church and Learning in the Byzantine Empire* (London, 1937)
ISN	S. Ćirković (ed.), *Istorija Srpskog Naroda*, i (Belgrade, 1981)
Janin, *Les Églises et les monastères*	R. Janin, *Les Églises et les monastères des grands centres byzantins* (Paris, 1975)
Lemerle, *Cinq Études*	P. Lemerle, *Cinq Études sur le XIᵉ siècle byzantin* (Paris, 1977)
Meyendorff	J. Meyendorff, *Byzantium and the Rise of Russia* (Cambridge, 1981)
MGH	Monumenta Germaniae historica
Milev	A. Milev, *Grŭtskite zhitiya na Kliment Okhridski* (Sofia, 1966)
Ostrogorsky, *History*	G. Ostrogorsky, *History of the Byzantine State* (Oxford, 1968)

P   *Povest' vremennykh let*, ed. D. S. Likhachev and V. P.
                               Adrianova-Peretts, i (Moscow–Leningrad, 1950)
Pauly–Wissowa   A. Pauly, rev. G. Wissowa, *Real-Encyclopädie der classischer
                               Altertumswissenschaft* (Stuttgart, 1894–1980)
PG   *Patrologiae cursus completus*, series Graeco-Latina, ed. J.-P.
                               Migne (Paris, 1857–66)
PSRL   *Polnoe sobranie russkikh letopisey* (St Petersburg–Moscow,
                               1848–   )
Reader   *A Historical Russian Reader*, ed. J. Fennell and D. Obolensky
                               (Oxford, 1969)
Shabatin, *Vestnik*   I. N. Shabatin, 'Iz istorii Russkoy Tserkvi', *Vestnik Russ-
                               kogo Zapadno-evropeyskogo patriarshego Ekzarkhata*, xiii/
                               49–52 (Paris, 1965)
SNSS   *Sava Nemanjić—Sveti Sava: Istorija i predanje (Sava Nema-
                               njić—Saint Sava: Histoire et tradition)*, ed. V. Djurić (Bel-
                               grade, 1979)
SSS   *Spisi sv. Save*, ed. V. Ćorović (Belgrade–Sremski Karlovci,
                               1928)
Stephen Nemanjić   Stevan Prvovenčani, 'Žitije Simeona Nemanje', *SZ* ii. 1–76
Sveti Sava (1977)   *Sveti Sava: Spomenica povodom osamstogodišnjice rodjenja
                               1175–1975* (Izdanje Svetog Arhijerejskog Sinoda Srpske
                               Pravoslavne Crkve, Belgrade, 1977)
Symeon, *Pismata*   Metropolitan Symeon, *Pismata na Teofilakta Okhridski*
                               (Sofia, 1931)
SZ   *Svetosavski zbornik*, 2 vols. (Belgrade, 1936–9)
Tachiaos, Ἐπιδράσεις   A.-E. Tachiaos, Ἐπιδράσεις τοῦ ἡσυχασμοῦ εἰς τὴν ἐκκλη-
                               σιαστικὴν πολιτικὴν ἐν Ῥωσίᾳ (Thessalonica, 1962)
Teodosije   Teodosije Hilandarac, *Život svetoga Save*, ed. Dj. Daničić
                               (Belgrade, 1860; repr. Dj. Trifunović, Belgrade, 1973)
Théophylacte d'Achrida   *Théophylacte d'Achrida: Discours, traités, poésies*, introduc-
                               tion, texte, traduction et notes par Paul Gautier (Thessalo-
                               nica, 1980)
TM   Centre de recherche d'histoire et civilisation byzantines,
                               Travaux et mémoires (Paris, 1965–   )
TODRL   *Trudy Otdela Drevnerusskoy Literatury* (Leningrad,
                               1934–   )
Tunitsky   N. L. Tunickij (Tunitsky) (ed.), *Monumenta ad SS Cyrilli et
                               Methodii successorum vitas resque gestas pertinentia* (Lon-
                               don, 1972)
Turdeanu, *La Littérature   E. Turdeanu, *La Littérature bulgare et sa diffusion dans les
bulgare*   pays roumains* (Paris, 1947)
VC   *Vita Constantini*, in Grivec–Tomšič, 95–143
VM   *Vita Methodii*, in Grivec–Tomšič, 147–67

Introduction

SOME years ago, in a book entitled *The Byzantine Commonwealth*, I ventured the opinion that in the Middle Ages, despite notable differences in social and political life, those East European countries which owed their religion and much of their culture to Byzantium formed a single international community; its nature, I argued, is revealed in a common cultural tradition shared and contributed to by their ruling and educated classes. They were bound by the same profession of Eastern Christianity; they acknowledged the primacy of the Constantinopolitan Church; they recognized that the Byzantine emperor was endowed with a measure of authority over the whole of Orthodox Christendom; they accepted the principles of Romano-Byzantine law; and they held that the literary standards and artistic techniques of the Empire's schools, monasteries, and scriptoria were universally valid models. This international community I rather intrepidly called the Byzantine Commonwealth.

The existence of this community was questioned at the time by one or two critics, but the majority of my colleagues responded favourably, judging the concept a helpful look-out point for viewing international relations in Eastern Europe during the Middle Ages. The present collection of essays is a biographical sequel to the earlier book; its aim is to assess the contribution of six men to the history of this Byzantine commonwealth between the ninth and the sixteenth centuries. They lived very different kinds of lives, in widely separated regions of Eastern Europe. One thing, however, they did have in common: through their birth, their professions, or their personal circumstances, they all belonged simultaneously to the different worlds of the Greeks and the Slavs, and acted as bridges between the two. With one exception they were men of standing and authority in their societies, and this made their contribution to Europe's cultural history all the more significant.

The encounter between Byzantium and the Slavs which these six mediators exemplified or promoted is part of the wider phenomenon which social anthropologists and some historians call acculturation; it occurs when societies with different cultures come into direct and prolonged contact. The process is complex and seldom easy to grasp completely, and both its motives and its results are often ambiguous. Byzantine expansion in the Balkans and on the northern shores of the Black Sea, and in Russia, for example, was prompted in part by the missionary energies of the Church of Constantinople, but it owed at least as much to the Empire's need for military security: the 'barbarians' thrusting south towards the Aegean and Adriatic Seas, and threatening to invade and settle on imperial territory, had to be brought under the civilizing control of Byzantium. To the Empire's statesmen the taming of monsters seemed the first stage in this process. A similar ambiguity can be seen in the impulses which brought the Slavs into the orbit of Byzantium. To their land-hungry communities invading the Balkans in the sixth and seventh centuries the Empire appeared as an object of plunder; later, when they began to be absorbed, they came to regard it as the way to a career; and, as they acquired a more distinct consciousness of themselves as a group, their leaders reached out for the material and spiritual fruits of Byzantine civilization.

The ambivalence in the early contact between Byzantium and the Slavs affected the image they formed of each other. The Byzantines, true to the Hellenic heritage of which—at least in the literary field—they regarded themselves as the trustees, never freed themselves completely from the conviction that the Slavs, even when they had accepted Greek Christianity, were still tainted by their 'barbarian' origins. This opinion was in obvious conflict with the belief, which many Byzantines probably sincerely held, that Christianity had abolished all essential distinction between Greek and barbarian; in particular, all languages were equally acceptable to the Lord. Yet this ambiguity remained to the end, reflecting a tension between the Greek classical tradition and the Christian teaching which was never wholly resolved in Byzantine society.[1]

The same ambiguity appears in the image of the Byzantines which

---

[1] See the arresting contrast drawn by M. Mollat du Jourdin between the egocentric projection on to the Other of a counter-image of Self, and the readiness to accept the Other on his own terms: 'L'image de l'Autre dans la mentalité occidentale à la fin du Moyen Âge', in *Rapports du XVIe Congrès international des sciences historiques,* i (Stuttgart, 1985), 105.

the Slavs created for themselves. Individually, the Byzantines were seldom popular among their East European neighbours: faced with the superior skill and the dubious methods of the Empire's diplomacy, the Slavs came to believe that its agents in the field were untrustworthy intriguers. The saying 'Greeks have remained deceivers to the present day', uttered about 1100 by a Russian chronicler, was no doubt current in medieval Eastern Europe. Yet this feeling, rooted in distrust and wounded pride, paled before the vision of what Byzantium stood for in the world of the mind and spirit. The extent of the debt which the Orthodox Slavs owed to its civilization was apparent wherever they might look: religion and law, literature and art, all bore witness to the fact that their educated classes were the pupils of Byzantium. Nor was the attitude of simpler folk any less respectful: it found striking expression in their reverence for the city of Constantinople, which the Slavs called Tsarigrad or Tsar´grad, the Imperial City. For the whole of Eastern Christendom, Constantinople was a holy city, and not only because it was the seat of the *basileus* and his spiritual partner, the oecumenical patriarch. Its chief claim to holiness lay in the supernatural forces believed to be present within its walls: the memorials of Christ's passion and the innumerable relics of saints; the churches and monasteries, renowned shrines of Christendom; above all, the patronage of its heavenly protectors: Divine Wisdom, whose temple was St Sophia, and the Mother of God, whose robe, preserved in the church of Blachernae, was venerated as the city's palladium. In the aura of sanctity which surrounded it, Constantinople was often thought of as the New Jerusalem, its only rival.

Some of these conflicts affected the lives of the six figures who sit for the following portraits. Two—Theophylact and Maximos—were Greeks by birth. Three others—Clement, Sava, and Cyprian—were Slavs closely identified with Byzantium. The odd man out, at first sight, is Vladimir Monomakh, whom the written records portray as belonging wholly to Russian history. Yet this Russian prince had several significant points of contact with the Byzantine world: through the inheritance of his mother, a princess of imperial descent; through his vivid autobiography, and its debt to Greek models; and through works of art he commissioned, which were fully intelligible only within the context of the Byzantine tradition.

To be really fruitful, the Byzantine–Slav encounter required more than imperial diplomacy and missionary zeal, or merely an East

European quest for culture. It had to take place within an ambience somehow common to both worlds and capable of acting as an intermediary and a catalyst. This ambience needed a creative energy strong enough to leave its mark on religious beliefs, literature, and social and political ideas. It also needed a cosmopolitan character, capable of crossing state boundaries and linguistic frontiers and of being seen as a common East European tradition; and it would have to attract and command the loyalties of men of different nations, and link them to each other by common discipleship and the ties of friendship.

In the period covered by this book, two such ambiences fostered the encounter between Byzantium and the Slavs: the Cyrillo-Methodian tradition, and the religious and cultural movement which originated in the monasteries of Mount Athos.

The Cyrillo-Methodian tradition played a leading role in the lives of several of the men in this book. It was born in the second half of the ninth century out of the Byzantine need to evangelize the Slavs beyond the frontier in their native language, and in 862 the need became urgent and specific. Envoys from the ruler of Moravia, a Slav principality in central Europe, arrived in Constantinople asking for a Slav-speaking Christian missionary. Moravia had already been partly converted by German priests under Frankish sway; but its ruler, fearful for his country's independence, wished to counter their influence by that of a Slav-speaking clergy owing allegiance to Byzantium.

The emperor's choice fell on two brothers from Thessalonica, Constantine (later known as Cyril) and Methodius. Distinguished public servants and experienced diplomatists, they had the added advantage of knowing the Slavonic language, which, alongside Greek, was widely spoken in their native city. Before leaving Constantinople, Constantine invented an alphabet for the use of the Moravian Slavs, which he adapted to a dialect of southern Macedonia, in the Thessalonica neighbourhood. This alphabet is known today as Glagolitic. With its help he translated a selection of lessons from the Gospels into Slavonic and later, with the assistance of Methodius after their arrival in Moravia in 863, the Byzantine liturgical offices.

Thus a new literary language was brought into being, modelled on Greek in its syntax and abstract vocabulary, and—because the different Slavonic tongues were still very close to each other—

intelligible to all the Slavs. It is known today as Old Church Slavonic.[2] Its range was gradually broadened and its vocabulary enriched by further translations of Christian scripture, theological writings, and Byzantine legal texts, and also by the composition of original works. In this way Old Church Slavonic became, after Greek and Latin, the third international language of Europe and the common literary idiom of the Bulgarians, the Serbs, the Russians, and the Rumanians, who through their conversion to Christianity gained entry into the Byzantine cultural commonwealth. In opening up the religious and cultural world of Byzantium to the peoples of Eastern Europe, Old Church Slavonic simultaneously enabled them to make their own distinctive contribution to that world.

Some of the episodes in the history of this Byzantine mission to the Slavs will be discussed later.[3] But the term 'Cyrillo-Methodian tradition', which will often be encountered on the following pages, calls for a brief definition here. It will be used in two distinct but related senses: firstly, to designate the translated and original body of writings produced in Old Church Slavonic in the early Middle Ages; and secondly to describe a specific outlook, partly religious and partly political, which served to determine the place now allotted to the Slavs within the Christian community. This outlook rested on the belief that a language which serves as a medium for the Christian liturgy becomes a sacred one, and that the nation speaking it is raised to the status of a people consecrated to the service of God. Hence every nation with a native liturgical language and literature has its own particular mission and its own legitimate place within the Christian *oikoumene*. A joyful optimism seems to bring to many of the early writings of the Cyrillo-Methodian tradition the breath of a cultural springtime; it comes from the Slavs' awareness that they have acquired a distinct historical identity by receiving the Christian 'letters' in their own language.[4] The nature of the Cyrillo-Methodian tradition—Slavonic in form and at first largely Greek in content— thus made it an admirable channel for the diffusion of Byzantine culture in Eastern Europe.

Two of our characters were associated with this tradition, one of

[2] By the year 1100, in the different areas where it was used, Old Church Slavonic had developed local features. This led to the rise of different 'recensions' (e.g. Bohemian, Bulgarian, Russian) of 'Church Slavonic'.

[3] See Ch. 1.

[4] See R. Jakobson, 'The Beginning of National Self-determination in Europe', in *Selected Writings*, vi (Berlin–New York–Amsterdam, 1985), 115–28.

them intimately, the other by adoption. In the late ninth century Clement of Ohrid, a disciple of Methodius, transplanted it from central Europe to the Balkans, where it put out new shoots and flowered in the soil of Macedonia. In the late eleventh and early twelfth century Archbishop Theophylact, a Greek scholar from Byzantium, toiled at the administration of a large tract of the Balkans which the Empire had recently conquered from Bulgaria. I believe that the Cyrillo-Methodian tradition helped him to face up to the problems of his quasi-colonialist situation, and gave him a key to the complex bilingual society with its two cultures, over whose Church he was called to preside.

Mount Athos was another of the sinews of the Byzantine cultural commonwealth. The first of the monasteries on this mountainous peninsula in northern Greece was founded in 963, and in the Middle Ages they belonged to several nations. The most numerous were the Greeks; but by the year 1200 Georgians, Italians, Bulgarians, Russians, and Serbs had acquired their own establishments on the 'Holy Mountain', sharing a common experience of the spiritual and ascetic life. Some of these monasteries, often in co-operation between Greeks and Slavs, became major literary centres where Byzantine religious writings were translated into Slavonic, and then carried to the sister and daughter foundations in Eastern Europe. In the late Middle Ages the international role of Mount Athos became more important still: it was from there that the movement known today— not altogether appropriately—as hesychasm,[5] of which the revival of contemplative monasticism in the fourteenth century was the original and most characteristic feature, spread to the Balkans, Rumania, and Russia. Led by a series of outstanding patriarchs of Constantinople, fostered locally by a confraternity of devoted Slav and Rumanian monks, and overflowing into literature and art, this movement linked together, more closely perhaps than ever before, the different parts of the Byzantine cultural commonwealth. Its interme-diary role between the Greek and the Slav worlds proved no less important than that played by the Cyrillo-Methodian tradition three or four centuries earlier.

Three characters of this book were intimately associated with Mount Athos. In the closing years of the twelfth century Sava Nemanjić founded there, together with his father, the former ruler of

---

[5] See J. Meyendorff, *Byzantine Hesychasm* (London, Variorum Reprints, 1974); id., 'Is "Hesychasm" the Right Word?', *Harvard Ukrainian Studies*, vii (1983), 447–57.

Serbia, the monastery of Hilandar, which became for many centuries the fountain-head from which the Serbs drank at the source of Byzantine spirituality and culture. In the second half of the fourteenth century a Bulgarian monk called Cyprian, trained on Athos and then primate of the Russian Church, succeeded thanks to his 'hesychast' connections in rekindling among the Slav Orthodox peoples a common loyalty to their mother-Church of Constantinople. Finally, for much of his life, Mount Athos was the spiritual home of Maximos Trivolis, a Greek expatriate who spent his early years absorbing Platonic philosophy in the schools of Renaissance Italy and the latter part of his life—from 1518 to 1556—as a monk in Russia. The fate of this versatile and tragic figure, whose cultural roots lay in post-Byzantine Greece and who came to grief in the Muscovy he went to serve, illustrates Russia's turning away, in the century that followed the fall of Constantinople, from her ancient Byzantine heritage.

These portraits of six men whose lives surely deserve to be more widely known to students of medieval history are offered in the hope that, through the study of their achievements and failures, the reader will gain insight into the cosmopolitan world of Eastern Europe in which they lived, and into the role which these outstanding Greek and Slav personalities—four of them acknowledged saints—played in the history of the Byzantine cultural commonwealth.

I

Clement of Ohrid

ON a winter's day, late in 867 or early in 868, a group of Roman citizens, carrying lighted candles, went out to meet a company of foreigners on the last stage of their journey to Rome. At the head of the reception-party was the pope. The strangers had travelled, via Venice, from Moravia, a Slav principality which lay on both banks of the middle Danube, in the heart of central Europe. They were of mixed nationality: some were Greeks, others Slavs. Their leaders were two brothers, both distinguished citizens of the Byzantine Empire, Constantine (later known as Cyril), and Methodius.

Their names, and reputation, were well known in Rome. For the past four years, as envoys of the Byzantine emperor to Moravia, Constantine and Methodius had been translating the Byzantine liturgy and Christian scriptures from Greek into Slavonic, and training a native clergy capable of building a Slav-speaking Church in central Europe. Moravia, the centre of their activity from 863 to 867, belonged to western Christendom and came under papal jurisdiction. The Moravians had already been converted, earlier in the century, to Latin Christianity by Frankish missionaries from Salzburg and Passau. Understandably these Frankish clerics regarded the envoys from Byzantium as trespassers on their own missionary domain. In the tense situation that followed the arrival in the autumn of 863 of Constantine and Methodius in Moravia, only the pope was in a position to encourage and support their work. The insubordinate tendencies of the Frankish bishops were causing anxiety and irritation in Rome. Constantine and Methodius, because of their Byzantine affiliations, their conflict with the Franks, and the strong support given them by the Slav princes of central Europe—Rastislav of Moravia and Kotsel of Pannonia—had involved themselves in some of the principal concerns of the ninth-century papacy. It is not surprising that the progress of Slav vernacular Christianity in central Europe was monitored with some care in Rome. In 867 an invitation reached Constantine and Methodius from Pope Nicholas I to visit him. By the time they reached Rome Nicholas was dead; and it was his successor, Hadrian II, who welcomed them and their companions on the outskirts of the city.

One of these companions is the subject of the present biographical sketch. A Bulgarian Slav called Clement—this was perhaps his clerical, not his original name—he came to occupy in the history and immediate aftermath of the Cyrillo-Methodian mission a position second only to that of its two leaders. His early life is virtually unknown: it is not until the death of Methodius in 885 that the limelight in the sources begins to fall on him. So for his early years we are forced to rely on circumstantial evidence, and on the statement by his medieval biographer that he was a disciple and companion of Methodius 'since his tender youth'.[1]

The history of the Cyrillo-Methodian mission to the Slavs is thus a necessary prelude to Clement's early career; and we may be reasonably sure that he was in his masters' retinue as it entered Rome in the winter of 867/8.

The signal honour paid to the visitors by the presence of the pope in the reception-party was not due to the personal deserts, nor even to the missionary achievements, of its two leaders. The excitement provoked in Rome by their arrival was caused not by them, but by what they carried. In the place of honour in their baggage were the relics believed to be those of St Clement, bishop of Rome, one of the early successors of St Peter.

The circumstances in which these relics were discovered are described in several contemporary, or near-contemporary, sources. Chief among them are the Old Church Slavonic Life of Constantine, the *Vita Constantini*,[2] and a Latin document, variously known as the *Legenda Italica* or *Vita cum translatione sancti Clementis*, and based on the evidence of Constantine's Roman friend Anastasius the Librarian, the pope's secretary.[3] The relics were found near the town of Cherson in the Crimea during the winter of 860/1, when Constantine was on a diplomatic mission to the court of the Khazar ruler, in the foothills of the Caucasus. Brought to Constantinople, they were carried by

---

[1] See below, p. 12.
[2] F. Grivec and F. Tomšič, *Constantinus et Methodius Thessalonicenses: Fontes* (Zagreb, 1960), 95–143.
[3] Ibid. 59–64.

Constantine and Methodius to Moravia, and from there to their final resting-place in Rome.

We know today that these relics were not genuine. In its written form, the tradition that Clement was banished to the Crimea in the reign of the Emperor Trajan, and thrown into the Black Sea tied to an anchor, goes back no further than the fourth century, and is now generally regarded as apocryphal. Yet it was firmly believed in the Middle Ages; and Constantine was certainly convinced that the discovery was genuine, and due to divine intervention. The Romans shared this belief. Their sense of history as well as their local pride were rekindled by the posthumous return of St Clement, pope and martyr, to the city of which he had been one of the first bishops. Since the seventh century the custom of 'translating' the relics of Christian martyrs to sanctuaries within the city of Rome had been growing. This revival of the cult of Roman martyrs was encouraged by the great popes of the late eighth and early ninth centuries, Hadrian I, Leo III, and Paschal I, who restored their churches and lavishly adorned their shrines.[4] By the mid-ninth century, through this combination of saintly antiquarianism and architectural display, Rome had come to be seen, as perhaps never before, in the threefold guise of the city of martyrs, a goal of pilgrims, and the patrimony of St Peter. No pope worked harder to implant this image in western Christendom than Nicholas I; and it is hard to imagine an event which provided more striking endorsement for his policy than the arrival in Rome, shortly after his death, of the relics of St Clement.

The pope, we have seen, had several reasons for showing a friendly interest in the bearers of these relics. Constantine's friendship with Photius, the former patriarch of Constantinople who was then regarded in Rome as a sworn enemy of the papacy, was no doubt a liability. But the prestige he enjoyed in the Greek monasteries in Rome was a point in his favour. In February 868 Hadrian II gave a banquet in honour of the local Greek monks.[5] It is likely that Constantine and Methodius, and perhaps their disciples, attended this feast. By early March at the latest the pope had decided to authorize the use of the Slavonic language in the liturgy. It cannot have been an easy decision, for it meant departing from the well-established tradition

    [4] See R. Krautheimer, *Rome: Profile of a City, 312–1308* (Princeton, NJ, 1980), 109–42.
    [5] See F. Dvornik, *Byzantine Missions among the Slavs: SS. Constantine-Cyril and Methodius* (New Brunswick, NJ, 1970), 138.

which had secured for Latin an almost total liturgical monopoly throughout the Western Church; and, by actively supporting the work of Constantine and Methodius, the pope was risking a major conflict with the Frankish clergy. But the fruits of Slavonic vernacular Christianity now being offered him were clearly too valuable to be declined, and the popularity Constantine and Methodius enjoyed in the Slavonic courts of central Europe was a strong additional argument. Solemn liturgical celebrations, in three successive stages, followed in the principal churches of Rome. The Slavonic liturgical books were deposited in S. Maria Maggiore and a mass was then sung. Next the Slav disciples of Constantine and Methodius were ordained to the priesthood by two Roman bishops; and finally with the help of these newly ordained disciples the liturgy was celebrated in Slavonic on successive days in St Peter's, in the churches of St Petronilla and St Andrew, and in St Paul's *fuori le mura*. In St Paul's an all-night vigil in Slavonic was followed by a liturgy in the same language sung over the apostle's tomb, with the assistance of two high-placed clerical officials of the Roman Church; one of them was Constantine's friend, Anastasius the Librarian.[6] The importance which the *Vita Constantini* attaches to the celebrations in the church of St Paul is significant: for the Apostle of the Gentiles could be regarded in a special sense, together with St Clement, as the patron saint of the Slavonic mission.

The ordination in Rome of several of its members was an important event. It was, indeed, for the very purpose of having his disciples ordained that Constantine had travelled south from Moravia. According to the *Vita Methodii*, the pope himself ordained Methodius to the priesthood soon after the mission's arrival in Rome;[7] while the disciples of the two brothers were ordained by two Roman bishops, Formosus of Porto and Gauderic of Velletri.[8]

None of the contemporary sources mention the names of these newly ordained disciples. A late medieval document, however, tells us that one of them was called Clement.[9]

Our knowledge of him comes mainly from two medieval Greek documents. The earliest and much the more detailed, known as the 'Long Life', is generally, and rightly, ascribed to Theophylact,

---

[6] *Vita Constantini* (hereafter *VC*), xvii. 5–9 (Grivec–Tomšič, 139).
[7] *Vita Methodii* (hereafter *VM*), vi. 2 (ibid. 156).
[8] *VC* xvii. 6 (ibid. 139).
[9] I. Ivanov, *Bŭlgarski starini iz Makedoniya* (Sofia, 1970), 312.

archbishop of Ohrid in the late eleventh and early twelfth centuries.[10] The second, the 'Brief Life', written in the first half of the thirteenth century, is attributed on equally solid grounds to another archbishop of Ohrid, Demetrios Chomatianos.[11]

The 'Brief Life' is the only one to mention Clement's nationality. 'He drew his origin', its author tells us, 'from the European Moesians, who are also known to most people as Bulgarians.'[12] This, in the thirteenth century, could mean only one thing: that Clement was a Slav inhabitant of the Kingdom of Bulgaria. The precise region of this kingdom from which his family stemmed is unknown, but it was probably Macedonia. It was there, we shall see, that Clement was sent by the Bulgarian ruler, with the task of setting up a Slav vernacular Church: a mission in which a native could be expected to succeed better than a foreigner. Moreover, Clement's command of Greek, apparent in the quality and range of his translations, suggests that he acquired a knowledge of that language early in life: this again points to Macedonia, some of whose Greek-speaking towns and villages had been incorporated into the Bulgarian kingdom in the middle of the ninth century. Clement is more likely to have grown up in a bilingual milieu in Macedonia than in any other province of that kingdom.

The earliest recorded fact of Clement's biography connects him closely with Methodius. The author of the 'Long Life' tells us that he 'set the great Methodius as the model of his own life . . . , for he knew his [Methodius'] life as no one else did, as he had followed him since his tender youth, and saw with his own eyes all the things that his master did'.[13] How literally we are entitled to take this imprecise statement is a matter of opinion. Clement is generally believed to have been born around 840: according to the 'Long Life' he died in old age in 916. If we accept the date 840, and take the words 'tender youth' to refer to an age between sixteen and eighteen, we may tentatively date his association with Methodius from the years 856–8.

[10] The text of the 'Long Life' (hereafter *Vita*) was published by N. L. Tunickij (Tunitsky), *Monumenta ad SS Cyrilli et Methodii successorum vitas resque gestas pertinentia* (London, 1972), 66–140 (hereafter Tunitsky) and by A. Milev, *Grŭtskite zhitiya na Kliment Okhridski* (Sofia, 1966), 76–146 (hereafter Milev). There is an English translation (hereafter ET) by S. Nikolov in *Kiril and Methodius, Founders of Slavonic Writing: A Collection of Sources and Critical Studies*, ed. I. Duichev (Boulder, Colo., 1985). Theophylact's authorship of this work is defended by D. Obolensky, 'Theophylaktos of Ohrid and the Authorship of the *Vita Clementis*' in *Byzantium: Tribute to Andreas N. Stratos*, ii (Athens, 1986), 601–18.
[11] Published by Milev, *Grŭtskite zhitiya*, 174–82.
[12] Ibid. 174.
[13] *Vita*, xxii. 65 (Tunitsky, 124; Milev, 130).

This was a decisive period in the life of Methodius. About 856, his biographer tells us, he gave up a promising career in the Byzantine provincial administration and entered a monastery on the Bithynian Mount Olympus, in north-western Asia Minor.[14] This mountainous region, which lay immediately south of the Sea of Marmara, known in antiquity and the Middle Ages as the Mysian Olympus—today the Turks call it Keşiş (or Ulu) Dağ—was in the ninth century a leading monastic centre. We do not know for certain in which of its many monasteries Methodius was tonsured: most probably it was the one of which he became abbot several years later, and which his Slavonic biographer called Polikhron.[15]

If we can accept the view that Clement's association with Methodius began in 856–8, we may conclude that he became his disciple in one of the monasteries of Mount Olympus. Methodius remained a member of its community, continuously we may suppose, from about 856 to 860. Soon after his arrival he was joined there by his brother Constantine, who had recently given up a chair of philosophy in Constantinople. However, unlike his elder brother, Constantine did not at this stage become a monk. If Clement was then living with Methodius, his first encounter with Constantine, who already then enjoyed a formidable reputation as a scholar and diplomat, must have made a powerful impression on the young man who was probably still in his teens. Clement was later to write an encomium of Constantine, praising him for his work for the Slavs, and saluting him as his teacher.

The years which Constantine and Methodius spent together on Mount Olympus (*c.* 856–60) are described by their biographers with tantalizing brevity. Each biographer, however, seems to drop the same significant hint. The *Vita Constantini* tells us that during his stay in the monastery Constantine spent his time 'conversing with books' in the company of his brother.[16] The *Vita Methodii*, using an almost

---

[14] *VM* iii. 3 (Grivec–Tomšič, 154).

[15] Some scholars have identified Polikhron with Polichnion (or Polychronia), a monastery known from Byzantine sources and believed to have been located in the foothills of the Sigriani Mountains, known today as Kara Dağ. See F. Dvornik, *Les Légendes de Constantin et de Méthode vues de Byzance* (Prague, 1933), 115, 210–11, and C. Mango and I. Ševčenko, 'Some Churches and Monasteries on the Southern Shore of the Sea of Marmara', *Dumbarton Oaks Papers*, xxvii (1973), 259–70. The identification is regarded with scepticism by R. Janin, *Les Églises et les monastères des grands centres byzantins* (Paris, 1975), 207–9.

[16] *VC* vii. 5 (Grivec–Tomšič, 108).

identical phrase, states that on Mount Olympus Methodius 'devoted himself to books'.[17] What was the nature of this joint literary activity? It can hardly have been the mere reading of Scripture: had that been the case the biographers, who seldom miss an opportunity of praising their heroes' piety, would surely have said so. Nor is it likely that the two brothers spent the whole of their leisure time studying works of theology: Constantine would hardly have chosen a provincial monastery as a place of scholarly retreat, when he had all the books he needed in the libraries of Constantinople. It is hard to resist the impression that the brothers' 'conversation with books' on Mount Olympus had another, more specific, purpose; and it is tempting to speculate that this purpose had to do with the invention of the Slavonic alphabet and with early attempts to translate Greek texts into Slavonic.[18] The arguments in favour of this hypothesis are tentative, and largely based on chronology. We know that the Slavonic alphabet was in existence by 863 at the latest. Its invention, however, must have required years of labour. We can confidently discount the claim of Constantine and Methodius' biographers that it was invented in Constantinople during the weeks or months of 862 which followed the arrival of the embassy from Prince Rastislav of Moravia, requesting from the Byzantine government a teacher capable of giving Christian instruction to his subjects in their own Slavonic tongue. Both biographers tell us that Constantine was assisted in the task of inventing the Slavonic alphabet.[19] One of his collaborators was surely Methodius. And it is worth noting that between *c.* 843, when Constantine, a boy of sixteen, arrived in the imperial capital from his native Thessalonica, and 862, when the Moravian envoys came to Constantinople, the only period during which the two brothers were together for any length of time (except for the Khazar mission of 860–1, when they were on active diplomatic service) were the years they spent on Mount Olympus.

Are we entitled to conclude that Constantine and Methodius invented the Slavonic alphabet in the late 850s in one of the monasteries of Mount Olympus, and then essayed with the help of this

---

[17] *VM* iii. 3 (ibid. 154).

[18] This hypothesis is advanced by A.-E. Tachiaos, 'Sozdanie i deyatel'nost' literaturnogo kruga Konstantina-Kirilla do Moravskoy missii', in B. St. Angelov *et al.*, *Konstantin-Kiril filosof:Dokladi ot simpoziuma, posveten na 1100-godishninata ot smŭrtta mu* (Sofia, 1971), 288.

[19] See below, p. 15.

alphabet the first translations from Greek into Slavonic? We cannot state this with any confidence, given the tentative nature of the evidence. But the view that at least the first experiments leading to the new alphabet were made in this period on Mount Olympus by a group of scholars and translators under Constantine's direction may be put forward as a plausible hypothesis.

If Clement, probably still a layman, was then living as Methodius' disciple in the same monastery, he would naturally have joined this group. His knowledge of the Slav and Greek languages—both, we have seen, probably acquired in childhood in his native Macedonia—would have made him a useful member of Constantine's linguistic seminar.

Then, for the next few years, we lose sight of him. It has been supposed[20] that in 860-1 he accompanied Constantine and Methodius on their mission to the land of the Khazars, and that he took part in, or at least witnessed, the discovery of the relics of the pseudo-Clement in the Crimea. But no convincing evidence has been found to support this view.

The next piece of evidence, pointing to Clement's presence in Constantine's linguistic circle, comes from Constantinople. The *Vita Constantini* tells us that, after the arrival of the Moravian mission, the Emperor Michael III asked Constantine to invent a Slavonic alphabet; whereupon 'he gave himself over to prayer together with his other collaborators'.[21] The *Vita Methodii*, recording the same event, calls these assistants of Constantine and Methodius 'others, who were of the same spirit as they.'[22] This same group is mentioned also by Theophylact, in the 'Long Life' of Clement, who tells us that after inventing the Slavonic letters Constantine and Methodius 'took pains to impart the divine knowledge [of these letters] to the sharper-witted of their disciples'.[23] He mentions five of them by name: Gorazd, Clement, Naum, Angelarius, and Sava. What we know of Clement's later activity as a teacher, writer, and translator certainly suggests that he belonged to this chosen group. The statements in the *Vita Constantini* and the *Vita Methodii* that Constantine 'composed' or

---

[20] See E. Georgiev, *Raztsvetŭt na bŭlgarskata literatura v IX–X v.* (Sofia, 1962), 91. Some have been tempted to conclude, from the coincidence of names, that Clement assumed his name in honour of St Clement, either in the Crimea or at his ordination in Rome.

[21] *VC* xiv. 13 (Grivec–Tomšič, 129).   [22] *VM* v. 10 (ibid, 155).

[23] τοῖς ὀξυτέροις τῶν μαθητῶν: *Vita*, ii. 7 (Tunitsky, 70; Milev, 80).

'formed' the Slavonic letters in 862 could well, in that case, refer to
the final stage in the development of the Glagolitic alphabet.[24] To this
final stage at least Clement can hardly have failed to make some
contribution.

During the next five years (863–8) the sources make no mention of
him. However, the fact that in 868 he was with his masters in Rome,
where, as we have seen, he was ordained priest, makes it virtually
certain that he had accompanied them to Moravia; and we may
suppose that he supported their efforts to provide the Moravians with
a complete cycle of liturgical offices in Slavonic translation, to train a
local Slav-speaking clergy, and to repel the Frankish assaults on the
Byzantine mission. These were the years of his apprenticeship in the
service of Slav vernacular Christianity.

After spending some three and half years in Moravia, it will be
recalled, Constantine and Methodius travelled south to have their
disciples ordained. It is a moot point whether they intended to go for
this purpose to Rome or Constantinople.[25] One of the prospective
ordinands was certainly Clement. The different stages of their journey
to Rome are recorded in the *Vita Constantini*. It included a break of
several months in Mosaburg near Lake Balaton in present-day
Hungary, whose Slav ruler, Kotsel, was persuaded to support the
cause of the Slavonic vernacular liturgy; and a stopover in Venice,
where Constantine made a spirited defence of the Slavonic liturgy
against the local clergy, who argued that only in three languages—
Hebrew, Greek, and Latin—was it permissible to offer public worship
to God.

Clement's ordination to the priesthood in Rome has already been
mentioned. We know nothing precise about his sojourn in the city,
which probably lasted from the winter of 867/8 to the summer or
autumn of 869. His contacts with influential circles of the Roman
Church, Latin as well as Greek, may have been almost as wide as those
of Constantine and Methodius. He was ordained by two leading
Roman bishops, Gauderich of Velletri and Formosus of Porto, and
must have personally known Constantine's friend and admirer,
Anastasius the Librarian.[26] He surely had close links with Greek
monasteries in Rome, and may well have lived in Santa Prassede, one
of them.[27]

---

[24] On the Glagolitic alphabet invented by Constantine-Cyril see A. P. Vlasto, *The
Entry of the Slavs into Christendom* (Cambridge, 1970), 38–44, and below, pp. 29–30.

[25] See Dvornik, *Byzantine Missions*, 132–7.   [26] Ibid. 138–42.

[27] Ibid., 141.

Constantine died in Rome on 14 February 869, soon after becoming a monk under his now more familiar name of Cyril. Later in that year Hadrian II appointed Methodius archbishop of Pannonia, and sent him to Kotsel's court as papal legate to the Slavs of Central Europe. We can be fairly sure that Clement accompanied him.

In obedience to his brother's last wish, Methodius renounced the intention of returning to his monastery on Mount Olympus, and chose to continue their common work for the Slavs. It was a fateful decision. His old enemies, the Frankish clerics, enraged at the thought that their prerogatives in Pannonia and Moravia had been annulled by his new appointment, secured his arrest and trial by a synod of local bishops. Condemned as a usurper of episcopal rights, Methodius was imprisoned for two and a half years in Swabia, and it was not until 873 that Pope John VIII, having learned of his legate's fate, forced the Frankish bishops to release him.[28]

The last years of Methodius' life were spent fighting to defend the Slavonic liturgy in his archdiocese. He had to contend simultaneously with the hostility of the Franks, the inconstancy of the new Moravian ruler Svatopluk, and the growing indifference of Rome. Only in Byzantium, which he visited in 881, did he receive encouragement from the Emperor Basil I and the Patriarch Photius. He now devoted all the time he could spare to the work of translation. In times gone by he had helped his brother to render into Slavonic the Greek liturgical offices and some at least of the New Testament. In his last years he translated most of the Old Testament, selected writings of the great Christian theologians (the 'Fathers of the Church'), and a Byzantine manual of canon law. In this he was helped by two disciples, described by his biographer as priests 'expert in shorthand'.[29] One of them may well have been Clement: we may suppose that he spent the last fifteen years of Methodius' life by his master's side.

The sources, however, are silent on Clement's activity during those years. It was only after Methodius' death on 6 April 885 that he grows to his full stature in the documents. Methodius had designated as his successor his pupil Gorazd, who enjoyed the double advantage of being a native Moravian and of knowing Latin. But he failed to secure the pope's approval of his appointment; and Methodius' old adversary, Wiching, the Frankish bishop of Nitra, now seemed set to obtain the suppression of the Slavonic liturgy in central Europe.[30]

---

[28] *VM* x. 1–3 (Grivec–Tomšič, 160).   [29] *VM* xv. 1 (ibid. 164).
[30] See F. Dvornik, *Les Slaves, Byzance et Rome au IXe siècle* (Paris, 1926), 286–98.

In addition to these vexatious problems, an important theological issue divided the disciples of Methodius from the Frankish clerics under his authority. The Frankish Church was now firmly committed to the doctrine of the *Filioque*, according to which the Holy Spirit 'proceeds' not from the Father alone, as is stated in the Nicene Creed, but from the Father and the Son. In Rome the *Filioque* was not formally accepted until the early eleventh century; the popes held that, though the addition of the words 'and from the Son' was theologically justified, it was not desirable to tamper with the version of the creed accepted by the whole of Christendom. The Byzantine Church strongly objected to the *Filioque*, partly on the grounds that any alteration to the creed had been forbidden by the oecumenical councils, and partly because it regarded the clause as theologically erroneous. Methodius, who, despite his position as papal legate, remained in outlook a Byzantine, could not fail to regard the Frankish doctrine, recently condemned by Patriarch Photius, as heretical. The *Filioque* was to become the main doctrinal issue in the medieval disputes between the Greek and the Latin Churches.[31]

It is as a disputant in this theological debate that we gain our first clear picture of Clement. It was to him and to Gorazd that fell the task of publicly arguing the case against the *Filioque*. The Orthodox, we are told in the 'Long Life', 'spoke through the mouth of Gorazd and Clement'.[32] On two occasions they expounded the Greek doctrine of the Trinity: the first homily, a lengthy one, was addressed to the Frankish clergy, the second, much the shorter, to Prince Svatopluk.

The dispute soon turned into violence. At first, Theophylact tells us, Wiching's men almost came to blows with the followers of Gorazd and Clement. Svatopluk tried to arbitrate; but his ham-fisted methods only played into the hands of the Frankish party. Methodius' disciples, numbering some two hundred priests and deacons, now faced state persecution. The younger ones were sold by the Moravian authorities into slavery and taken to Venice; others were driven out of their homes and beaten up, while their leaders were cast into prison.[33]

Theophylact cites the names of five of these imprisoned champions of the Slavonic liturgy: Gorazd, Clement, Naum, Laurence, and Angelarius.[34] Except for one, Laurence, the list is identical with that of the 'sharper-witted' students of Constantine and Methodius men-

[31] See below, pp. 42–5.
[32] *Vita*, viii. 26, ix. 29–30 (Tunitsky, 94, 98, 102; Milev, 100, 104, 108).
[33] *Vita*, xi. 34 (Tunitsky, 104 Milev, 110).   [34] *Vita*, xii. 35 (ibid.).

tioned earlier. In both lists, Clement occupies the second place, immediately after Gorazd. The latter's subsequent fate is unknown.[35] Laurence and Angelarius are also shadowy figures, though we know that the second went with Clement to Bulgaria, and died there soon afterwards. At this point all but two of the disciples of Cyril and Methodius fade into a hazy background, and the main focus in the sources is now brought to bear on Clement, and to a lesser degree on his friend and companion Naum.

The 'Long Life' is distressingly vague on geography. Some historians believe that Clement and his companions were imprisoned in Nitra, one of Svatopluk's residences, in present-day Slovakia.[36] Their period of detention, however, was brief; sentenced to perpetual exile, they were escorted, probably to the borders of the Moravian state, by what seems to have been a detachment of Svatopluk's German soldiers. Three of them, Clement, Naum, and Angelarius, came to the Danube, crossed the river on a makeshift raft made of the trunks of three lime-trees tied together with ropes of bark, and during the winter of 885–6 reached Belgrade, which was then on Bulgarian territory.[37]

The expulsion of Clement and his companions from Moravia signalled the final collapse of the Cyrillo-Methodian mission in that country. It took, however, two centuries more to wipe out the last traces of the Slavonic liturgy from central Europe. In neighbouring Bohemia, where some of Methodius' disciples must have taken refuge, it survived until the late eleventh century, when the Roman policy of linguistic uniformity finally enforced the liturgical use of Latin. But the future of Slavonic vernacular Christianity lay elsewhere. The Cyrillo-Methodian linguistic and cultural tradition, banned from Moravia after Methodius' death, was saved for Europe and the Slavs by the Bulgarians.[38] Their achievement was to enrich this tradition on their own soil and, in the fullness of time, to transmit it to other nations which formed part of the Byzantine cultural common-wealth—the Russians, the Serbs, and the Rumanians. In the initial stages of this work Clement played the leading role.

[35] Some scholars believe that Gorazd on his release from prison went into hiding, perhaps in the castle of some Moravian nobleman, and may later have found refuge in southern Poland: see Dvornik, *Byzantine Missions*, 197–9; Vlasto, *The Entry of the Slavs into Christendom*, 82, 138.

[36] F. Grivec, *Konstantin und Method, Lehrer der Slaven* (Wiesbaden, 1960), 151.

[37] *Vita*, xvi. 47 (Tunitsky, 114; Milev, 120).

[38] Dvornik, *Les Slaves, Byzance et Rome*, 282–322.

On their release from their Moravian prison Clement and his companions longed to go to Bulgaria, hoping to find 'solace' there.[39] It is unlikely that, in attributing these expectations to them, the hagiographer is simply being wise after the event. Clement was a Bulgarian by birth: after the torments he had endured in Moravia, it was natural enough that he should seek 'solace' in his native land. But there may well have been other reasons as well for his choice of Bulgaria: indeed, the author of the 'Long Life' seems to hint, even then, at a meeting of minds between Clement and the Bulgarian ruler Boris.

Boris had been baptized into the Byzantine Church in 864; by 870 his newly converted country, after a brief flirtation with Rome, seemed firmly set on a pro-Byzantine course. One obstacle, however, remained before Bulgaria could be peacefully absorbed into the Byzantine cultural commonwealth. Its church was still mostly staffed, at least in the higher echelons, by Greeks, few of whom could have had an adequate command of the Slavonic language spoken by their flocks. They conducted the services in Greek, of which the native parish priests were largely ignorant. The problem posed by the linguistic gap between the higher clergy and the people was aggravated by a cultural and political dilemma which faced the ruling classes of every East European nation converted to the Empire's Christian faith. It arose from the need to reconcile the demands of local independence with Byzantine universalist claims. These claims required the ruler of every country which adopted the religion of Byzantium to accept not only the spiritual jurisdiction of the patriarchate of Constantinople but also, if only theoretically, the paramount authority of the emperor. By the late ninth century it must have been apparent to more than one East European ruler that the rigour of these Byzantine hegemonistic claims could be tempered by adopting the Cyrillo-Methodian vernacular tradition. Certainly Boris was not slow to realize that by acquiring a native clergy and a Slav-speaking Church the Bulgarians could continue to borrow and adapt the values and products of Byzantium without the risk of losing their cultural autonomy. He was presumably well informed from neighbouring Moravia about the achievements of Cyril and Methodius, several of whose leading disciples were now at hand to help him

---

[39] *Vita*, xiv. 42 (Tunitsky, 110; Milev, 116).

resolve his cultural and political dilemma. No wonder that, in the words of the 'Long Life', Boris 'thirsted after such men'.[40]

The military governor of Belgrade was doubtless aware of his sovereign's preoccupation: when Clement, Naum, and Angelarius had rested from their exertions and sufferings, he sent them on to Pliska, the Bulgarian capital.

The last chapter in Clement's life—he must have been then in his middle or late forties—was about to begin. It is by far the best-documented, for both Theophylact and Chomatianos provide valuable information on this period.

Boris was delighted at the arrival of the Slavonic missionaries in Pliska, and received them warmly. They were billeted on local grandees, and had regular consultations with the sovereign and his advisers. Theophylact hints at a certain secrecy surrounding these meetings.[41] It seems that Boris wished to discuss the main lines of his future policy with Clement and his companions without the risk of antagonizing the opposition. The identity of these potential adversaries of the Cyrillo-Methodian tradition is not clear. They could have been members of the old Bulgar aristocracy, still loyal in the main to their Turkic ancestry and pagan traditions, who only twenty years earlier had led a powerful if abortive revolt against Boris's decision to impose Christianity on his country; or they might have belonged to the Greek clergy in Bulgaria, jealous of their prerogatives and resentful of the sudden appearance of a distinguished group of rival missionaries. Whatever the truth, we may be sure that Boris and his collaborators recognized that their plan to expand the work of Cyril and Methodius in Bulgaria required cautious handling and careful preparation.

Before long the three Slavonic missionaries went their separate ways. Angelarius died in the months following their arrival in Bulgaria, Naum remained in Pliska, while Clement, probably in 886, was sent as a missionary to Macedonia.[42]

The reasons why Clement, now the undisputed leader of the disciples of Cyril and Methodius, was dispatched to this remote south-western province of the Bulgarian kingdom have been much debated. It has rightly been argued that, by contrast with north-eastern Bulgaria—the country's political centre, which seems to have still

---

[40] *Vita*, xvi. 47 (Tunitsky, 114; Milev, 120).
[41] *Vita*, xvi. 49 (Tunitsky, 116; Milev, 122).
[42] *Vita*, xvi. 50–1, xvii. 53 (Tunitsky, 116; Milev, 122–4).

retained at that time a sizeable minority of Turkic 'Proto-Bulgars'—
the population of Macedonia was predominantly Slavonic; the region
had only recently been incorporated into the Bulgarian realm. An
experienced pupil of Cyril and Methodius, who was in addition
probably a Macedonian by birth, could be expected to minister
effectively to the spiritual needs of the people of this province and to
hasten their cultural assimilation into Boris's kingdom.

There has been much discussion, too, about the whereabouts of the
centres of Clement's new activity. On this point the 'Long Life ' is not
very helpful. Boris, we are told, 'detached [the territory of] Koutmitsinitsa from [that of] Kotokios', and appointed Dometas governor and
Clement 'teacher', *didaskalos*, of this territory.[43] Kotokios (or Kotok-
ion) has so far eluded all attempts at identification. Koutmitsinitsa, on
the other hand, can be located, at least approximately. The pointers
are provided by the 'Long Life', which tells us that Boris bestowed on
Clement three comfortable houses in Diabolis, as well as 'places of rest'
near Ohrid and Glavinitsa.[44] It is clear from the context that these
three towns—Ohrid, Diabolis, and Glavinitsa—were situated on the
territory of Koutmitsinitsa. Ohrid, on the north-eastern shore of the
lake of that name, in the heart of western Macedonia, was Clement's
favourite residence; and, in large measure thanks to him, it now
became one of the principal centres of the new Byzantine–Slav culture
in the Balkans. Diabolis, the second centre of Clement's teaching, has
been plausibly located in the upper valley of the Devolli river, not far
from the southern shore of Lake Ohrid, in what is today south-eastern
Albania.[45] As for Glavinitsa (Κεφαληνία in Greek), the 'Brief Life' tells
us that Clement often resided there, and that he left behind some
'monuments'.[46] These 'monuments' were probably the stone col-
umns which, according to the 'Brief Life', could still be seen in
Glavinitsa in the early thirteenth century: on one of them was carved
an inscription mentioning the conversion of the Bulgarians to
Christianity.[47] By a striking coincidence, a votive stone was discovered in 1918 by the Austrian army in the town of Ballsh, south-
west of Berat, in southern Albania, inscribed with a text which refers
to the baptism of King Boris and his subjects.[48] The location of

[43] *Vita,* xvii. 53 (Tunitsky, 116–18; Milev, 124).
[44] *Vita,* xvii. 54 (Tunitsky, 118; Milev, 124).
[45] See A. Ducellier, *La Façade maritime de l'Albanie au Moyen Âge* (Thessaloniki,
1981), 18–20.
[46] Milev, 176.   [47] Ibid. 178.   [48] Ibid. 171–2.

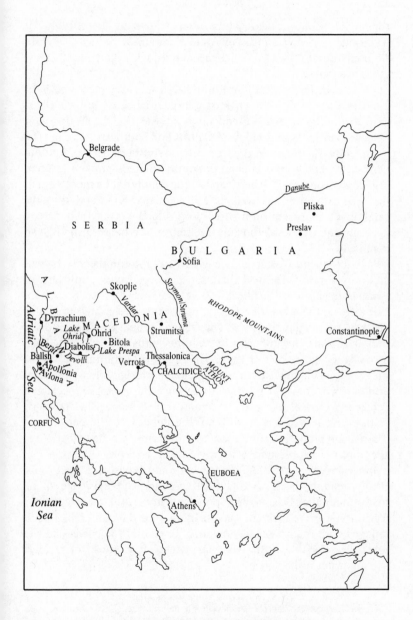

Map. 1—Macedonia and adjacent lands, 900–1000

Glavinitsa between Berat and Valona, close to the Adriatic, is confirmed in two passages of Anna Comnena's *Alexiad*.[49] Ballsh, situated in that very area, is hence identified with Glavinitsa by most modern scholars.[50]

We may thus conclude that Koutmitsinitsa, over which Boris gave Clement licence to teach, covered a large area between Lake Ohrid and the Adriatic Sea. It encompassed the region of the west Macedonian lakes and much of central and southern Albania. The indigenous Albanians, in the western and southern parts of Koutmitsinitsa, probably lived in close proximity to Slavs, the more recent invaders of this area.[51] There can be little doubt that Clement's pupils included Albanians as well as Macedonian Slavs, and that the brighter alumni from both these groups later played their part in fostering the Cyrillo-Methodian tradition in the heart of the Balkan peninsula.

When Clement was appointed *didaskalos* of Koutmitsinitsa he was still only a priest. He held this post for seven years, until he was consecrated bishop. The title *didaskalos*, later held by some prominent members of the Byzantine clergy, apparently designated priests or deacons specifically entrusted with teaching and preaching. It was only in the late eleventh century that the status of the *didaskaloi* was formally recognized within the patriarchate of Constantinople; and by an imperial edict of 1107 it was made to correspond to a particular ecclesiastical rank. In the twelfth century the *didaskaloi* became a privileged clerical order with administrative as well as teaching duties, and also the right of reporting directly to the patriarch.[52] There is no proof that this function, thus formally defined, existed in the ninth century; and Theophylact, in asserting that Clement belonged to the 'order' ($\tau\acute{\alpha}\xi\iota\varsigma$) of teachers, may have been anachronistically reading back to the ninth century the existence of an institution which became widespread and important in his own time. Yet the nature of Clement's commission, and the close relations he enjoyed with the provincial governor, show that the powers he was given by Boris in 886 were far wider than those of a mere schoolmaster or preacher.

---

[49] *Alexiad*, iii. 12, xiii. 5. Cf. Ducellier, *La Façade maritime*, 23.

[50] See T. Popa, 'La Glavenice médiévale et le Ballsh actuel', *Studia Albanica*, 1964, no. 2, 124; A. Ducellier, 'L'Arbanon et les Albanais au XIᵉ siècle', *TM* iii (1968), 365.

[51] Ducellier, ibid. 356–8.

[52] J. Darrouzès, *Recherches sur les ὀφφίκια de l'Église byzantine* (Paris, 1970), 66–78.

However, it is as a preacher and teacher that Clement is depicted in the sources during the years (886–93) of his ministry in Koutmitsinitsa. He seems to have moved frequently between his three residences of Ohrid, Diabolis, and Glavinitsa. Part of his time was spent preaching the Gospel to the pagans, of whom there must have been many among the Slav and Albanian peasants of this region. The area had only recently been annexed to the Bulgarian kingdom; and the influence from neighbouring Byzantine missionary centres, such as Thessalonica and Dyrrachium, had probably been slow in penetrating to the interior. The author of the 'Brief Life' writes of the 'spell' (ἴυγξ) which Clement's words cast on those who heard them;[53] this may well be more than a mere hagiographical cliché.

In a particularly arresting passage, the 'Long Life' describes Clement's teaching methods. We can hardly doubt that this vivid account was borrowed by Theophylact from one of his principal sources—an early biography of Clement, written in Old Church Slavonic by one of his personal disciples. The children were taught to write in three stages. First Clement would make them draw the shape of individual letters; then he would explain the 'meaning' of what they had written; and finally he would guide their hands in a motion of consecutive writing.[54] The alphabet he used was almost certainly Glagolitic, the creation of Constantine-Cyril. The dialect of southern Macedonia, to which its inventor adapted his alphabet, must have been close to, and perhaps identical with, the spoken vernacular of Clement's Slavonic pupils in Koutmitsinitsa.

Onlookers were struck by Clement's ability to do more than one thing at a time: thus, while he was teaching children, he would simultaneously read and 'write books'.[55] By 'writing books' his biographer probably meant copying manuscripts, an occupation in which—especially if we accept that he had been one of Methodius' shorthand secretaries—he was no doubt highly proficient.

The more promising of Clement's pupils went on to join the ranks of his chosen disciples, who were given more advanced theological training and no doubt singled out for ordination. To them, 'he unveiled the more profound scriptures'.[56] According to the 'Long Life', they numbered 3,500. Measured against the fact that the Slavonic literary tradition was still in its infancy, this represents a

---

[53] Milev, 178.   [54] *Vita* xviii, 58 (Tunitsky, 120; Milev, 126).
[55] Ibid.
[56] *Vita* xviii. 57 (Tunitsky, 120; Milev, 126).

remarkable achievement. 'By any standards', a distinguished authority on Byzantine education has written, Clement's teaching results
'represented an educational undertaking almost without parallel in
the Middle Ages'.[57] After seven years in Koutmitsinitsa, Clement had
done much to further Boris's plan to replace the Greek clergy by native
Slavs.

Both biographers tell us that Clement was strongly drawn to the
monastic life. We do not know when he received the tonsure, but his
close association with Methodius suggests that it was early in life.
During the years he taught in Koutmitsinitsa he founded a monastery
in Ohrid, dedicated to St Panteleimon. He cared for his foundation
with deepening love; and in his later years, burdened with episcopal
duties, he retired to it whenever he could for rest and prayer. St
Clement's monastery, not far from the shores of Lake Ohrid, became a
major centre for the training of a native clergy.[58] It contributed to
Ohrid's fame as the cradle of Slavonic Christianity in the Balkans.

Three years after Clement's arrival in Koutmitsinitsa, an event
occurred in Pliska which was to have a profound effect on his life and
work. In 889 Boris abdicated and entered a monastery, appointing as
his successor his eldest son Vladimir. There followed a complete
reversal of Boris's policy. Doubtless in agreement with the 'Proto-
Bulgar' aristocratic party, Vladimir renounced his father's special
relationship with Byzantium, encouraged a revival of paganism, and
began a persecution of the Christian clergy. One of his targets was
probably the Slavonic literary and liturgical centre founded in Pliska
by Naum, Clement's friend and companion.[59] For four years Bulgaria
remained in the throes of this pagan and anti-Byzantine movement.
In 893, seeing his life-work threatened, Boris emerged from his
monastery, and appeared in the capital. He rallied the faithful,
resumed power, and had Vladimir blinded and imprisoned. He then
summoned an assembly of the land, which ratified the following

[57] R. Browning, *Byzantium and Bulgaria* (London, 1975), 155; Cf. P. Lemerle, *Le
Premier Humanisme byzantin* (Paris, 1971). According to the 'Long Life' (xviii. 59)
Clement ordained from among these chosen disciples readers, subdeacons, deacons,
and priests. This must be a confusion with his later activity as bishop, since as a priest he
would not have had the right to ordain.

[58] Two churches of this monastery have been excavated on the site of the Imaret
Mosque in Ohrid: D. Koco, 'Klimentoviot manastir "Sv. Pantelejmon" i raskopkata pri
"Imaret" vo Ohrid', *Godišen zbornik*, i (Filozofski fakultet na Univerzitetot, Skopje,
1948), 129–80.

[59] For this literary movement see Vlasto, *The Entry of the Slavs into Christendom*,
176–9.

decisions: Boris's third son Symeon became the new ruler, Slavonic replaced Greek as the official language of the Bulgarian state and Church, and the capital of the realm was transferred from Pliska (where paganism, as recent events had shown, was still a powerful force) to the neighbouring city of Preslav.

We do not know whether the pagan revival directly affected Clement's work in distant Koutmitsinitsa. The outbreaks of violence were probably confined in the main to the country's north-eastern provinces. We may be sure, however, that the years of Vladimir's reign were a period of tension and uncertainty for Clement, and that he welcomed the decisions of the assembly of 893. It is not impossible that he secretly inspired them; and it is tempting to speculate on the links that may have existed between Clement and Boris in his monastic retreat. On several matters, we have seen, they tended to think alike; and on one at least of the decrees of the 893 assembly—the proclamation of Slavonic as the official language of the Bulgarian Church—they must have been in total agreement.

With Boris back in his monastery, there seemed to be every prospect of the same understanding between Clement and the new Bulgarian ruler. Symeon had been educated in Constantinople, where he earned the qualified approval of his Greek mentors. He had not yet succumbed to his fateful ambition to usurp the throne of Byzantium. He shared, moreover, his father's enthusiasm for Slavonic letters, and proved eager to foster them by royal patronage. His reign (893–927) has been described by some modern scholars as 'the golden age of Bulgarian literature'. One of his first acts was to summon Clement to Preslav, and to appoint him bishop. He is generally portrayed in iconography with the episcopal *omophorion* (Plate 1).

The name and whereabouts of the diocese to which Clement was appointed in 893 have been endlessly debated by scholars. The 'Long Life' calls it 'Dragvista or Velitsa'.[60] None of the attempts to identify these two place-names has met with general acceptance. Most modern historians have tended to favour for both names one of three locations: central Macedonia (in and around the Vardar valley); southern Macedonia (north of a line drawn between Thessalonica and Verroia); and the western slopes of the Rhodope Mountains. Their views rest largely on divergent interpretations of 'Dragvista' and 'Velitsa'. Some scholars have connected 'Velitsa' with the name of the

---

[60] See P. Gautier, 'Clément d'Ohrid, évêque de Dragvista', *Revue des Études byzantines*, xxii (1964), 199–214.

bishopric of *Velikeia*, probably situated on the northern slopes of the Rhodope Mountains, mentioned in a list of sees within the patriarchate of Constantinople dating from the reign of Leo VI (886–912). It is far from clear, however, whether in 893 this area was part of the Bulgarian realm. As for 'Dragvista', it has been identified with Dragovitia, a name thought to be derived from the Slavonic tribe of the Drougouvitae. A bishop of *Drougouvitia*, in southern Macedonia, appears in Leo VI's list of dioceses. The Drougouvitae, however, are known to have lived in the Middle Ages not only in Macedonia, but also in the Rhodope region of Thrace. These arguments may support the view that Clement's diocese was somewhere in the vicinity of the Rhodopes; but the question remains an open one.[61]

Whatever the exact location and extent of Clement's diocese, it was presumably at some distance from Ohrid. His new flock is described in the 'Long Life' as 'thick-witted' and 'wholly ignorant of the divine Word and Scriptures'.[62] Even if we allow for a measure of exaggeration on the part of the hagiographer—whose purpose, no doubt, was to extol Clement's achievements in evangelizing his diocese—it is hard to reconcile this picture of brutishness with the success of his pedagogic and apostolic work in Koutmitsinitsa. It seems likely, therefore, that his bishopric was situated in a more remote and primitive area. Nevertheless, his personal links with his monastery in Ohrid remained strong: he loved the natural beauty of the place, and visited it repeatedly.

Clement remained bishop of Dragvista or Velitsa for twenty-three years (893–916). Both his biographers describe the last period of his life rather sketchily. The picture that emerges is of a man alive to the practical duties of his new office, yet mindful too of his earlier teaching vocation. As a bishop—the first one, as Theophylact puts it, in the Bulgarian (i.e. Slavonic) language[63]—he could now continue with new authority the work of his masters, Cyril and Methodius. The most urgent need remained the training of a native clergy, capable of celebrating the offices in Slavonic, and he now ordained priests,

[61] For a recent discussion of the location of Clement's bishopric, see I. G. Iliev, 'La mission de Clément d'Ohrid dans les terres sud-ouest de la Bulgarie médiévale, *Études historiques* (Académie Bulgare des Sciences, Institut d'Histoire: A l'occasion du XVIe Congrès International des sciences historiques), xiii (1985), 63–4. A survey by P. Koledarov of older views will be found in the anniversary volume, B. St. Angelov *et al.* (eds.), *Konstantin-Kiril Filosof* (Sofia, 1969), 141–4.

[62] *Vita*, xxi. 63 (Tunitsky, 122–4; Milev, 130).

[63] *Vita*, xx. 62 (Tunitsky, 122; Milev, 128).

deacons, subdeacons, and lay readers. His practical concerns were not confined to the spiritual needs of his flock. We can be grateful to Theophylact for telling us that 'since in the whole land of the Bulgarians the trees grew wild and there was a lack of cultivated fruits, he . . . brought from the land of the Greeks all manner of cultivated [fruit] trees, and made fruitful the wild trees by grafting'.[64] It is a gracious picture of a provincial pastor cast in the traditional mould.

An enigmatic and much discussed sentence of the 'Brief Life' states that Clement 'skilfully devised other shapes of letters with a view to making [them] clearer than those which the wise Cyril invented'. With the help of these new letters he 'wrote down all the scriptures, panegyrics, and lives of martyrs and holy men, as well as sacred hymns'.[65] How is this passage to be understood? Did Clement invent a new alphabet, or merely simplify an existing one? The question acquires special interest in the light of the fact that the earliest Old Church Slavonic manuscripts are written in two different scripts, the Glagolitic and the Cyrillic. Glagolitic, the more complex, is a highly distinct and original creation. Cyrillic, except for half a dozen letters, is little more than an adaptation of the Greek alphabet. It is widely accepted today that Glagolitic was invented by Constantine-Cyril, while Cyrillic, which bears his monastic name, was the result of an attempt by Methodius' disciples, probably in Bulgaria, to adapt Greek uncial writing of the ninth century to the phonetic peculiarities of the Slavonic tongue. The comparative simplicity of Cyrillic, and its close resemblance to the Greek script, whose range and prestige were unrivalled in Eastern Europe, account for its greater historical importance. To the present day, the church books of the Orthodox Slavs—the Bulgarians, the Serbs, and the Russians—are printed in a slightly simplified form of Cyrillic, and the modern alphabets of these three peoples are based upon it. The Rumanians, too, adopted this alphabet in the Middle Ages, and their liturgical books were written and printed in Cyrillic until the late seventeenth century.

Can one conclude from the passage of the 'Brief Life' cited above that the inventor of Cyrillic was Clement? It will be recalled that he took some part, quite possibly an active one, in the invention of

---

[64] *Vita*, xxiii. 68 (Tunitsky, 128; Milev, 134).
[65] Milev, 180.

Glagolitic. Can the authorship of the second Slavonic alphabet be ascribed to him? A number of scholars believe that it can.[66]

These scholars, however, face several difficulties. For one thing, Macedonia, one of the principal areas of Clement's activity, remained in the early Middle Ages the main centre of Glagolitic scriptoria in the Balkans. Cyrillic, on the other hand, became the standard alphabet of the Preslav school in eastern Bulgaria. Furthermore, no reliable tradition connects Clement's name with the Cyrillic alphabet. Finally, several blatant historical errors have been detected in the 'Brief Life';[67] they counsel caution in accepting all of its statements. These observations have led most present-day scholars to reject the view that Clement invented the Cyrillic alphabet. The prevalent opinion is that he consistently used the Glagolitic script which he and his companions had brought from Moravia, and that the 'other shapes of letters' which he is said to have devised in Bulgaria (probably already in Koutmitsinitsa) were a refinement, perhaps a simplification, of Constantine's Glagolitic, and not a new alphabet. This complex and technical question, however, may still be regarded as an open one.

Theophylact, in his account of Clement's episcopacy, records his literary activity. He ascribes to him three types of writing: hymns, lives of saints, and sermons.[68] Clement's major contribution to hymnography was the translation of the Greek *Pentekostarion*, a collection of hymns sung in the Orthodox Church between Easter and Whitsun.[69] His hagiographical writings included panegyrics of saints, a number of which are extant. But his favourite literary form was the sermon. A recent edition of his writings includes fifty-nine sermons and eighteen panegyrics.[70] Not all these works can be ascribed to him with assurance; but he was almost certainly the author of at least fifteen.

[66] For example, D. Angelov in B. St. Angelov *et al.* (eds.), *Kliment Okhridski* (Sofia, 1966), 21.

[67] See Milev, 170.

[68] *Vita*, xxii. 66 (Tunitsky, 126; Milev, 132). The editors of a recent edition of Clement's writings—*Kliment Okhridski: Sŭbrani Sŭchineniya*, ed. B. St. Angelov *et al.* (Sofia, 1970–7)—believe that he wrote the *Vita Constantini* and the *Vita Methodii*. Their arguments (iii. 5–9) have failed to convince me.

[69] *Vita*, xxvi. 73 (Tunitsky, 132–4; Milev, 140). A number of original hymns in Old Church Slavonic are now also ascribed to Clement. See G. Popov, 'Novootkriti khimnografski proizvedeniya na Kliment Okhridski i Konstantin Preslavski', *Bŭlgarski ezik*, xxxii (1982), 3–26; id., *Triodni proizvedeniya na Konstantin Preslavski* (Sofia, 1985), 43–60. For these two references I am indebted to Dr Mary MacRobert.

[70] *Sŭbrani sŭchineniya*, i–ii. See also *Sv. Kliment Okhridski; Slova i poucheniya*, tr. into Bulgarian by A. Bonchev (Sofia, 1970), 35–111.

Theophylact writes of Clement's sermons with a touch of condescension. 'Knowing', he declares, 'the thick-wittedness of the people and their complete obtuseness in comprehending the Scriptures, and aware that many Bulgarian priests, understanding with difficulty what was written in Greek, were trained only to read by spelling out [the words] and were hence beast-like, and because there existed no festive sermons in the Bulgarian language . . . he composed sermons for all the feast-days, simple and clear and containing nothing profound or elaborate, and not beyond the grasp of the most stupid Bulgarian'.[71]

The origins of this supercilious attitude to the Bulgarians will be discussed in the next chapter. But we must record here that, as an overall judgement on Clement's sermons, Theophylact's words are unjust. It is true that many of these sermons contain little more than a paraphrase of some Gospel text, accompanied by moral exhortations. Yet they also reveal an extensive and pertinent knowledge of the scriptures, and an acquaintance with masterpieces of Greek liturgical art, such as the Akathistos Hymn; some of them can still attract by their verbal sophistication and their command of poetic rhythm. These qualities are particularly apparent in the panegyrical sermon devoted to the Archangels Michael and Gabriel—one of Clement's most popular writings, to judge from the large number of manuscripts in which it has survived.[72]

To the modern reader the most interesting of Clement's works are those in which personal undertones can be detected. Thus his panegyric of St Demetrios,[73] which eulogizes the heavenly protector of Thessalonica, echoes the devotion so movingly paid to this martyr-saint by a distinguished native of the city, Clement's teacher Methodius. Similarly, his encomium of his namesake, St Clement of Rome,[74] despite a somewhat florid style and conventional content, recalls an important moment in his life when, still a young man, he probably accompanied his masters carrying the saint's relics from Moravia to Rome.

[71] *Vita*, xxii. 66 (Tunitsky, 124–6; Milev, 132).

[72] *Sŭbrani sŭchineniya*, i. 238–86. German tr. by W. Baumann, *Die Faszination des Heiligen bei Kliment Ochridski* (Munich, 1983), 139–45.

[73] *Sŭbrani sŭchineniya*, i. 221–37; German tr. 135–9. See D. Obolensky, 'The Cult of St Demetrius of Thessaloniki in the History of Byzantine–Slav Relations', *Balkan Studies*, xv (1974), 3–20, repr. in id., *The Byzantine Inheritance of Eastern Europe* (London, Variorum Reprints, 1982).

[74] *Sŭbrani sŭchineniya*, i. 287–305; German tr. 145–51.

But perhaps the most remarkable of Clement's writings is his encomium of Constantine-Cyril.[75] Of all his extant works it is the warmest and most personal. The intensity of his devotion to his master's memory repeatedly breaks through the sober etiquette of conventional hagiography. Based in part on the *Vita Constantini*, it illustrates, with the help of techniques borrowed from medieval Greek rhetoric, the underlying features of the Cyrillo-Methodian tradition: an awareness of its Byzantine origins; veneration for the apostolic city of Rome; recognition of the immense debt owed by the Slavs to Constantine, who, by giving them a liturgy and scriptures in their own language, placed them among the chosen peoples of the earth; and a Christian universalism seeking to unite Byzantium and the Slavs within a single religious and cultural community. Fittingly enough, Constantine's achievement of teaching 'all nations' is likened by Clement to that of St Paul, the Apostle of the Gentiles, whose work was brought to fulfilment by 'Cyril the philosopher, the teacher of the Slavs', who 'overflew all countries, from east to west, and from north to south'.

Clement's panegyric of his master shares two further traits with the early works of the Cyrillo-Methodian tradition, composed in Bulgaria in the late ninth and early tenth centuries. The first is a sense of triumph springing from the knowledge that the Slavs, by acquiring the scriptures and the liturgy in their own language, have gained direct access to the knowledge of God. This heritage is seen as an outpouring of divine bounty, which Clement, together with other writers of the Cyrillo-Methodian school, makes concrete through the image of rain: thanks to St Cyril, he writes, 'the rain of divine understanding came down upon my people'. The idea of ethnic self-determination implicit in these words provides the second ideological link between Clement's encomium and other works of the Cyrillo-Methodian school. All of these, in one form or another, echo the joyful assurance of the *Vita Constantini* that the Slavs, by acquiring the vernacular liturgy and scriptures, have 'been numbered among the great nations which praise God in their own languages'.[76] By entering this community the Slavs underwent a spiritual rebirth, became 'a new people'. The author of the 'Long Life' was aware of the role played by Clement in this spiritual renaissance. This awareness is evident in his description of Clement as 'the first bishop in the

[75] *Sŭbrani sŭchineniya*, i. 415–42; German tr. 157–61.
[76] *VC* xiv. 16 (Grivec–Tomšič, 129).

Bulgarian language', and in the composite quotation from the Psalms with which he begins the biography of his hero: 'Come, ye children, hearken unto me, come and hear, all ye that fear God, that the generation to come might know them, even the children which should be born, and the people which shall be created shall praise the Lord.'[77]

In old age, Clement, exhausted, tried to resign his bishopric. King Symeon, however, who admired him greatly, would not hear of it. After visiting his sovereign in Preslav, Clement returned to his diocese, which he now governed, no doubt largely nominally, from his monastery in Ohrid. He died there, aged almost eighty, on 27 July 916. The city of Ohrid, which he had made into a leading centre of Slavonic Christianity, became permanently associated with his name. The Bulgarians, who profited most from his labours, still hold him in special regard. Next to his masters, Constantine-Cyril and Methodius, he was one of the chief architects of the Byzantine cultural commonwealth.

---

[77] *Vita*, i (Tunitsky, 66; Milev, 76). The quotation is from Pss. 34: 11, 66: 16, 78: 6, 102: 18 (AV).

2

Theophylact of Ohrid

BYZANTINE officials, clerical and lay, who served abroad faced a problem familiar to representatives of empires with a claim to world hegemony: that of reconciling the imperial ideology which they were expected to propagate with the cultural and political aspirations of the peoples among whom they worked. Their education and training, and the constraints of their mission, filled these Byzantine expatriates with the belief that the Empire they represented was immeasurably superior to all other societies and nations of the earth. Over these nations, which the Byzantines, like the ancient Greeks, called 'barbarians', the emperor in Constantinople was held to exert a God-given authority; and if some of them still lived outside the realm of his direct jurisdiction, this was the result of God's permissive will, and in the fullness of time they would be induced or persuaded to accept the authority of their legitimate sovereign. Such was the Byzantine theory; any discrepancy between ideology and reality could be eliminated, or at least reduced, by the use of persuasion and tactful diplomacy; and in this the accredited agents of Byzantium—missionaries, bishops, ambassadors in the field—were expected to play an important role.

The subject of this chapter is one of the more notable of these Byzantine expatriates. Theophylact Hēphaistos, a native of the Greek island of Euboea, was appointed in the late eleventh century archbishop of Bulgaria, with his see in the Macedonian town of Ohrid, and in this Slav environment he laboured for his Church and Empire for at least twenty years, and possibly longer.

He has several claims on our interest. In the first place, his writings were an important channel through which Greek theology reached the West at the time of the Renaissance; and, through his commentaries on the Gospels and on St Paul's Epistles, Theophylact exerted a strong influence on the thought of Erasmus. This influence has been detected in the latter's *Annotations on the New Testament* and in his *Paraphrases*; but it is especially evident in Erasmus' most popular work, *The Praise of Folly*. The notion of 'divine folly' (μωρία) which we find in its theological passages was, on Erasmus' own showing, directly taken over from Theophylact's Pauline commentaries. It conforms to the tradition, particularly stressed in the Eastern Church, which is anchored in St Paul's first Epistle to the Corinthians: 'For the preaching of the cross is to them that perish foolishness . . . For the wisdom of this world is foolishness with God' (I Cor. I: 18; 3: 19). Curiously enough, at the time he was writing *The Praise of Folly*, Erasmus was unaware of the identity of the author whose commentaries in manuscript he was using, and believed some of them to be the work of a certain 'Vulgarius'. It was not until 1519, long after *The Praise of Folly* was published, that he realized his error and became aware that 'Vulgarius' was no more than a designation of Theophylact's Bulgarian see.[1]

Secondly, Theophylact played a marginal but not insignificant role in the doctrinal strife which in his time was causing Eastern and Western Christendom to drift ever further apart. His role in these polemics was that of a clear-headed and fair-minded judge: he severely blamed the Latins for teaching the doctrine, which he regarded as heretical, of the Double Procession of the Holy Spirit (the *Filioque*); yet he reserved his severest strictures for his own Greek colleagues, whose lack of tolerance and understanding led them only too often to slander the legitimate customs of the Western Church.

Thirdly, Theophylact's career is a living illustration of the psychological and cultural problem mentioned in the opening lines of this chapter. A learned man with fastidious tastes, educated in the best schools of Constantinople and a professional teacher of rhetoric, in about 1090, as archbishop of Ohrid, he was sent to administer a remote Slav-speaking province of the Empire, which, barely seventy years earlier, had been part of an independent and strongly hostile Bulgarian state. This new position required him to reconcile two sets of apparently conflicting duties: he needed to ensure that his Bulgarian flock remained politically loyal to Byzantium, and at the same time to carry out his local pastoral obligations; and his consciousness of belonging to a master-race had to be in some measure adjusted to the need to understand the aspirations of the subject Bulgarians. Naturally, the contrary impulses generated by

---

[1] On Theophylact's influence on Erasmus, see M. A. Screech, *Ecstasy and the Praise of Folly* (London, 1980), pp. xxi–xxii, 144–52. For further parallels with St Paul's epistles, see *Collected Works of Erasmus*, xlii, ed. R. D. Sider (Toronto, 1984), index, p. 185.

this virtually colonial situation gave rise to tensions and ambiguities. To see how Theophylact faced and attempted to resolve them we must turn to his writings. The evidence they provide is fortunately abundant; the difficulty lies in the fact that much of it has to be fitted into its context, and then decoded.

Theophylact's biographer faces formidable problems of chronology. The external evidence concerning his life is so scanty that most of its events can only be roughly dated. He was probably born between 1050 and 1060; he tells us himself that he was a native of Euboea; and we may assume that he was born in Chalkis, the main city of this Greek island. It is virtually certain that he bore the surname Hēphaistos.[2] He probably came from a wealthy family: at any rate his parents managed to send him to one of the private schools in Constantinople, where he must have followed the normal course of secondary education—the *enkyklios paideia*, which usually included grammar, rhetoric, and philosophy.[3]

If we can tentatively date Theophylact's arrival in Constantinople to the 1060s, we may assume that in his student days he saw the last phase of the notable intellectual movement which began soon after the death of the Emperor Basil II in 1025, and came to an end during the third quarter of the eleventh century; this marked renewal of interest in teaching and scholarship, especially in the fields of philosophy, rhetoric, and law, let to a further concentration of intellectual life in the capital, spearheaded by a group of outstanding scholars actively engaged in teaching who eventually occupied commanding posts in the state or the Church.[4] The leaders of this learned circle were John Mauropous, the poet and polymath and metropolitan of Euchaita; Constantine Leichoudes, the rhetorician and lawyer, first minister in the reign of Constantine IX Monomachos (1042–55) and later patriarch of Constantinople; John Xiphilinos, the head of the state Law School,[5] which was set up in the 1040s, and

---

[2] P. Gautier, 'L'épiscopat de Theóphylacte Héphaistos, archevêque de Bulgarie', *Revue des études byzantines*, xxi (1963), 165–8; *Théophylacte d'Achrida; Discours, traités, poésies*, introduction, texte, traduction et notes par Paul Gautier (Thessalonica, 1980) (hereafter *Théophylacte d'Achrida*), 12–15.

[3] *Théophylacte d'Achrida*, p. 22. On the education available in Constantinople in Theophylact's time see P. Lemerle, *Cinq Études sur le XIe siècle byzantin* (Paris, 1977), 227–48; cf. id., *Le Premier Humanisme Byzantin*, 100–2.

[4] On this movement see J. M. Hussey, *Church and Learning in the Byzantine Empire 867–1185* (London, 1937); Lemerle, *Cinq Études*, 193–248; M. Angold, *The Byzantine Empire, 1025–1204* (London, 1984), 43–5.

[5] The traditional view that a real university was established (or reopened) in

later Leichoudes' successor as patriarch; and, finally, Michael Psellos, philosopher, historian, orator, and politician, the dominant figure in the intellectual history of the age.

We do not know whether Theophylact ever met Mauropous, Leichoudes, or Xiphilinos,[6] but Psellos was his teacher, and the only master whose influence he explicitly acknowledged. Admittedly the terms in which one of his letters refers to Psellos, though full of praise, are rather vague.[7] But Psellos is known to have taught for a long time in one of the schools of Constantinople, and he died in 1078 or 1096;[8] so it seems likely that Theophylact had been in every sense of the word his pupil.

After finishing his higher studies, Theophylact stayed on in the capital, where he was ordained deacon, attached to the clergy of St Sophia, and appointed *rhētōr*, or teacher of rhetoric, like his teacher Psellos before him. He seems to have been promoted before long, for in one of his letters he tells us that he later became 'chief rhētōr'.[9] He taught for some years in a school dependent on the patriarchate; but this was not a clerical establishment, and many of his pupils became teachers, doctors, soldiers, civil servants, and judges, as well as churchmen. The most eminent was Constantine Doukas, heir presumptive to the Byzantine throne.[10] This prince, son of the former Emperor Michael VII and of a Caucasian princess, Maria of Alania, was entrusted to Theophylact's care, probably in 1084 or 1085, by

Constantinople in 1045 (Hussey, *Church and Learning*, 51–72; G. Ostrogorsky, *History of the Byzantine State* (Oxford, 1968), 328) is increasingly challenged today; see Lemerle, *Cinq Études*, 210; C. Mango, *Byzantium, the Empire of New Rome* (London, 1980), 142–3.

[6] Mauropous is generally believed to have died in 1060. Hussey, however, believes that he may have lived until the early 1080s: *Church and Learning*, 69; ead., 'The Byzantine Empire in the Eleventh Century: some Different Interpretations', *Transactions of the Royal Historical Society*, xxxii (1950), 84. The same view is advanced tentatively by A. D. Karpozilos, Συμβολὴ στὴ μελέτη τοῦ βίου καὶ τοῦ ἔργου τοῦ Ἰωάννη Μαυρόποδος (Ioannina, 1982), 49–50; cf. E. Follieri, 'Canoni paracletici di Giovanni Mauropode', *Archivio italiano per la storia della pietà*, v (1980), 17–19. Leichoudes died in 1063; Xiphilinos was patriarch of Constantinople from 1064 to 1075. See J. M. Hussey, *The Orthodox Church in the Byzantine Empire* (Oxford, 1986), 138–40. Theophylact taught in a school under the patriarchate's jurisdiction, possibly before 1075.

[7] *Théophylacte d'Achrida*, 22–3.

[8] See N. G. Wilson, *Scholars of Byzantium* (London, 1983), 157.

[9] κορυφαῖος ῥητόρων: *Patrologia Graeca* (hereafter PG) cxxvi, cols. 309, 509. In the superscription to one of the medieval manuscripts of the Life of St Clement of Ohrid, its author, Theophylact, is described as μαΐστωρ τῶν ῥητόρων: *Théophylacte d'Achrida*, 24 n. 11. For this function see Darrouzès, *Recherches sur les ὀφφίκια de l'Église byzantine*, 78–9.

[10] See D. I. Polemis, *The Doukai* (London, 1968), 60–3.

the Emperor Alexius I Comnenus. He was then about ten years old, and had just become engaged to Anna Comnena, the new-born daughter of Alexius, who appointed his prospective son-in-law co-emperor: this seemed to assure Constantine's eventual succession to the throne. But in 1087 his hopes were dashed, when Alexius' consort bore him a son, and Constantine's prospects were shifted to the infant John Comnenus. Alexius remained fond of him and he was still engaged to Anna until he died in about 1095. As a further sign of official goodwill, Anna's education was entrusted to his mother, the former *basilissa* Maria of Alania.

By then Maria, a Georgian princess whose physical beauty was later extolled by Anna in lyrical tones,[11] had become a nun. She remained keenly interested in public life, and was not averse to political intrigue.[12] Her relations with Theophylact were friendly and close: later on, when he became archbishop of Bulgaria, he tried to visit her on the island of Prinkipo, but rough seas forced him to turn back;[13] and on another occasion she visited him when he was ill.[14] It was at the *basilissa*'s request that he wrote—probably during his life in Ohrid—his extensive and influential commentaries on the Gospels.[15]

About 1085, while Constantine Doukas was still co-emperor, Theophylact delivered a formal address to his imperial pupil. It was made in the presence of his mother, and this *logos basilikos*, inaccurately known to western scholars as *Institutio regia*,[16] opened on a complacent note: 'I take wing', the orator exclaimed, 'at the thought that I am your teacher, and I grow to the height of ten cubits

[11] *Alexiad*, iii. 2.   [12] *Théophylacte d'Achrida*, 58–67.

[13] PG cxxvi, cols. 501–5.

[14] Ibid., col. 469. See, however, B. Skoulatos, *Les Personnages byzantins de l'Alexiade* (Louvain, 1980), 123 n. 31, who believes that Theophylact's imperial visitor was Irene Doukainē, wife of Alexius I.

[15] PG cxxiii; cf. *Théophylacte d'Achrida*, 66–7. On Maria's relationship with Theophylact see M. Mullett, 'The "Disgrace" of the Ex-Basilissa Maria', *Byzantinoslavica*, xlv (1984), 202–11.

[16] The correct superscription, as its recent editor, P. Gautier, has pointed out, is Λόγος εἰς τὸν πορφυρογέννητον κῦρ Κωνσταντῖνον (*Théophylacte d'Achrida*, 48–67, 178–9). The title under which it has long been known, Παιδεία βασιλική (*Institutio regia*), was a fraudulent invention of its first editor, who in 1650 dedicated his edition to the young king of France, Louis XIV (*Théophylacte d'Achrida*, 48–9). Louis was then about the same age as Constantine had been when Theophylact delivered his encomium and, like Constantine, was under his mother's tutelage. Gautier's critial edition (ibid. 179–211) has superseded Migne's text (PG cxxvi, cols. 253–85). An abbreviated English translation was published by E. Barker, *Social and Political Thought in Byzantium* (Oxford, 1957), 146–9.

when I am called the emperor's tutor.' He waxes lyrical on the marvellous climate of Constantinople—mild in winter and temperate in summer—extols the delicious flavour of the fruit that grows there, then bursts into fulsome praise of the prince's prowess in riding and hunting, but slides rather perfunctorily over his intellectual attainments. A warm panegyric of his mother comes next. In the second, the didactic, part of the *logos* Theophylact discusses different forms of government, contrasting, in true classical fashion, monarchy, aristocracy, and democracy with their counterparts, tyranny, oligarchy, and 'ochlocracy'; and ends up with a list of qualities needed in a true emperor: these include the readiness 'not to yield the first place, even to priests', refusal to consort with actors and other theatre folk, and the practice of the godlike virtue of 'philanthropy'.

At court Theophylact was undoubtedly acclaimed as a master of such rhetorical encomia. His last recorded feat of eloquence, and his greatest, was an address to the Emperor Alexius, delivered most probably on 6 January 1088.[17] This *logos basilikos* glorifies the emperor's military and diplomatic achievements and his services to the Church; it contains valuable evidence on the Empire's relations with its northern foes in 1086 and 1087, the Pechenegs and Cumans, and ends with a panegyric of Alexius' mother. Like Maria of Alania, Anna Dalassena had become a nun, but she still lived in the palace and exerted a powerful influence on the affairs of state.[18]

A year or two later, in the Macedonian town of Ohrid, Theophylact was enthroned archbishop of Bulgaria. The exact date of his nomination is unknown, and has been much debated.[19] Paul Gautier, the most recent editor of Theophylact's writings, dates it to between 6 January 1088—the day of his address to the Emperor Alexius—and the spring of 1092;[20] the most likely dates are 1089 or 1090.

There has been much otiose speculation about why Theophylact was chosen for this post. It has been argued that his appointment by the emperor to this distant archbishopric was a punishment for his friendship with the *basilissa* Maria, allegedly out of favour with

---

[17] The date has been established fairly firmly by Gautier, *Théophylacte d'Achrida*, 68–96.

[18] For the text, see ibid. 215–43; on Anna Dalassena see ibid. 87–96.

[19] See R. Katičić, "Βιογραφικὰ περὶ Θεοφυλάκτου, ἀρχιεπισκόπου Ἀχρίδος", Ἐπετηρὶς Ἐταιρείας Βυζαντινῶν Σπουδῶν, xxx (1960–1), 370–3; Gautier, *L'Épiscopat de Théophylacte Héphaistos*, 159–60.

[20] *Théophylacte d'Achrida*, 29–36.

Alexius I at the time;[21] or that he was chosen as a promising instrument for the Hellenizing of the Bulgarians.[22] These theories, in my view, are wholly without foundation. In the eleventh and twelfth centuries appointment to high ecclesiastical posts in the provinces was often a reward for distinguished service on the patriarchal staff in Constantinople.[23] The Byzantine authorities looked on the see of Ohrid as a key post. Basil II had annexed Bulgaria to the Empire in 1018, and in an attempt to appease the Bulgarians had allowed them to keep several of their cherished national institutions. Chief among these was their Church. In three charters, between 1019 and 1025, the emperor declared the archbishopric of Ohrid (which replaced the Bulgarian patriarchate of the years of independence) to be autocephalous—independent, that is, of the patriarchate of Constantinople; and he placed under its authority all the bishoprics which, in the tenth century, had belonged to the Bulgarian state. These covered a huge area in Macedonia, Albania, Serbia, and northern Greece, as well as central and northern Bulgaria. The archbishop was to be appointed by the emperor, and consecrated by his suffragan bishops: this was both a sure sign of the hold the Byzantine government had now gained over the Bulgarian Church, and a concession to local susceptibilities. Ohrid's autocephalous status was meant as a safeguard against direct interference by the patriarch of Constantinople. Its incumbent ranked high in the hierarchy of the Eastern Church. He won, and held for several centuries, a commanding position in the central and northern Balkans. Theophylact's intellectual gifts and his reputation, enhanced no doubt by his recent address to the Emperor Alexius, fully explain his rapid promotion and appointment to this important see.

Between 1025, the year of Basil II's death, and 1089–90, when Theophylact took up his appointment in Ohrid, many changes had occurred in Bulgaria. Though it retained many of its suffragan

---

[21] Symeon, Metropolitan of Varna and Preslav, *Pismata na Teofilakta Okhridski* (Sofia, 1931), pp. xiv–xviii. Maria could hardly have been out of favour at the time, since the Emperor Alexius entrusted her with the education of his daughter Anna: see *Théophylacte d'Achrida*, 65.

[22] V. N. Zlatarski, *Istoriya na Bŭlgarskata Dŭrzhava prez srednite vekove*, ii (Sofia, 1934), 264–9.

[23] See R. Browning, 'Unpublished Correspondence between Michael Italicus, Archbishop of Philippopolis, and Theodore Prodromos', *Byzantinobulgarica*, i (1962), 279–97; repr. in id., *Studies on Byzantine History, Literature and Education* (London, Variorum Reprints, 1977).

dioceses in Macedonia, Albania, Greece, and central Bulgaria, and on the Danube, the territory of the archdiocese had shrunk.[24] More ominously, Basil II's moderation towards the conquered lands of Bulgaria was abandoned by his successors. Ruthless taxation was launched; and this precipitated a Bulgarian military revolt in 1040, followed in 1072 by another, a more dangerous one, which was supported by the Serbs. This, too, was forcibly suppressed by the Byzantines, and by the time Theophylact arrived in Ohrid the growing disaffection of the Slavs of the Balkan peninsula must have been only too apparent.

Next to the military governor of the province, or 'theme', of Bulgaria, who mostly resided in Skoplje[25], the archbishop was the principal representative of Byzantine authority in the newly annexed land. Though the first incumbent, placed there by Basil II, had been a native Bulgarian, his successors were all Greeks. The first of these, Leo, was appointed about 1037 by Michael IV from among the deacons of St Sophia. He has the melancholy distinction of helping to provoke the schism between the Churches of Constantinople and Rome which broke out in 1054. At the behest of the Patriarch Michael Cerularius, Leo of Ohrid wrote a letter to the patriarchal representative in Italy, to be handed on to the pope and all the bishops of the Western Church. The letter intemperately attacked the Latin Church for its use of unleavened bread in the Sacrament and the custom of fasting on Saturdays.[26] The resulting anger and resentment in Rome stirred up a violent conflict between the two Churches; this culminated in the events of 16 July 1054, when the papal legates laid a bull of excommunication on the altar of St Sophia, in which Leo of Ohrid, alongside Michael Cerularius, was personally named.

It fell to Theophylact, fourth in succession to Leo, to make amends for the self-righteous bigotry of his predecessor. About 1090, or perhaps in 1112, he wrote to a former pupil called Nicholas, who was a deacon of St Sophia, a long reply to the latter's request for a ruling on 'the errors of the Latins in ecclesiastical matters'.[27] It is clear that Theophylact was writing in his capacity as archbishop. He rejected his pupil's claim that these errors were very numerous. Many of the

---

[24] See Theophylact's letter to the bishop of Corfu, PG cxxvi, cols. 388–9.

[25] See G. Litavrin, *Bolgariya i Vizantiya v XI–XII vv.* (Moscow, 1960), 265–93.

[26] *Leonis Bulgariae archiepiscopi epistola de azymis et sabbatis*, PG cxx, cols. 836–44.

[27] Gautier's critical edition (*Théophylacte d'Achrida*, 247–85) has superseded Migne's text (*Liber de iis quorum Latini incusantur*, PG cxxvi, cols. 221–49).

charges made by the Greeks against the Latins, he observed, relating
to minor differences in ritual or custom, were childish and trivial.
Two, the use of unleavened bread in the Sacrament and the Saturday
fast, were rather more serious. But these practices, which his
predecessor Leo had stigmatized with such violence, however repre-
hensible, were in his view not important enough to sunder the body of
Christendom. In both these matters, Theophylact urged, tolerance
and charity were needed.

In his opinion, only one issue was capable, unless resolved, of
causing a schism between the Churches.[28] This was the addition by
the Latins of the *Filioque* clause to the Nicene Creed. The addition
expressed the belief that the Holy Spirit 'proceeds' not from the Father
alone (as the Greek Church, following the oecumenical councils, has
always affirmed) but from the Father and the Son. Since 867, when
the Patriarch Photius denounced Latin missionaries for spreading this
doctrine in Bulgaria, the *Filioque* had been the main bone of
contention between the Eastern and Western Churches.

Theophylact strongly objected to the *Filioque* on two grounds. In
the first place it was an innovation (καινοτομία) introduced into a
creed which 'should be free of the slightest alteration'.[29] Secondly, it
was theologically untrue, for it distorted the true relations between
the Three Persons of the Holy Trinity. Both points had already been
made by Photius, but Theophylact introduced an argument which
had been largely lacking in Photius' anti-Latin polemic.[30] Greek
theologians, arguing against the Latin belief that the Holy Spirit
'proceeds' from the Son as well as from the Father, faced the task of
interpreting the passage in St John where the risen Christ bestows
the Spirit upon his disciples: 'he breathed on them, and saith unto
them, Receive ye the Holy Ghost' (John 20: 22). Theophylact argued
that the Latins, in citing this text in support of their doctrine, were
guilty of a confusion between the eternal 'procession', and the
temporal 'mission', of the Holy Spirit. 'Procession', he points out, 'is
the mode according to which the Spirit has his being from the Father',
while 'the mode of being sent, bestowed, and distributed . . . indicates
an enrichment and an outpouring of a goodness which has its being
in the Father, but which is poured out to those who are worthy from
the Son'.[31] In other words 'procession' (τὸ ἐκπορεύεσθαι) relates to the

---

[28] *Théophylacte d'Achrida*, 247.   [29] Ibid. 251.
[30] Theophylact claimed in this matter to be following no earlier authority: ibid. 261.
[31] Ibid. 255.

fundamental mystery of Trinitarian theology. On this plane the Spirit 'proceeds' eternally from the Father alone. But on the temporal plane the concepts of 'mission' (τὸ πέμπεσθαι), 'bestowal' (τὸ χορηγεῖσθαι), and 'communication' (τὸ μεταδίδοσθαι) relate to the 'outpouring' (χύσις) of grace from the Son. Theophylact maintains that the Latins ignore this essential distinction between eternal 'procession' and temporal 'mission', and returns to it again and again.

But even in this doctrinal matter, on which he would brook no compromise, Theophylact was willing to show a measure of personal understanding. The error of the Latins, he conceded, 'comes not so much from wickedness of judgement as from ignorance of the truth'.[32] They cannot be held wholly responsible for the regrettable confusion between 'mission' and 'procession': it is due to the poverty of Latin vocabulary.[33] If, Theophylact states—without, it seems, a trace of irony—the Latins are really incapable of distinguishing 'procession' from 'communication', and its synonyms, so be it: let them use these various terms as their language allows, provided they accept the creed without the *Filioque*.

At first sight it is surprising that Theophylact has little to say about the other issue which, since the ninth century at least, had loomed large in the polemics between Rome and Constantinople: the papal primacy. He seems to regard it, on the whole, as a kind of corollary of the *Filioque*; and he objects above all to the popes' claim that they have the right to impose this doctrine on the whole Church. On the theoretical aspects of the papal claims, Theophylact is neither clear nor explicit.[34] No doubt, in agreement with most 'liberal' Byzantine churchmen, he recognized that the Roman see had primacy over all other Churches and that the pope was the first bishop in Christendom. This primacy, which the Byzantines never defined precisely, was ascribed by them less to the apostolic origin of the Roman see than to its location in the former capital of the Roman Empire; and also to its record of doctrinal orthodoxy, virtually unblemished. Probably more than a mere primacy of honour, it sometimes implied a recognition by the Byzantines of the right of any cleric condemned by his own

[32] Ibid. 253.

[33] πενία λέξεων καὶ Λατίνου γλώττης στενότητι: ibid. 257.

[34] In his commentaries on the New Testament he interprets the primacy of Peter in the early Church in complete agreement with the Roman position: PG cxxiii, col. 1073; PG cxxiv, col. 309. But he draws no conclusion regarding the later Roman claims to primacy.

Church authorities to appeal to Rome. But they never recognized the privilege, claimed by the medieval popes, of summoning any cleric to the Curia, or of retrying in Rome cases affecting the vital interests of the Eastern Church. Believing that a monarchical government of the universal Church is contrary both to the canons and to tradition, the Byzantines held that doctrinal truth is not expressed through the mouth of a single bishop, however exalted his office, but by the corporate Church, represented by its bishops gathered in council.

Despite his cursory treatment of the Roman claims, there is little doubt that Theophylact implicitly subscribed to this view. In common with his compatriots and contemporaries, he seems to have been unable to develop a coherent doctrinal response to Roman ecclesiology. This is why he attributed the pope's claims to direct jurisdiction over the whole Church to the simple desire to subject all Christians to his authority: with undisguised sarcasm, he declared himself unwilling to accept a teaching as true just because it has been proclaimed from the papal throne: not even if the Latins 'shake the keys of the kingdom in our faces'.[35]

It is clear from the contents of Theophylact's treatise that he did not believe that the Churches of Rome and Constantinople were actually in schism. Provided the Latins 'record a vote in accordance with the laws of the Church Fathers, nothing', he asserted, 'can divide us from the Western Churches''.[36]

Sadly, however, Theophylact admits that few of his compatriots saw things in the same way.[37] Many Byzantines, he complains with bitterness, puffed up with pride, condemn and slander perfectly legitimate Latin usages which differ from the practice of the Byzantine Church. By giving way to 'contentiousness' and 'self-love'[38] these latter-day Pharisees are putting their own souls in danger; and Theophylact solemnly warns them that in excluding their Latin brethren from the Church, they may find themselves excluded from the kingdom of heaven.[39]

Theophylact's conciliatory and generous stance on the divergences between the two Churches has been compared with the position taken on the same issue by his contemporary, Archbishop Anselm of Canterbury.[40] There is indeed a distinct similarity between their

[35] *Theóphylacte d'Achrida*, 275.   [36] Ibid. 279.
[37] Ibid. 247.   [38] Ibid. 271.   [39] Ibid. 281.
[40] See S. Runciman, *The Eastern Schism* (Oxford, 1955), 76–7.

respective attitudes to the principal doctrinal problem. In 1098, at a council convened in Bari by Pope Urban II to settle the differences between the Latin and the Greek Churches of southern Italy and Sicily, Anselm, who was in exile from England, was invited to address the assembly on the *Filioque*. He spoke in calm and measured tones, arguing that by adopting this clause the Latins were not innovating, but merely adding clarity to a doctrine already latent in the creed. He implied that there was no need for the Greeks to add the disputed word to the creed, provided they did not criticize the Latins for doing so. The Greek bishops from Italy and Sicily acquiesced in this position.[41] It is not without interest to the historian of the Christian Church that, about the year 1100, the archbishops of Canterbury and Ohrid, who had never met, professed their belief that despite the bitterness created by the events of 1054, Christendom was still a single body.

Theophylact's rhetorical and theological writings can teach us something about their author, and it is perhaps not too fanciful to detect traces of two distinct tendencies which can also be seen in his life and in his literary works: a natural conservatism of outlook, on the one hand, reinforced no doubt by his career as a rising star in the court and the patriarchal chancery of Byzantium; and, on the other, an ability to achieve a sympathetic understanding of societies and ideologies which were alien to him. The conservative tendency is apparent in the two *logoi basilikoi* addressed to Constantine Doukas and Alexius Comnenus: they follow the conventions of imperial panegyrics traced by his Byzantine predecessors,[42] and not least by his teacher Psellos. The other characteristic, which inspired him with considerable fellow-feeling for western Christians, was far less common in Byzantine society: we might describe it today as a remarkable gift of empathy. Both these tendencies are amply shown in Theophylact's letters.

We possess some 130 published letters of Theophylact written during his tenure of the see of Ohrid.[43] Scholars have combed them for

---

[41] See B. Leib, *Rome, Kiev et Byzance à la fin du XIe siècle* (Paris, 1924), 287–97.

[42] In one respect, however—by laying great stress on military prowess—Theophylact seems to have departed from the traditional ideal of the 'Mirrors for Princes'. See A. Kazhdan and S. Franklin, *Studies on Byzantine Literature of the Eleventh and Twelfth Centuries* (Cambridge, 1984), 39, 108.

[43] Published by Migne, PG cxxvi, cols. 308–557; a critical edition has recently appeared, *Théophylacte d'Achrida: Lettres*; introduction, texte, traduction et notes par

information on a wide variety of subjects: the Byzantine command-structure in Bulgaria; the Empire's fiscal policy in the provinces; the social and economic history of Macedonia; medieval heresies; and the *Who's Who*, as it were, of Byzantine officials. Relatively little attention has been paid to a more personal kind of evidence: few have scrutinized Theophylact's letters for the light they shed on his personality, and on the ways he faced his personal and professional duties.[44] The following pages, without claiming to be exhaustive, may help to fill this gap.

The reader of these letters faces several difficulties. In the first place Theophylact's Atticizing Greek is not made easier to understand by the deliberate obscurity of his style. Relying heavily at times on riddles and enigmas, it owes much to the elliptic manner of contemporary Byzantine letter-writers, and something at least to the 'parabolic-figurative style' prevalent at the time in several European literary genres.[45] Theophylact referred to this manner of writing on several occasions, somewhat unconvincingly disclaiming any intention of following it. The technique 'weaves riddles',[46] 'recounts puzzles',[47] 'speaks in obscure words',[48] and leads his correspondent into the labyrinth where he would need Ariadne's thread to find his way out.[49] The effect of this style is well described by Margaret Mullett:

'Reading one of Theophylact's letters often seems like touching on the edge of a great historical scandal, or like being told a joke so strange that it does not seem funny, or trying to crack a code where the cipher is composed in an alphabet of which only a few characters are familiar'.[50]

Secondly, this 'deconcretization' of the literary material,[51] as a

---

Paul Gautier (Thessalonica, 1986). In Migne's edition the letters are grouped, and separately numbered, within the three collections published earlier by Finetti, Meurs, and Lami. For ease of reference these collections will be cited in the notes as F, M, and L, together with the number of each letter. In reference to Gautier's edition (cited as G) the number of the letter will be followed by that of the page.

[44] A notable exception is the unpublished doctoral thesis of Margaret Mullett, 'Theophylact through his Letters: the Two Worlds of an Exile Bishop' (Birmingham, 1981). The following pages, in which his correspondence is discussed, owe much to her perceptive study, and to her articles concerned with Theophylact (n. 65, 86, 136, 142).

[45] On this style see R. Jakobson, 'The Puzzles of the Igor Tale', *Speculum*, xxvii (1952), 44–5; repr. id., *Selected Writings*, iv (The Hague–Paris, 1966), 380–3.

[46] γρίφους πλέκοντα: M 56, PG cxxvi, col. 473 = G 111: 535.

[47] Ἄρα μή σοι γρίφους κατέλεξα καὶ αἰνίγματα: M 10, col. 376 = G 71: 383.

[48] Εἰ δέ σοι σκοτεινοὺς λόγους λαλῶ καὶ αἰνίγματα: M 36, col. 437 = G 91: 471.

[49] M 10, col. 376 = G 71: 383.   [50] 'Theophylact through his Letters', 19.

[51] For this literary convention see G. Karlsson, *Idéologie et cérémonial dans*

modern scholar has called it, coupled with the fact that we do not possess the other side of Theophylact's correspondence, make the dating of many of his letters exceedingly difficult.[52] In keeping with this abstract convention, he passes over the sometimes earth-shaking historic events of his archdiocese in almost total silence. He barely mentions, and only fleetingly in a single letter, the passage through Ohrid, in the spring of 1097, of the largest army of the First Crusade.[53] His allusions to the appearance in the autumn of 1107, between Lake Ohrid and the Adriatic Sea, of Bohemond, the Norman prince of Antioch, who was preparing to besiege Dyrrachium,[54] are even more opaque. His references to both these Western invasions are highly uncomplimentary.

Sometimes his letters shake off abstract literary convention. Personal feeling, intense and articulate, bursts through both the fashionable rhetoric and the cares of his archdiocese, most strikingly, once, soon after his arrival in Ohrid, in a letter to an anonymous friend in Constantinople, recording his first impressions. Ohrid, on the north-eastern shore of the large mountain-lake of the same name, was not exactly a backwater: for the ancient Lychnidus had a distinguished Roman past, and under Bulgarian rule, in the late ninth century—largely thanks to St Clement—it became an important centre of Slavonic Christianity. At the end of the tenth Ohrid was the capital of Samuel, tsar of the Bulgarians. Under Byzantium, one of Theophylact's predecessors set the crown on its many churches and monasteries by reconstructing the monumental church of St Sophia, which became the cathedral of the archdiocese. Moreover, the Via Egnatia, the Roman road, linked Constantinople, through Thessalonica, Ohrid, and the Macedonian interior, to Byzantium's Adriatic outposts at Apollonia and Dyrrachium, and laid his bishopric open to international traffic.

---

l'épistolographie byzantine: Textes du Xe siècle analysés et commentés (Uppsala, 1962), 14–17; H. Hunger, *Die hochsprachliche profane Literatur der Byzantiner*, i (Munich, 1978), 214, 221.

[52] The most thorough attempt hitherto is by S. Maslev, *Fontes Graeci Historiae Bulgariae* vol. ix: *Theophylacti Achridensis, Archiepiscopi Bulgariae, Scripta ad historiam Bulgariae pertinentia*, part 1 (Sofia, 1974).

[53] Φραγγικὴ διάβασις, ἢ ἐπίβασις: F 11, cols. 324–5 = G 52: 303.

[54] Many, though not all, scholars believe that Bohemond was one of the three monsters by whom Theophylact felt threatened (M 17, col. 389 = G 75: 401); 'Sennacherib the Assyrian' (M 22, col. 397 = G 77: 407); and 'the slave and rebel' (δοῦλος καὶ ἀποστάτης) who plundered the lands to the west of Lake Ohrid (M 65, col. 484 = G 120: 555).

Yet Theophylact was not impressed by his new home, or by its
inhabitants. He had not set foot inside the town, he wrote to his friend,
when he was assailed by 'a deathly stench'. Worse still, the people of
Ohrid greeted their new archbishop with jeers and insults, and
evidently to spite him, sang a 'victory song' in the streets of the city,
pointedly hymning the past glories of independent Bulgaria.[55]

Understandably this unfriendly reception turned Theophylact's
thoughts back to the imperial city he had so recently left, and in the
same letter—one of the very first he wrote from Macedonia—he
yielded to an onslaught of homesickness: 'I have hardly set foot in
Ohrid, but I already long for the city that holds you, like an infatuated
lover'.[56]

Throughout his sojourn in Ohrid this homesickness never left him.
The longing for Constantinople—'the city of the world's desire'[57] for
so many of its exiled or expatriate citizens—runs through Theophylact's correspondence like a constant theme. Occasionally he begged
exalted friends, or acquaintances at court, to release him from the
burden of his office.[58] His visits to Constantinople seem to have been
few and short: only two are recorded in his letters.[59]

Rather than desert his post, Theophylact tried valiantly to exorcize
his agonizing homesickness by sublimation. As an educated Byzantine, he was heir to a long and rich literary tradition; and he drew on it
in his searching for models to give form and expression to his
nostalgia. Two themes in this tradition were particularly relevant to
his predicament: the yearning for Constantinople, a feeling shared by
all Byzantine provincial officials; and recourse to letter-writing as a
spiritual kind of expression of friendship. The first theme was in high
favour in the tenth, eleventh, and twelfth centuries;[60] the second had

---

[55] F 1, col. 308 = G 6: 147 (παιᾱνά τινα ἐπινίκιον); cf. L 2, col. 508 = G 5: 145.

[56] L 2, col. 508 = G 6: 147.

[57] Ἡ κοσμοπαμπόθητος αὐτὴ . . . πόλις: Constantine of Rhodes (10th c.) in *Revue des
études grecques*, ix (1896), 38; ὀφθαλμὸς ἄρα τῆς οἰκουμένης ἐστὶ τὸ Βυζάντιον: M. Psellos,
Scripta Minora, ed. E. Kurtz and F. Drexl, ii (Milan, 1941), 219. On the role of
Constantinople in 11th-c. Byzantine society, see H. Ahrweiler, 'Recherches sur la
société byzantine au XIᵉ siècle: Nouvelles hiérarchies et nouvelles solidarités', *TM* vi
(1976), 99–124.

[58] L 2, col. 508 = G 5: 145; cf. *Théophylacte d'Achrida*, 17.

[59] Zlatarski, *Istoriya*, ii. 511–15. Zlatarski's dating of these journeys (1095 and
1107) has been disputed: see I. Bozhilov, 'Pismata na Teofilakt Okhridski kato
istoricheski izvor', *Izvestiya na Dŭrzhavnite Arkhivi*, xiv (1967), 81–2; Maslev, op. cit.
44.

[60] See Browning, *Unpublished Correspondence*; I. Ševčenko, 'Constantinople Viewed
from the Eastern Provinces in the Middle Byzantine Period', *Harvard Ukrainian Studies*,

remained popular in medieval Byzantium ever since its heyday in the patristic age.[61] A letter to a friend was seen as a spiritual gift, an 'icon of the soul'; it brought with it 'the illusion of presence', and, in a striking and oft-recurring metaphor from Plato, was styled 'the second voyage'[62] the best alternative to actual physical presence. St John Chrysostom gave wide currency to the metaphor;[63] Psellos, too, shared this idealized concept of friendship with his disciple Theophylact.[64]

Though, as far as I am aware, Theophylact used none of these expressions, except the comparison of the letter with a gift, his letters contain more than a trace of this spiritualized concept of friendship. It shows clearly in a letter to his friend the bishop of Corfu: 'If we are orphaned from one another, this is true only of our faces, and not of our hearts: we converse with each other through the mouth of our letters'.[65]

The warmth of Theophylact's friendship is equally apparent in his letters to a certain Nicholas Anemas. This otherwise unknown figure seems to have been an administrator recently posted somewhere, though not to Ohrid, in the archdiocese of Bulgaria.[66] Theophylact could not contain his joy at the news that his friend was not far away. Jubilant quotations jostled each other in his mind: and it is interesting to note that the first two are from Euripides[67] and Aristophanes;[68] the Scriptural quotation, more appropriate no doubt to an archbishop, only comes later: 'My soul doth magnify the Lord.'

Most of Theophylact's letters deal with business matters: requests, instruction, and information. The ones to his suffragan bishops are

---

iii–iv (1979–80), 737–41; repr. in id. *Ideology, Letters and Culture in the Byzantine World* (London, Variorum Reprints, 1982).

[61] See Karlsson, op. cit. 21–138; Hunger, *Hochsprachliche profane Literatur*, i. 224.
[62] Ὁ δεύτερος πλοῦς: *Phaedo*, 99 C–D.   [63] *Epis.* 27 (PG lii, col. 627).
[64] *Epis.* 3 (*Michaelis Pselli Scripta Minora*, ed. E. Kurtz, ii (Milan, 1969), 3). Cf. F. Tinnefeld, 'Freundschaft in den Briefen des Michael Psellos', *Jahrbuch der österreichischen Byzantinistik*, xxii (1973), 151–68.
[65] M 22, col. 397 = G 77: 407. See M. Mullett, 'Byzantium: a Friendly Society', *Past and Present*, forthcoming.
[66] It is not clear whether he belonged to the same family as the four Anemas brothers whose abortive conspiracy against the Emperor Alexius is related by Anna Comnena (*Alexiad*, xii, 5–6). Cf. G 39.
[67] *Orestes*, 211–12: ὦ φίλον ὕπνου θέλγητρον, ἐπίκουρον νόσου,/ὡς ἡδύ μοι προσῆλθες ἐν δέοντί γε. As a concession to Christianity, Theophylact altered ὕπνου to λόγου: M 19, col. 392 = G 32: 237.
[68] *Plutus*, 288: ὡς ἥδομαι καὶ τέρπομαι καὶ βούλομαι χορεῦσαι. Χορεῦσαι is changed to χορεύειν, perhaps because Theophylact is quoting from memory (ibid.).

friendly and paternal in tone, though none of them equals in warmth his letters to the bishop of Corfu.[69] To the patriarch his attitude is deferential: he is grateful for his encouragement and support, thanks him for his gift of twelve pairs of walking-shoes, and begs protection from local tax-collectors who allege that he has a large undeclared income.[70] But on one occasion his relations with the patriarch turned sour. Without consulting Theophylact, the patriarch had given permission to an unnamed monk to open 'a house of prayer' in Macedonia , and the archbishop, who jealously guarded the independence of his Church, regarded this as an uncanonical act and responded angrily. 'What rights has the patriarch of Constantinople in the land of Bulgaria,' he wrote to a high-placed cleric in Constantinople, 'he who has no authority to ordain anyone here, nor any other privilege in this land, which has acquired an autocephalous archbishop?'[71] Theophylact had written, no doubt in more measured tones, to the head of the patriarch's chancellery to protest against this infringement, but had received no reply.[72] The results of this canonical clash are unknown; but it is hard to believe that Ohrid could have prevailed against Constantinople.[73]

Another conflict, which caused Theophylact much annoyance and anxiety, broke out with the bishop of Sofia. This elderly prelate had been bullying the abbot of a monastery in his diocese, and the abbot appealed to Theophylact, who took his side. However, no amount of pressure from the archbishop—even from the emperor himself— could move the stubborn bishop. Summoned to appear before a synod of the bishops of the archdiocese, he declined to attend, on various

---

[69] F 11, cols. 324–5=G 52: 303–5; F 15, col. 336=G 56: 321; F 16, cols. 336–7=G 57: 323–5; M 58, cols. 476–7=G 113: 539; M 66, cols. 485–8=G 121: 559; M 67, col. 488=G 122: 561; L 10, col. 520=G 15: 179–81.

[70] F 4, cols. 313–17=G 45: 281–7; F 13, cols. 329–33=G 54: 313–15. The patriarch was Nicholas III Grammatikos. He too was a learned man: see Lemerle, *Cinq Études*, 232.

[71] M 27, col. 417=G 82: 437.

[72] The letter is not extant. Theophylact mentions it in his letter to the Constantinopolitan cleric (see n. 71).

[73] Theophylact was protesting against the exercise by the patriarch of the prerogative of *stavropēgia*, i.e. the right of founding a monastery in another bishop's diocese and retaining jurisdiction over it. Imperial legislation of the 8th and 9th cc. gave the Byzantine patriarch this right, not only within the dioceses belonging to the patriarchate, but also in those of independent Churches. This right, though sometimes disputed, remained theoretically in force throughout the Middle Ages. In strict canonical terms, therefore, Theophylact's protest was invalid. See Symeon, *Pismata*, 91–3.

specious pretexts. Theophylact then laid his suffragan under an interdict, which was to take effect fifteen days after its receipt; and followed it with a personal letter, roundly rebuking him for the insolence and illiteracy of his letters; he said they were so full of solecisms that school children at the sight of them would split their sides with laughter. The final episode showed the opponents ready for reconciliation. The bishop, claiming to be seriously ill, surrendered. Theophylact wrote to say that he was willing to forgive him, to overlook the fact that he had been hypocritically slandering his archbishop in Constantinople, and to exhort his colleagues to lift the interdict.[74]

Theophylact's relations with the local Byzantine military and political officials, with the prominent ones at least, seem on the whole to have been friendly. No doubt the compliments in his letters are not always disinterested: the most fulsome were reserved for two successive military governors of Bulgaria, stationed at Dyrrachium. The first was John Doukas, the Emperor Alexius' brother-in-law, who was in Dyrrachium when Theophylact arrived in Ohrid, and was recalled to Constantinople in 1092. Theophylact praises his military exploits and, no doubt recalling his own earlier bonds with the family, says that he unites in his person all the virtues of 'the blessed house of Doukas'. In one letter Theophylact solicits unspecified favours for his relatives in Euboea, and in another requests that a Macedonian village near Bitola should return to his jurisdiction.[75] Doukas' successor as governor was John Comnenus, the emperor's nephew. Theophylact's letters to him contain specific and urgent requests: to lift exorbitant taxation from the Albanian bishopric of Diabolis; to end the conscription of infantrymen in the Ohrid region; and to see that the imperial exemption of the priests in the Vardar valley from all dues except land-tax is honestly applied.[76]

---

[74] Theophylact's letters to the bishop of Sofia are found in F 17, cols. 337–44 = G 58: 327–35; F 18, cols. 344–9 = G 59: 337–41; F 19, cols. 349–53 = G 60: 343–9; and M 32, cols. 429–32 = G 87: 457–9. For an account of this affair see Zlatarski, *Istoriya*, ii. 337–46, and G 63–6.

[75] F 2, cols. 309–12 = G 8: 153–5; L 12, cols. 521–4 = G 17: 187–9. The second letter was written after John Doukas had left Dyrrachium. Cf. Polemis, *The Doukai*, 66–70.

[76] L 6–8, cols. 513–17 = G 10: 161, 11: 163–5, 12: 167–9; L 16–18, cols. 529–33 = G 22–4: 203–11. Cf. A. Leroy-Molinghen, 'Prolégomènes à une édition critique des "Lettres" de Théophylacte de Bulgarie', *Byzantion*, xiii (1938), 253–62, and G 48–53.

Theophylact was not averse to sweetening these petitions with modest gifts. These *douceurs* are not necessarily to be thought of as outright bribes—Byzantine letters were often accompanied by presents. Fish was his favourite gift: a Lenten delicacy particularly becoming to an archbishop and a monk. He seems to have sent two consignments to the Caesar Nicephorus Melissenos, lord of Thessalonica: fifty fish, some salted, and some baked inside small loaves of bread;[77] and on another occasion, two hundred little fish, all salted.[78] To the governor and *dux* John Comnenus he sent a hundred salted fish.[79] Small amounts were dispatched to Constantine Doukas, governor of the Vardar region,[80] and to Nicephorus Bryennios, *dux* of Dyrrachium.[81] Some of these were probably the famous trout of Lake Ohrid (*Salmo ohridanus*), which has always been prized by gourmets. Whenever Theophylact mentions the numbers of the fish he is sending, he comments with complacency on their happy symbolism: fifty fish is five times ten, the five senses multiplied by the perfect number,[82] two hundred fish symbolizes the five senses multiplied by the four virtues, and then multiplied by ten.[83]

His letters to Constantinople are more varied and, from the standpoint of this study, more instructive. They are addressed to friends, pupils, colleagues and officials whose patronage he thought important. The most powerful of these were Gregory Kamateros, the head of the imperial chancellery, and Adrian Comnenus, the emperor's brother and commander-in-chief of all Byzantine forces in Europe. To judge from the mixture of fatherliness and respect in Theophylact's address, Gregory was either a former pupil or a spiritual son.[84] The tone is congratulatory: the new governor, appointed through Gregory's good offices, could not be better;[85] a village in the lower Vardar region is in danger of being ruined by the tax-collectors: Gregory is thanked for defending the Church's inter-

---

[77] M 12, col. 380=G 73: 391–3. Nicephorus Melissenos, Alexius Comnenus' brother-in-law, had been his rival for the imperial throne in 1081. Alexius made a deal with him, and ensured his loyalty by granting him the title of Caesar and the lordship over Thessalonica: *Alexiad*, ii. 8. Cf. G 84–6.

[78] L 9, cols. 517–20=G 13: 171–3.

[79] ἰχθύας ταρίχους ἑκατόν: L 8, col. 517=G 12: 169.

[80] μικράν τινα ἰχθύων ἀποστολήν: M 64, col. 481; G 119: 551.

[81] M 50, col. 468=G 105: 521.   [82] M 12, col. 380=G 73: 391–3.

[83] L 9, col. 520=G 13: 173.

[84] Πανυπέρλαμπρέ μοι ἐν Κυρίῳ υἱὲ καὶ αὐθέντη: L 23, col. 537= G 31: 233 (who has δέσποτα). On Theophylact's relations with Gregory, see G 73–9.

[85] M 6, cols. 368–9=G 67: 369–71.

ests, but Theophylact's enemies are sharpening their weapons and trying to persuade the emperor to reverse his decision: so let Gregory beware, and stand fast.[86]

Theophylact's letters, written before 1105, to the Grand Domestic Adrian, deal mainly with the imperial tax-collectors' exactions in Bulgaria, from whom the archbishop sought protection.[87] Bitter complaints against the tax-collectors—*praktores*—constantly recur, and one can hardly fail to sympathize. The stringent fiscal policy of Alexius Comnenus' government, aimed at milking the provinces to the benefit of the capital and compounded by the now regular system of farming out the taxes, weighed heavily on the outposts of the Empire.[88] 'The *praktores*', Theophylact lamented, 'are always robbing us.'[89] One of these, the chief tax-official in Bulgaria, skulks like an evil genius through the pages of his correspondence. His name was Iasites, and he belonged to an aristocratic Byzantine family.[90] Like Theophylact, he had influential friends in Constantinople, and he was able to block the archbishop's efforts to have him removed.[91] The latter owned large estates in Macedonia, and raised a special tax (the *kanonikon*) from all the dioceses under him: this made him fair game for Iasites and his rapacious myrmidons. In a letter to the emperor's son-in-law Theophylact complained with withering sarcasm of the rumours of his alleged wealth that his enemies spread abroad. One of them, he maintained, slandered him to the emperor, stating under oath 'that my roads exude cheese, that milk flows from my

---

[86] L 30, cols. 549–52=G 38: 259–61. See M. Mullett, 'Patronage in Action: the Problems of an Eleventh-century Bishop', in R. Morris (ed.), *Byzantine Church and People* (Manchester, 1987), forthcoming.

[87] M 24, cols. 404–8=G 79: 419–23; M 30, cols. 421–5=G 85: 445–51; M 34, cols. 433–6=G 89: 465–7; M 43, cols. 453–60=G 98: 499–505. Cf. G 44–7.

[88] The view, expressed by Ostrogorsky (*History*, pp. 369–70), that Byzantium had been plagued by a severe financial crisis since the 1070s is being challenged today. See A. Kazhdan and A. W. Epstein, *Change in Byzantine Culture in the Eleventh and Twelfth Centuries* (Berkeley and Los Angeles, 1985), 24–73.

[89] L 29, col. 549=G 37: 255. A grievance, it would seem, not uncommon at the time in the provinces. In the late 12th c. Michael Choniates, metropolitan of Athens, bitterly reproached the authorities of Constantinople for their indifference to the countryside, to which they sent only 'tax-collectors with their bestial fangs': *Tὰ σωζόμενα*, ed. S. Lampros, ii (Athens, 1880), 83. Cited in Kazhdan and Epstein, op. cit. 46.

[90] On the Iasites family see P. Gautier, *Revue des études byzantines*, xxviii (1970), 217–18, xxix (1971), 251; A. P. Kazhdan, *Sotsial'nyi sostav gospodstvuyushchego klassa Vizantii XI–XII vv.* (Moscow, 1974), *passim*.

[91] See in particular M 33, cols. 432–3=G 88: 461–3; L 7, cols. 513–16=G 11: 163–5.

mountains, that . . . I am fabulously rich and live like a satrap . . . and that the royal palaces of Susa and Ecbatana are mere huts compared to the many-storeyed and airy dwellings where I spend my sum-mers.[92] Theophylact was so obsessed by the malignancy of the tax-collectors that, even in lamenting the death of his own brother, he was unable to forget them: 'Who', he wrote in a poem bewailing his departure, 'will [now] restrain the violent onslaught of the *praktores*? Who will close the mouths of these office-frogs?'[93]

It would be wrong to conclude that Theophylact's strife with the tax-collectors sprang only from self-interest. He reserved his most biting anger for their attacks on the property of the Church and their persecution of the defenceless. He openly accused them of 'leading off into slavery one child out of every five',[94] maintained that public officials[95] were held in bondage by Satan, and bade them cease from 'slaughtering and destroying, and robbing parents of their chil-dren'.[96]

The issue of the many battles between Theophylact and the taxmen is unknown, but there is little doubt that he suffered financially and personally from their assaults. This guerrilla warfare may well have undermined his constitution. His health, at least while he was in Ohrid, seems to have been rather poor; he often complained of sickness. He was certainly something of a hypochondriac, for the illnesses of which he complained—gout,[97] sciatica,[98] catarrh, and a dry cough[99]—were scarcely terminal diseases, though they some-times confined him to his bed;[100] and on one occasion he feared the onset of a chest infection.[101]

His interest in symptoms and cures bordered on obsession. To judge from the lively correspondence he carried on with several leading physicians in Constantinople, he possessed a fair amount of medical knowledge.[102] He wrote ten letters—the largest extant number to a

---

[92] M 41, col. 445=G 96: 487.   [93] *Théophylacte d'Achrida*, 377.
[94] F 16, col. 337=G 57: 323.
[95] Οἱ τὰ δημόσια πράττοντες—an expression Theophylact uses repeatedly to designate the tax-collectors: F 15, col. 336=G 56: 321; M 24, col. 405=G 79: 419.
[96] F 15, col. 336=G 56: 321.   [97] F 1, col. 309; G 6: 149.
[98] 'Sciatica is wearing me out', in a poem addressed to Michael Pantechnes: *Théophylacte d'Achrida*, 351.
[99] F 7, col. 321=M 55, col. 472=G 48: 295; 110: 531.
[100] M 48, col. 465=G 103: 517.
[101] M 55, col. 472=G 110: 531.
[102] See J. Kohler, *Der medizinische Inhalt der Briefe des Theophylakt von Bulgarien* (Inaugural-Dissertation zur Erlangung der Doktorwürde in der Medizin, Leipzig, 1918).

single person—to his former pupil, who was one of the emperor's doctors, Michael Pantechnes. He was fond of this pupil who had made his way in the world: he urged him to beware of intriguers at court ('scorpions', as he called them), chided him for neither writing nor visiting him, and promised him a present of some garlic if he would come and see him.[103]

Theophylact's most unforgettable 'medical' letter is addressed to the *magister* John Pantechnes, probably Michael's father.[104] It describes in horrifying detail an attack of seasickness lasting all four days of a sea voyage, probably from Constantinople to Thessalonica. We are spared no gruesome detail: nausea, vomiting, an outflow of saliva and bile, and of an 'undigested and sloppy liquid'.[105] Theophylact was obviously scared of voyages and, given the choice, would have shunned the open sea; he favoured 'just scraping the land with the oars'.[106] More vivid still is his account, on a vain attempt to visit the *basilissa* Maria, of a storm between Nicomedia and the Princes' Islands. The ship was prevented from reaching port by the concerted action of a howling north wind and a 'murderous' one from the south.[107] But in deference, no doubt, to the *basilissa* to whom the letter is addressed, we are spared embarrassing physical details.

Another batch of letters on medical subjects was written to the *archiatros* Nicholas Kallikles, the chief physician of the Emperor Alexius. Several are concerned with the deteriorating health of Theophylact's younger brother Demetrios. Some time between 1097 and 1105, strife with the tax-collectors became so fierce that Theophylact was forced to leave Ohrid for a while and retire to Pelagonia (Bitola). Seeking redress against Iasites, he sent Demetrios on a winter journey to Constantinople with two letters to Nicholas Kallikles.[108] It was probably then that Demetrios contracted the tuberculosis from which he eventually died. Soon afterwards

---

[103] M 47, col. 464=G 102: 515; col. 500=G 129: 583. 'Twelfth-century [Byzantine] writers were continually addressing letters to medical doctors': Kazhdan–Epstein, *Change in Byzantine Culture*, 155.

[104] On Michael Pantechnes see A. Kazhdan, 'The Image of the Medical Doctor in Byzantine Literature in the Tenth to Twelfth Centuries', *Dumbarton Oaks Papers*, xxxviii (1984), 44. Cf. *Théophylacte d'Achrida*, 120.

[105] M 65, col. 484=G 120: 553.

[106] L 1, col. 501=G 4: 139. On the perils of the sea as viewed by Byzantine writers see Kazhdan–Franklin, *Studies on Byzantine Literature*, 263–78.

[107] L 1, cols. 501–5=G 4: 137–41.

[108] M 38–9, cols. 440–1=G 93–4: 477–9. Cf. *Théophylacte d'Achrida*, 17–18; G 69–73.

Theophylact wrote to Nicholas again, with his brother's greetings,
and the news that he was gravely ill.[109] He asked for some books of
Galen and other commentaries on Hippocrates,[110] probably hoping to
trace the causes of the illness. He gave more precise medical details in
a letter to the bishop of Kitros in Pieria. To save Demetrios from the
summer heat in Ohrid, Theophylact had him taken to a village in the
valley of the Vardar. Once there, however, he missed the mountain
air, and the light wine, and the wholesome food of Ohrid; beset with
acute anorexia, headaches, and humours of the stomach, his health
went quickly downhill. The only medicine he could take, and that
very sparingly, was called ὀξυσάκχαρι, probably based on a mixture of
honey and vinegar.[111] He died in Ohrid, probably about 1107.[112]

The relations between the two brothers were clearly very close, but
unfortunately no letters from Theophylact to Demetrios survive.
Demetrios was of great help to his brother, both as a messenger for his
letters, and as an ally against Iasites. Theophylact claimed that he was
loved by the emperor and honoured by the senate and the court,[113]
and his loss was the saddest event recorded in the correspondence. In
a letter to the bishop of Kitros, full of sorrow and discouragement,
Theophylact, writing of his brother, refers to him as 'the breath of my
breath, and everything to me';[114] and it was probably soon after
Demetrios' death that he wrote two poems lamenting him.[115] The
first begins with these lines:

> I long for a sea of tears
> So I may weep for my brother.
> He was a light shining before me
> On my road fated to darkness.

---

[109] M 56, col. 476=G 111: 535. As the wording of this passage shows,
Theophylact's love of classical imagery has once again worsted the expected Christian
phraseology: Ὁ ἀδελφός μου προσαγορεύει σε, ἀλλ' ἐκ τοῦ Ταινάρου, δι' οὗ πρὸς τὸν ᾅδην
κατάγεται.

[110] M 57, col. 476=G 112: 537.

[111] M 58, cols. 476–7; G 113: 539. A. Leroy-Molinghen argues that ὀξύσακχαρ (or
ὀξυσάκχαρι) was identical with, or a substitute for, ὀξύμελι, mentioned by Galen as a
remedy for fever and lung diseases: 'Médecins, maladies et remèdes dans les *Lettres* de
Théophylacte de Bulgarie', *Byzantion*, lv/2 (1985), 491.

[112] See Maslev, *Fontes Graeci Historiae Bulgaricae*, ix/1. 76–7; *Théophylacte
d'Achrida*, 20.

[113] *Théophylacte d'Achrida*, 16–20, 375.

[114] M 66, col. 485=G 121: 559: ἀδελφοῦ τῆς ἐμῆς ἐξηρτημένου πνοῆς καὶ πάντα ὄντως
ἐμοί.

[115] *Théophylacte d'Achrida*, 369–77.

I grope an unlit path
Now death has extinguished him.
Grief like Niobe's
Grips my whole heart.
Were God to turn me to stone
Still would I weep my misfortune:
Time is no healer of grief:
It lasts and remains ever fresh.[116]

These dignified and moving anacreontic verses are among fifteen
poems by Theophylact, composed at various times and for different
occasions;[117] he seems to have been much admired as a poet in his
day.[118] One of his letters describes his efforts to take his mind off the
heat and sirocco of the Ohrid summer by composing iambic verses.[119]
Two poems extol the hymns of the Byzantine mystic St Symeon the
New Theologian:[120] 'Everyone should read this book', he states in the
opening line of one of them. No doubt his enthusiasm for Symeon's
hymns was rooted in his poetic sensitivity and his awareness of
spiritual values. This is revealing: the reader of Theophylact's letters
would not immediately suspect that this busy, worried, and sometimes irascible prelate could find communion of spirit with that great
master of the contemplative life, whose writings bear continual
witness to the vision of divine light.

What we have so far learnt of Theophylact may help us to approach
the central problem of the present inquiry: how did he reconcile the
mission to further Byzantine interests in Bulgaria, with which he was
entrusted by the emperor, with his pastoral duties towards his
Bulgarian flock? How, in other words, was he able to inhabit two such
widely different worlds—Constantinople, the focus of his memories
and longings and the home of his friends, and Ohrid, that remote
Macedonian frontier town where, for reasons of duty, he may well
have been virtually banished for half his life?
    We know that he did not find this easy. His first impressions of
Ohrid, we have seen, were depressing. They did not change very

---

[116] Δακρύων θέλω θαλάσσας/τὸν ἀδελφὸν ὡς δακρύσω,/ὃν ἔχον φάος προλάμπον,/ἐν ὁδῷ
ζόφον λαχούσῃ·/σκότιον τρίβω τὸν οἶμον,/θανάτῳ σβέσιν παθόντος./Νιόβης ἔμοιγε πένθος/
κραδίην ἔχει κατ' ἄκρας·/λάαν ἂν πλάσῃ Θεός με/τὸ πάθος πάλιν δακρύσω·/χρόνος οὐ λύει τὸ
πένθος,/νεαρὸν μένει χρονίζον: ibid. 369.
[117] *Théophylacte d'Achrida*, 347–77.   [118] Ibid. 118.
[119] M 20, cols. 393–6 = G 76: 403–5.   [120] *Théophylacte d'Achrida*, 353–5.

much with the passing of time. He may have preferred the mountain air of Ohrid, and the wine and the food, to the dismal resources of his Vardar village; but the poverty and remoteness of the Ohrid region continued to torment him: 'small and wholly destitute' is how he describes it, 'of all provinces of the Empire the most pitiable'.[121] In size it cannot hold a candle to the wide Pelagonian plain in central Macedonia; and can only be compared to the proverbially puny and boorish isle of Mykonos.[122] Books are hard to get, and at best they reach him only once a year.[123] Even the beauty of Lake Ohrid (Plate 2) leaves him cold: he describes it as a 'lake of ill fortune'.[124] But Theophylact's complaints about Ohrid and its inhabitants are mostly abstract and literary. He compared them, for instance, to frogs among which, like Zeus' eagle, he is condemned to live.[125] In this barbarous land, he wails, reason is worse hated than myrrh by dung-beetles.[126] The people of Ohrid, he declares, adapting an ancient proverb, listen to his song like asses to the lyre.[127] He likens Bulgaria to the barbarian tents of Kedar, mentioned so dismissively in the Psalms.[128] Worst of all, as he admits to his friend Anemas, probably about 1105, through contact with his environment he is becoming a barbarian himself. 'Now that we have lived for years in the land of the Bulgarians', he writes in the same letter, 'the bumpkin way of life has become our daily companion'[129]

This seeming contempt for his surroundings comes out in Theophy-

---

[121] L 18, col. 532=G 24: 209.

[122] L 18, col. 533=G 24: 211. Mykonos already had this unenviable reputation in antiquity. See Athenaeus, *Deipnosophistae*, 1. 7–8; Julian, *Misopogon*, 20. 349 D; 'Plutarch', *Prov.* 1. 17 (*Corpus Paroemiographorum Graecorum*, ed. E. Leutsch and F. Schneidewin, i (Göttingen, 1839), 324). I am indebted for these references to Professor G. W. Bowersock.

[123] L 29, col. 549=G 37: 255.

[124] τὴν ἐνταῦθα τῶν κακῶν λίμνην: F 1, col. 309, L2, col. 509=G 6: 149.

[125] F 1, col. 308=G 6: 147.

[126] F 14, col. 333=G 55: 317. A dung-beetle figures prominently in the opening section of Aristophanes' *Peace*. Line 169 alludes to its inverse relation to myrrh.

[127] F 9, col. 324=G 50: 299. Cf. e.g. Menander, *Misoumenos*, 295, ed. F. H. Sandbach (Oxford, 1972); Lucian, *Adversus indoctum*, 4.

[128] M 35, col. 436=G 90: 469: παρῴκησα μετὰ σκηνωμάτων Κηδάρ. The reference is to Ps. 119: 5 (LXX; 120: AV): Οἴμοι, ὅτι ἡ παροικία μου ἐμακρύνθη, κατεσκήνωσα μετὰ τῶν σκηνωμάτων Κηδάρ. The unflattering parallel is repeated in one of Theophylact's poems: ἡ Κηδάρ, ἡ Βουλγάρων: *Theophylacte d'Achrida*, 349.

[129] M. 21, col. 396=G 34: 243. The terms he uses to describe this lack of refinement are ἀμουσία and ἀγροικία. Theophylact's ἐκβεβαρβαρῶσθαι λέγων . . . ἐν μέσοις Βουλγάροις (ibid.) goes back to Euripides' βεβαρβάρωσαι, χρόνιος ὢν ἐν βαρβάροις (*Orestes*, 485). Cf. Hunger, *Hochsprachliche profane Literatur*, i. 228; Wilson, *Scholars of Byzantium*, 205.

lact's attitude to the local names. With overt snobbery he makes a show of despising all place-names of Slavonic origin. He writes of the chief river of Macedonia, 'the ancient Greeks called it the Axios, and in the new barbarian language it is the Vardar'.[130] His fastidious request to a correspondent not to mock his use of the Slavonic name of a Macedonian town is more disagreeable still.[131] These local names are 'an unpleasantness (ἀηδία), which one has to put up with; one cannot always rejoice in the delightful sound of the Greek.[132] This literary game becomes all the more obvious in the light of Theophylact's readiness to use a 'barbarian name' whenever he feels a professional need to do so.[133]

Not surprisingly, the textbook image of Theophylact as an inveterate Bulgar-hater became solidly entrenched. The strongest champion of this view was the leading Bulgarian medievalist V. N. Zlatarski.[134] He went as far as to argue that the main task laid upon Theophylact by his imperial master was the extirpation of the Bulgarian language and literature from the archdiocese, and the Hellenization of the Bulgarian people.[135]

Our verdict on this matter must be postponed until the concluding pages of this chapter. But a few preliminary remarks will perhaps not come amiss. First, those who emphasize Theophylact's hostility to the Bulgarians base their arguments almost exclusively on the evidence of his letters; they do not always realize that the 'anti-Bulgarian'

[130] M 55, col. 472 = G 110: 531.

[131] M 27, col. 416 = G 82: 435. The town in question is Kichevo, a name he renders as Κίτζαβα.

[132] F 7, col. 321 = G 48: 295.

[133] As he does invariably in the case of his own see, which he calls Ἀχρίς; though he once refers to Lake Ohrid by its classical name Λυχνιδός, comparing it with erudite irony to the Acherusian Lake near the estuary of the Acheron: M 71, col. 497 = G 127: 579. Cf. A. Leroy-Molinghen, 'Trois mots slaves dans les Lettres de Théophylacte de Bulgarie', *Annuaire de l'Institut de Philologie et d'Histoire Orientales et Slaves*, vi (1938), 111–17.

[134] See n. 22. His belief that Theophylact was assigned the task of Hellenizing the Bulgarians was recently revived by A. W. Epstein, 'The Political Content of the Paintings of Saint Sophia at Ohrid', *Jahrbuch der österreichischen Byzantinistik*, xxix (1980), 322–4. Similarly, and in the teeth of all the evidence, J. V. A. Fine, following V. Mošin, *TODRL* xix (1963), 60, asserts that Theophylact 'closed Slavic schools' (*The Early Medieval Balkans* (Ann Arbor, Mich., 1983), 220).

[135] Another frequently quoted anti-Bulgarian outburst of Theophylact is his assertion that 'the Bulgarian nature is the nursery of all evil' (M 41, col. 444 = G 96: 485). These are harsh words, certainly, but they should be read in context. In the letter in question, addressed to the emperor's son-in-law, Theophylact is driven to fury by the knowledge that a group of Macedonian malcontents is ganging up against him in an unholy alliance with the tax-collector Iasites.

ones are a small minority in the collection.[136] Secondly, these
'xenophobic' letters should be interpreted with Theophylact's idiosyn-
crasy in mind, and also the general tradition of Byzantine letter-
writing.

In denouncing the vices of Ohrid, Theophylact often seeks literary,
classical, or biblical parallels. Generally speaking, when ruing his
plight as a foreign exile in Bulgaria, he draws heavily on classical
mythology. In this world of semi-make-believe, where by force of
association the imagery acquires an almost autonomous existence,
Theophylact's enemies appear in the guise of mythological monsters,
while he himself becomes one of the heroic monster-slayers of ancient
times. He hazardously steers between Scylla and Charybdis,[137] battles
with Odysseus' fearsome enemies, the Laestrygones and the Cyc-
lopes,[138] and slashes away at the ever-multiplying heads of the
Lernaean Hydra;[139] he becomes Tantalus, condemned to thirst and
hunger for ever,[140] and Herakles, toiling as a slave for Omphale, the
Lydian queen.[141]

It has been observed[142] that these classical allusions and reminis-
cences are generally reserved for the inner circle of his correspondents: his intellectual equals and companions, that is, and pupils,
colleagues, and intimate friends. In writing to them in this vein,
consciously or not, he probably had several aims in view. The ancient
world and its intimations of a golden age were a means of escape from
the drabness of every day; the classical imagery made manifest the
links between Theophylact and his Constantinopolitan friends by
pointing to their common education and to the 'old boy network' that
still bound them together; and dangling before them, with a virtuosity
that would not have disgraced his teacher Psellos, these well-worn
fragments of the ancient world, he could show his friends that in exile
he had not forgotten the intricate rules of the game, and at the same
time reassure himself that he was not really about to become a

---

[136] They number no more than about ten (out of a total of some 130 letters): Cf. M.
Mullett, 'Byzantium and the Slavs: the Views of Theophylact of Ochrid', forthcoming.
[137] L 22, col. 537=G 30: 229; L 23, col. 540=G 31: 233.
[138] M 8, col. 372=G 69: 377.   [139] M 30, cols. 424–5=G 85: 449.
[140] M 21, col. 396=G 34: 243.   [141] L 2, col. 505=G 5: 143.
[142] By Margaret Mullett, op. cit. 174–6; see ead., 'The Classical Tradition in the
Byzantine Letter', in M. Mullett and R. Scott (eds.), *Byzantium and the Classical Tradition*
(University of Birmingham, Thirteenth Spring Symposium of Byzantine Studies, 1979
(Birmingham, 1981)), 93; ead., 'Aristocracy and Patronage in the Literary Circles of
Comnenian Constantinople', in M. Angold (ed.), *The Byzantine Aristocracy: Ninth to
Thirteenth Centuries* (Oxford, 1984), 173–201.

barbarian. The psychological value of mythological fantasies is not a proper subject for the present study; but we can conclude that Theophylact indulged in them freely, and that they helped him bridge the chasm between the worlds of Constantinople and Ohrid. His outlook is unlikely to have differed very much from that of countless others who served their empires abroad.

Another tradition, as well as classical mythology, gave form and substance to Theophylact's feeling of estrangement from his Slav surroundings. The disdain for his Bulgarian flock that a few of his letters express stemmed in no small measure from the literary conventions of the time. Many a Byzantine mandarin serving in outlying regions felt driven by the rigours of provincial life to contrast his rude surroundings with the distant delights of Constantinople. In the eleventh and twelfth centuries this attitude was widespread among provincial bishops. One of them, John Mauropous, the metropolitan of Euchaita in northern Asia Minor, wrote repeatedly to his pupil Michael Psellos of his longing to return to the capital.[143] Another, Michael Choniates, the learned metropolitan of Athens, was so cast down by the discovery of how far short his demotic-speaking peasant flock fell from his shining vision of the ancient Greeks, that he wrote these remarkable words: 'I am becoming a barbarian by living a long time in Athens.'[144] When these men dwelt among non-Greek populations, their feelings of loneliness were all the greater. Isolation and longing made them take up their pens, and their letters to colleagues and friends who had the good fortune to live in Constantinople tended to echo the tradition of idealized friendship which has been noted above. Theophylact was no exception; and when we consider the unflattering references to the Bulgarians in a few of his letters, it is well to remember this.

We have seen that these anti-Bulgarian outbursts cannot merely be due to a simple dislike of the Slav society he lived in. Some at least were due to administrative exasperation, cultural snobbery, or literary fashion. They do not take us very deep into his thought-world. We can hope to penetrate further, and perhaps move towards a clearer

---

[143] See Hussey, *Church and Learning*, 69; E. Follieri, op. cit. 12.

[144] βεβαρβάρωμαι χρόνιος ὢν ἐν ᾿Αθήναις: Michael Choniates (Acominatus), *Works*, ed. S. Lambros, ii (Athens, 1880), 44. Cf. Wilson, *Scholars of Byzantium*, 204–5; Mullett, 'The Classical Tradition', 92. The reference, as in Theophylact's letter cited above (see n. 129) is to Euripides (*Orestes*, 485).

understanding of the relationship between his two worlds, by considering two other works, both of them hagiographical, which he wrote during his episcopate.

The first is the 'Long Life' of St Clement of Ohrid, frequently referred to in the first chapter of this book. It is the chief source of our knowledge of Clement's life between the death of Methodius in 885 and his own in 916. Theophylact's authorship of this work has sometimes been disputed; so it seems fitting briefly to rehearse the main arguments which, in my view, establish beyond reasonable doubt that the 'Long Life' of Clement was indeed written by Theophylact.[145]

These arguments are three: they relate to the manuscript tradition; the textual parallels between the 'Long Life' and other writings of which Theophylact is indubitably the author; and chronological evidence, which points to his lifetime as the period when the work was written.

Of the nine manuscripts of the 'Long Life' which we know, only three contain the full text; they are independent of each other, and in all three Theophylact is cited in the superscription as the author. Of the six remaining manuscripts, all of them fragmentary, five are anonymous, and the sixth cites Theophylact as the author. More compelling still is the argument from textual parallels: close similarities exist, in the passages dealing with the *Filioque*, between the Life of Clement on the one hand, and Theophylact's treatise on the errors of the Latins and his commentary on St John's Gospel, on the other. Moreover, in the Life, Clement and his companion Gorazd used the same key argument in their disputation with the Franks in Moravia—that the Latins confuse 'procession' and 'mission'—as the one Theophylact put forward in his theological writings.[146] These textual parallels and similarities of content are too close and numerous to be fortuitous: they clearly point to Theophylact as the author of Clement's biography. Finally, several references to historical events in this work settle the time of writing as the late eleventh or early twelfth century.[147]

---

[145] I have developed these arguments in my article 'Theophylaktos of Ohrid and the authorship of the *Vita Clementis*', in *Byzantium: Tribute to Andreas N. Stratos*, ii (Athens, 1986), 601–18.

[146] See above, pp. 42–3.

[147] Particularly the impression conveyed by the text that the days of Boris of Bulgaria (d. 907) belong to the remote past, and the fairly transparent reference in the concluding lines of the work to the Pecheneg invasions of the Balkans in the late 11th c. Even so hardened a sceptic as P. Gautier, who will not accept that Theophylact was the

However, several passages of the 'Long Life' must have been written long before Theophylact's time, and they betray the hand of an early Bulgarian disciple of Clement. It is generally accepted that the existing Greek text has incorporated these and possibly other passages from this earlier biography composed in Old Church Slavonic soon after Clement's death in 916, which has not come down to us. We do not know whether Theophylact learnt either Old Church Slavonic or indeed vernacular Bulgarian. If he did not, he could have had the text of the earlier Life of Clement translated for him by one of his staff in Ohrid; there must have been many such translators in the administrative heart of the archbishopric.

Theophylact's Long Life of Clement opens with a panegyric of Clement's teachers Constantine-Cyril and Methodius. These Byzantine missionaries to the Slavs are exalted as 'blessed fathers and teachers',[148] and saints.[149] Pope Hadrian II is said to have felt towards them as Moses felt towards God.[150] Methodius, no doubt because he was Clement's personal teacher, is given pride of place, and he is dignified several times with the epithet 'great'.[151] It is possible, though not certain, that Theophylact used the ninth-century Old Church Slavonic biographies of Cyril and Methodius;[152] but he certainly had other sources at his disposal, for he relates a number of facts which are not to be found in the *Vita Constantini* or the *Vita Methodii*.[153]

One of these sources at least must have been of local Bulgarian

author of the *Vita Clementis*, believes that it was written in Ohrid in the 11th or 12th century: 'Deux œuvres hagiographiques du pseudo-Théophylacte' (Thèse de Doctorat du 3ème cycle, Université de Paris, Faculté des Lettres et Sciences Humaines, Sorbonne, 1968), 35. Gautier's thesis is still unpublished.

[148] *Vita*, i. 3 (Tunitsky, 68; Milev, 78; ET 94).

[149] *Vita*, iii. 10; iv. 16 (Tunitsky, 74, 81; Milev, 82, 88; ET 96, 99).

[150] *Vita*, iii. 9 (Tunitsky, 72; Milev, 82; ET 95).

[151] Ὁ μέγας Μεθόδιος: *Vita*, iii. 10; iv. 15; v. 17 (Tunitsky, 74, 80, 82; Milev, 82, 88, 90; ET. 96, 98, 99).

[152] The problem has been much debated. See S. Maslev, 'Zur Quellenfrage der Vita Clementis', *Byzantinische Zeitschrift*, lxx (1977), 310–15. Maslev regards the view that Theophylact used these biographies as unproven. Gautier ('Deux œuvres hagiographiques', 154–8) considers it improbable. Those who believe that he did make use of them include Dvornik, *Byzantine Missions*, 245.

[153] Such as the names of the principal disciples of Cyril and Methodius; the *Filioque* controversy; the account of King Svatopluk's dealings with Methodius' disciples; and the fact that on his death in Moravia Methodius left two hundred, presumably Slav-speaking, clerics whom he had trained: *Vita*, ii. 7; vi. 22; viii. 25–8; ix. 29–34; xi. 34.

origin. When describing Methodius' efforts to teach Christianity to Rastislav of Moravia and Kotsel of Pannonia, Theophylact states that Methodius 'had previously made Boris, king of the Bulgarians, who lived in the reign of Michael [III], emperor of the Rhomaioi, his [spiritual] child . . . and continually lavished upon him the bounty of his words.[154] Neither the ninth-century biographers of Cyril and Methodius, nor any other early medieval source, so much as mention any personal contact between them and Boris. Clement himself, in his encomium of St Cyril, written in Bulgaria from first-hand knowledge, says nothing about it.[155] Surely, had such a connection existed, he would have mentioned it.

Theophylact is the first known author to have claimed that Methodius baptized and instructed King Boris. He implies that this occurred before the Moravian mission, that is, before 863.[156] This claim, which is at variance with the earliest authentic evidence on the lives of the two brothers, should be seen as an unhistorical attempt to annex the work of Cyril and Methodius to the Bulgarian national tradition. Similar claims were to be made with growing frequency by Bulgarian writers of the thirteenth and fourteenth centuries. In an official document of the Bulgarian church, the *Synodicon of the Tsar Boril*, drafted in 1211, Cyril is said to have translated the Christian scriptures 'from the Greek into the Bulgarian language' and to have 'enlightened the Bulgarian people'.[157] From here there was only a step to claiming that Cyril and Methodius were Bulgarians by birth. It was taken *c.* 1300 by the anonymous Bulgarian author of the abbreviated biography known as 'The Dormition of St Cyril'.[158]

Theophylact does not go as far as to describe Cyril and Methodius as Bulgarians, However, by designating Old Church Slavonic, the language of Cyril and Methodius, as 'the Bulgarian language',[159] he

---

[154] *Vita*, iv. 15 (Tunitsky, 80; Milev, 88; ET 98).

[155] *Sŭbrani sŭchineniya*, i (Sofia, 1970), 426–8. See also above, p. 32.

[156] Byzantine sources make it clear that Boris was baptized by priests sent from Constantinople in 864 or 865: see Zlatarski, *Istoriya*, 1/2 27–32.

[157] See A.-E. Tachiaos, 'L'origine de Cyrille et de Méthode. Vérité et légende dans les sources slaves', *Cyrillomethodianum*, ii (Thessalonica, 1972–3), 136. The medieval sources and the principal modern works relating to Cyril and Methodius are discussed in this valuable study. Unaccountably, however, the author fails to mention Theophylact.

[158] Ibid. 133–4.

[159] *Vita*, ii. 7; xxii. 66 (Tunitsky, 70, 124–6; Milev, 80, 132; ET 95, 118). The term 'Bulgarian language' (ἡ Βουλγαρικὴ γλῶττα) is balanced, however, by the expression 'Slavonic letters' (τὰ Σθλοβενικὰ γράμματα: *Vita*, ii. 7).

took a further step towards meeting the growing nationalism of his Bulgarian flock. The earliest works of the Cyrillo-Methodian tradition, not least the *Vita Constantini* and the *Vita Methodii*, are remarkable for their cosmopolitan outlook: the mission of the two brothers is seen to be directed to all the Slav peoples. In this ideological shift from the broad horizons of the ninth-century Cyrillo-Methodian writings to the more confined, nationalistic position of fourteenth-century Bulgarian authors Theophylact's biography of Clement represents an intermediate stage. The sources of the 'Bulgarophile' elements he inserted into his biography are unknown. They were almost certainly literary; and, because of the nascent nationalism they reveal, they must have arisen considerably later than the putative Old Church Slavonic biography of Clement, which, as we have seen, was probably written in the first half of the tenth century.

There is no reason to doubt that Theophylact's assertion that Boris was baptized by Methodius was made in good faith. His opinion of Boris, Clement's patron, was understandably high. He describes him as 'holy'[160] and 'of sound judgement, and receptive to the good',[161] and terms him 'God's true lieutenant-commander'.[162] He praises him for building seven cathedral churches in his realm,[163] a statement he repeats in a letter to John Comnenus, the military governor of Bulgaria.[164] What is more surprising is his positive, though more restrained, assessment of Boris's son Symeon, Byzantium's deadly enemy. It is true that he confines himself to the rather perfunctory opinion that Symeon inherited his father's 'goodness of heart',[165] and to an account of his friendly relations with Clement.[166] Most probably Theophylact found these value-judgements on Boris and Symeon in one of his Bulgarian sources, perhaps in Clement's Old Church Slavonic biography. What is significant is that he incorporated them into his own work.

Yet not everything in the *Vita Clementis* shows the Bulgarians in a favourable light. In describing the testamentary dispositions made by

[160] *Vita*, xix. 60 (Tunitsky, 120; Milev 128).

[161] *Vita*, iv. 16 (Tunitsky, 80; Milev, 88; ET 98).

[162] *Vita*, xvii. 53: Ὁ τοῦ Θεοῦ ὄντως ὑποστράτηγος (Tunitsky, 116; Milev, 124). The epithet ὑποστράτηγος is doubtless intended to distinguish Boris-Michael from his heavenly namesake and patron, the Archangel (ἀρχιστράτηγος) Michael.

[163] *Vita*, xxiii. 67 (Tunitsky, 126; Milev, 132; ET 119).

[164] L 16, PG cxxvi, col. 529 = G 22: 205.

[165] χρηστότης: *Vita*, xix. 60 (Tunitsky, 120–2; Milev, 128; ET 116).

[166] *Vita*, xx. 61; xxv. 71–2 (Tunitsky, 122, 131–2; Milev, 128, 136–40; ET 116, 120–2).

Clement shortly before his death (he left half his belongings to his diocese and the other half to his monastery in Ohrid), Theophylact tells us that he had acquired his property from local princes and tsars. Clement, he says, had accepted these gifts for fear of discouraging the royal donors by a show of indifference, 'especially as they were by nature comparatively barbarian'.[167] Here, for a brief moment, we recognize the Theophylact we have come to know from some of his letters: the scholar from the capital, proud of his superior Byzantine culture, and whose very admiration of the ancient Christian rulers of Bulgaria was tinged with condescension. Condescension turns into contempt in his references to the Bulgarian subjects of Boris and Symeon: 'wholly ignorant and beast-like' is his verdict[168]; and he also applies the second of these epithets to many Bulgarian priests of their time, who were scarcely able to read Greek.[169]

The reader who has absorbed the evidence and followed the argument presented so far in this chapter will probably have concluded that Theophylact's attitude towards his Macedonian environment and the Bulgarians in his spiritual care was ambiguous to a marked degree. For all his distaste for their rustic manners—some of it genuine, the rest a concession to literary fashion—he defended them with vigour when roused by administrative cruelty or injustice. He pined for Constantinople, his *alma mater*; perhaps he regarded his Ohrid appointment as a perpetual exile; yet he seems to have been highly conscientious in his pastoral duties. In his Life of St Clement, despite signs of a squeamish attitude towards the unsophisticated Bulgarians, he does not hide his admiration for the founders of their vernacular Christian culture.

How are we to explain this ambiguity? Did its causes lie in Theophylact's personal attitudes: in his intelligence, perhaps, which made him understand the need to conciliate the Bulgarians by concessions to their national susceptibilities? In his sense of natural justice, which led him to sympathize with the victims of an inhuman fiscal policy? Or in his strong and energetic character, which made him prefer the role of a conscientious and efficient administrator to that of an *évêque fainéant*? There may be an element of truth in each of these suggestions. Yet none of them seems sufficient to account for the

---

[167] καὶ μάλιστα πεφυκότας βαρβαρικωτέρους: *Vita*, xxvi. 74; (Tunitsky, 134; Milev, 140).

[168] *Vita*, xxi. 63 (Tunitsky, 124; Milev, 130; ET 117).

[169] *Vita*, xxii. 66 (Tunitsky, 124; Milev, 132; ET 118). See also above, p. 31.

apparent ease with which a man of Theophylact's background and prejudices could accept and identify himself with certain essential features of this alien culture. What was the secret of his strange adaptability?

It seems likely that a crucial event in Theophylact's intellectual and spiritual development was his encounter, while *en poste* in Ohrid, with the Cyrillo-Methodian tradition. Several features of this tradition have been described in the first chapter of this book. It will be recalled that Cyril and Methodius, the founders of the tradition, by inventing a Slavonic alphabet and translating the Greek liturgy and scriptures, created a new literary language modelled on Greek and, at this period, intelligible to all the Slavs. This language, Old Church Slavonic, a common patrimony of those peoples who gained entry into the Byzantine cultural commonwealth, became a channel which ensured a regular flow of influence from the Greek-speaking world; it was a potent cultural bond between Byzantium and the Slavs. It provided the Orthodox Slavs (and later the Rumanians as well) with an international medium for worship, writing, and literature; and through the work of Cyril and Methodius and Clement and their disciples, it became the foundation of a cultural tradition in which Greek and Slav elements were in some measure blended.

From its beginnings in the ninth century the Cyrillo-Methodian tradition acquired a coherent ideology. This ideology, which Roman Jakobson did so much to describe and analyse,[170] was founded on the belief that all languages are equal in the sight of God, and on the cognate notion that a language which serves as a medium for the Christian liturgy becomes thereby a sacred one. Hence every people which acquires a sacred tongue is raised to the status of a nation consecrated to the service of God, with its own legitimate place and particular mission within the family of Christendom.

This ideology was eloquently proclaimed in the early works of Cyrillo-Methodian literature. The masterpieces of the literature—the ninth-century Lives of Constantine-Cyril and Methodius, Constantine's poetic Prologue to his translation of the Gospels, and the Russian Primary Chronicle—seem to have been widely read by educated Slavs in the early Middle Ages. After Methodius' death in 885 and the collapse of his work in Moravia, the Bulgarians salvaged this heritage and, in the following century, made the major

[170] See, in particular, several studies recently republished in his *Selected Writings*, vi. 1 (Berlin–New York–Amsterdam, 1985).

contribution to the Cyrillo-Methodian tradition. The Ohrid scriptorium founded by Clement became the direct heir to the Moravian Old
Church Slavonic school. At the other end of the country, in north-
eastern Bulgaria, the same literary tradition was cultivated at the
capital, Preslav. The leading writers of the Preslav school were
Constantine the Priest (later bishop, whose acrostic Alphabetic
Prayer, together with Cyril's Prologue, is the outstanding example of
the earliest Old Church Slavonic poetry), and the monk Khrabr,
author of a remarkable apologia for the Slavonic alphabet. These
authors, who wrote in the late ninth and early tenth centuries, were
fervent exponents of the Cyrillo-Methodian ideology and devoted
disciples of this tradition's founders.[171] Two centuries later, writing in
the style of St Clement, whose distant successor he was, Theophylact
could draw on a rich tradition of Cyrillo-Methodian literature. To gain
access to it he did not need to know Church Slavonic: all he required
was the services of a competent translator.

The Life of St Clement contains several clues which suggest that
Theophylact admired the Cyrillo-Methodian tradition and was willing
in some measure to identify himself with it. A few examples will
illustrate this gift of empathy.

The word—*logos, slovo*—conceived as the 'source of man's ration-
ality and of his communion with God'[172] is a central concept in this
tradition. Cyrillo-Methodian writers applied this notion to divine
truth apprehended through the use of vernacular languages, and
they held that the Slavs, by acquiring the liturgy and the scriptures in
their mother-tongue, received the 'word', the gift that enabled them
to understand and proclaim the true faith. Nowhere is the sacred
value of the *logos*, thus understood, proclaimed with more eloquence
and force than in St Cyril's poetic Prologue to his translation of the
Gospels. One of its passages reads: 'Then hear now with your own
mind, listen, all you Slavs: hear the Word, for it came from God, the
Word which nourishes human souls, the Word which strengthens
heart and mind, the Word which prepares all men to know God'.[173]
The semantic and mystical link between the 'word', signifying the
sacred vernacular tongue, and the incarnate Word or *Logos*—that is

---

[171] See G. Soulis, 'The Legacy of Cyril and Methodius to the Southern Slavs',
Dumbarton Oaks Papers, xix (1965), 19–43; Vlasto, *The Entry of the Slavs into
Christendom*, 168–79.

[172] *A Patristic Greek Lexicon*, ed. G. W. H. Lampe (Oxford, 1961), s.v. λόγος II. D.

[173] R. Jakobson, *Selected Writings*, vi/1. 194.

Christ himself—is revealed several times in the *Vita Clementis*. In evoking the solemn moment when the pope, having given his blessing to the translations of Cyril and Methodius, offers up the Slavonic books on the altar of one of the churches in Rome, Theophylact comments: 'What is more pleasing to the Word than the word which releases intelligent beings from unintelligibility, since like rejoices in like?'[174] And he makes the same point in another passage of alliterative verbal play, suggesting—in common with the author of the *Vita Constantini*—that St Clement of Rome, whose putative relics the two brothers had brought back from the Crimea, was the supernatural patron of their mission to the Slavs: 'The philosopher [St Clement] receives the philosopher [St Cyril], the great teacher takes to himself the voice of the word, the tutor of nations receives in his dwelling him who enlightened the nations with the light of know-ledge.[175]

This is a far cry from the notion we find in other passages of the *Vita Clementis* that the principal beneficiaries of the work of Cyril and Methodius were the Bulgarians. In common with the earliest and most authentic spokesmen of the Cyrillo-Methodian tradition, Theophylact is aware of the universal dimension of the work of the apostles to the Slavs. The same cosmopolitan spirit breathes in other judgements by Theophylact. The two brothers are represented in the Cyrillo-Methodian tradition as the heirs of St Paul, the apostle of the Gentiles.[176] According to his *Vita*, Constantine-Cyril, when defending in Venice the fundamental equality of all languages, quoted from St Paul's First Epistle to the Corinthians, and the text was used as an ideological manifesto by the champions of the Slav vernacular tradition.[177] Theophylact repeatedly states that Cyril and Methodius imitated St Paul.[178] This, he shows, was also true of Clement; he became 'a new Paul to the new Corinthians, the Bulgarians'.[179]

---

[174] Τὶ γὰρ τῷ λόγῳ λόγου τοὺς λογικοὺς ἀλογίας λυτρουμένου τερπνότερον, εἴπερ τῷ ὁμοίῳ τὸ ὅμοιον ἥδεται; *Vita*, iii. 9 (Tunitsky, 74; Milev, 82; ET 96). I. Duichev has traced the source of the second part of Theophylact's sentence back to two passages in the book of Ecclesiasticus: Πᾶν ζῷον ἀγαπᾷ τὸ ὅμοιον αὐτῷ: 13: 15; ἑταῖρος φίλου ἐν εὐφροσύνῃ ἥδεται: 37: 4 (ET 96). But see also, as Professor Hugh Lloyd-Jones pointed out to me: ὡς αἰεὶ τὸν ὁμοῖον ἄγει θεὸς ὡς τὸν ὁμοῖον: *Odyssey* 17. 218.

[175] Δέχεται τὸν φιλόσοφον ὁ φιλόσοφος, ὁ μέγας διδάσκαλος τὴν τοῦ λόγου φωνὴν προσλαμβάνεται, ὁ τῶν ἐθνῶν καθηγητὴς τὸν τοῖς ἔθνεσι φωτίσαντα τὸ φῶς τῆς γνώσεως εἰσοικίζεται: *Vita*, ii. 11 (Tunitsky, 76; Milev, 84; ET 97).

[176] Jakobson, op. cit. 109.

[177] *VC* xvi. 21–58, citing 1 Cor. 14 (Grivec-Tomšič, 135–6).

[178] *Vita*, iii. 8, 9; vi. 22 (Tunitsky 70, 74, 88; Milev, 80, 82, 94; ET 95, 96, 101).

[179] *Vita*, xxii. 66 (Tunitsky, 126; Milev, 132; ET 118).

Another feature of the Cyrillo-Methodian tradition, which we find in works written by its followers in the early Middle Ages, was the belief that the late entry of the Slavs into the Christian community was no sign of inferiority: rather was it to be seen in the light of the parable in St Matthew's Gospel (20: 1–16) of the householder who went out early in the morning to hire labourers to work in his vineyard: those who were hired at the eleventh hour received the same wages as those who from the beginning had 'borne the burden and heat of the day'. In like manner Theophylact, in his account of the Bulgarians' conversion to Christianity, stated that they came to know Christ, 'although they entered the divine vineyard late in the day, around the eleventh or twelfth hour'.[180]

A final example of Theophylact's sensitive awareness of the basic themes of Cyrillo-Methodian apologetics takes us into the field of scriptural exegesis. An idea that runs through Cyrillo-Methodian literature is that the invention of the Slav letters was an extension of the miracle of Pentecost, when the Holy Spirit descended in tongues of fire upon Christ's apostles, and they all 'began to speak with other tongues, as the Spirit gave them utterance' (Acts 2: 4).[181] Theophylact used the same Pentecostal image; he tells us that Cyril and Methodius, before inventing the Slavonic alphabet, 'turned to the Comforter, whose first gifts are the tongues and the help of the word'.[182]

The Cyrillo-Methodian legacy, both in its original 'pan-Slav' form and in its later 'Bulgarophile' version, provided Theophylact with an ideological basis and justification for his attempt, through his writings, to bridge the gulf between the worlds of Constantinople and Ohrid. Slavonic in form, and much of it Greek in content, this legacy proved to be the most lasting of bonds between Byzantium and the Slavs. It is within the context of this bicultural, Graeco-Slav literary tradition that Theophylact's Life of St Clement can best be understood.

The same eagerness to enhance the status of his archdiocese by

---

[180] Vita. iv. 16 (Tunitsky, 82; Milev, 88; ET 99); cf. D. Obolensky, 'Cyrille et Méthode et la christianisation des Slaves', in La conversione al Cristianesimo nell'Europa dell'alto medioevo (Settimane di studio del Centro italiano di studi sull'alto medioevo, xiv, Spoleto, 1967), 604–5. Reprinted in the same author's Byzantium and the Slavs: Collected Studies (London, Variorum Reprints, 1971).

[181] Jakobson, op. cit. 109.

[182] Πρὸς τὸν Παράκλητον ἀποβλέπουσιν, οὗ πρῶτον δῶρον αἱ γλῶσσαι καὶ τοῦ λόγου βοήθεια: Vita, ii. 6 (Tunitsky, 70; Milev, 80; ET 95).

uncovering its early Christian roots and by painting the history of the Bulgarian church on a wide historical canvas is apparent in Theophylact's second hagiographical work. It is entitled, in the superscription to the sole surviving medieval manuscript, 'The martyrdom of the holy and glorious Fifteen Martyrs of Tiberiopolis, called Strumitsa in Bulgarian, martyred in the reign of the impious Julian the Apostate'.[183] It was published in the last century by Migne. In 1968 Paul Gautier prepared a critical edition, which is still unpublished.[184]

This comparatively little known work is of considerable interest. To the ancient historian, to the student of the medieval Balkans, and even (as we shall see) to the art historian it can still offer new material; it is no less important to the student of Theophylact. Its ideological similarities to the Life of St Clement are striking. We have seen that in the Life of Clement Theophylact attempted to place the history of Christian Bulgaria within the context of the Cyrillo-Methodian tradition. In the *Martyrion* (or *Passio*) his aim was similar, but more ambitious: it was to graft the history of his archdiocese, personified by the cult of its local saints, on to some of the earliest Christian traditions of the Roman Empire. A brief summary of the contents of this work should make his intentions clear.

The *Martyrion* opens with a lengthy historical preamble based on several ancient authors, chiefly the fifth-century church historian Socrates, and covers the reigns of Constantius I, Constantine the Great, and Constantius II. Then we come to Julian; we are told of his youth, his education, his pagan sympathies, his accession to the imperial throne (AD 361), and his persecutions of the Christians. At this point Theophylact takes leave of ancient guides and begins to

---

[183] Μαρτύριον τῶν ἁγίων ἐνδόξων ἱερομαρτύρων ιε΄ τῶν ἐν Τιβεριουπόλει [τῇ βερίου πόλει MS] μαρτυρησάντων [-ρισ- MS] ἐπὶ τῆς βασιλείας τοῦ δυσσεβοῦς Ἰουλιανοῦ τοῦ παραβάτου, τῇ Βουλγαρικῶς ἐπονομαζομένῃ Στρουμμίτζῃ [τῆς . . . -ης -ης MS], συγγραφὲν ὑπὸ Θεοφυλάκτου, τοῦ ἁγιωτάτου ἀρχιεπισκόπου πάσης [-σις MS] Βουλγαρίας, Oxford, MS Barocci 197, fols. 589ʳ–621ᵛ. Cf. PG cxxvi, cols. 152–221.

[184] 'Deux œuvres hagiographiques du pseudo-Théophylacte' (see n. 147). Gautier has conclusively demonstrated, largely from textúal parallels, that the *Martyrion* and the *Vita Clementis* were written by the same person (pp. 5–7). He is unwilling to accept, however, that this person was Theophylact. His principal argument, which I believe to be mistaken, is that a Byzantine author who in his letters shows a strong aversion to the Bulgarians could hardly have written lives of saints whose cult was part of Bulgaria's Christian heritage. I have given above some of my reasons for believing that Theophylact was the author of the *Vita Clementis*. The arguments are developed further in my article, 'Theophylaktos of Ohrid and the authorship of the *Vita Clementis*' (see n. 145).

draw on unknown sources. He describes a grisly, and apparently quite apocryphal, persecution in Nicaea: a group of local Christians fled from there to Thessalonica and thence, for greater security, to the hinterland of Macedonia. One of them, Theodore, is alleged by Theophylact to have been present at the Council of Nicaea in 325. They settled in a town Theophylact called Tiberiopolis, which was 'situated in the region to the north of Thessalonica, and marched with the land of the Illyrians'.[185] There they formed a Christian community which gained great influence in the neighbourhood. Their fame soon reached Thessalonica; two officials, zealous instruments of the emperor's policies, went to Tiberiopolis to investigate. Fifteen local Christians, with their leaders Timothy, Comasius, Eusebius, and Theodore, were arrested, tried, and, by order of the two Thessalonican officials, put to the sword. They were buried by the local Christians, each in his own sarcophagus, and before long miracles were reported over their graves. Their cult spread far and wide, and many pagans were converted. 'Tiberiopolis became a renowned beacon, illumining the cities of the west'—that is the Balkans—'with the light of the faith'.[186]

The hagiographical source, or sources, used by Theophylact for his account of the persecutions in Nicaea and Tiberiopolis are unknown. The martyrdom itself, and the names of the fifteen martyrs, are not inventions of the author, for, as we shall see, there is evidence of their cult in Strumitsa in the late ninth or early tenth century, and the names of some of them are mentioned in a Slavonic *menologion* of the late tenth or the early eleventh.[187] Strumitsa, a town in the valley of the river of the same name (a tributary of the Struma or Strymon), lies in eastern Macedonia. The fact that its former name was Tiberiopolis is reliably attested by several mid-fourteenth-century sources.[188]

We cannot be sure how far back this place-name goes. There is no

---

[185] *Historia Martyrii XV Martyrum*, cap. 17 (PG cxxvi, col. 176).

[186] Ibid., cap. 26: Gautier (op. cit. 256) emends πύργον ('tower') to πυρσόν ('beacon').

[187] *Evangeliarium Assemani*, ii (Prague, 1955), 310.

[188] These sources are: (1) The superscription to the unique manuscript of the *Martyrion* (Bodl. Barocci 197), copied *c.* 1343; see H. O. Coxe, *Bodleian Library Quarto Catalogues*, i: *Greek Manuscripts* (Oxford, 1969), cols. 341–51; A. Turyn, *Dated Greek Manuscripts of the Thirteenth and Fourteenth Centuries in the Libraries of Great Britain* (Washington, DC, 1980), 108–12. (2) The colophon of the same manuscript, written by another hand soon after the manuscript was completed: Turyn, 111–12. (3) A mid-14th-c. chrysoboullon of the Serbian Tsar Stephen Dušan: S. Novaković, *Zakonski spomenici srpskih država srednjega veka* (Belgrade, 1912), 695, no. 138.

record in antiquity of any Balkan town called Tiberiopolis, but a city of that name, called after the Emperor Tiberius, is mentioned in Phrygia in the early centuries of the Christian era, and was renowned for the vigour of its Christianity. It may be, as Zlatarski and others have surmised, that populations removed from this region of Asia Minor brought the name of their native or metropolitan city with them to Macedonia.[189] The most likely time for this toponymic transfer would have been the early ninth century: for we are told by the chronicler Theophanes that in 809 the Emperor Nicephorus I ordered Christian communities 'from every province' to be uprooted and resettled in Slavonic regions of the Empire.[190] The aim of this population-shift was to reassert Byzantine control over the areas occupied by the Slavs during the previous two centuries. Macedonia had been densely colonized by the Slavs: and Theophanes tells us that some of the communities transferred by Nicephorus I were settled on the banks of the Struma.[191] Strumitsa is no more than fifty miles from that river; and it is not impossible that the town was then renamed Tiberiopolis by some transplanted communities from Asia Minor.

Recent archaeological evidence has lent powerful support to the view that Tiberiopolis was identified with Strumitsa as early as the ninth century. Excavations carried out in Strumitsa in 1973 by Yugoslav archaeologists have uncovered a complex of buildings with evidence of several periods: at the lowest level was an early Christian basilica, with three naves and three crypts; these are thought to date from a somewhat later period, the sixth to eighth centuries. Over it was discovered a cruciform and probably five-domed church, built in the late ninth or early tenth century and dedicated to the Fifteen Martyrs of Tiberiopolis; in the same period the central crypt was painted with frescoes representing the Fifteen Martyrs, which, though only partially preserved, show evidence of a technique said to be reminiscent of the Byzantine metropolitan style of the period. Finally fragments of frescoes were found, dating from the late eleventh or early twelfth centuries and showing that the cruciform church was reconstructed in this period, that is in Theophylact's time.[192]

---

[189] *Istoriya*, i. 2. 236.
[190] Theophanes, *Chronographia*, ed. C. de Boor, i (Leipzig, 1883), 486.
[191] Ibid. 496.
[192] D. Koco and P. Miljković-Pepek, 'Rezultatite od arheološkite iskopuvanja vo 1973 g. vo crkvata "Sv. Tiveriopolski mačenici"—Strumica', *Arheološki Muzej na Makedonija*, viii. 9 (Skopje, 1978), 93–7; Ts. Grozdanov, *Portreti na svetitelite od*

These archaeological finds in Strumitsa, we shall see, strikingly confirm Theophylact's evidence on the cult of the Fifteen Martyrs in the reign of Boris; the discovery of the frescoes is particularly important for our purpose, being the only known medieval depiction of the Martyrs of Tiberiopolis.

Back to Theophylact's narrative. After the account of the martyrdom, we leave the ancient world and, after an interval of several centuries, enter the Middle Ages. After the sack of 'Tiberiopolis', probably in the 580s, by the Avars[193]—an event not mentioned in any other source—the coming of the Bulgars a century later gave Theophylact his point of transition between the first and the second part of the *Martyrion*. For the second part he must have used one or more Slavonic sources which seem to have been both accurate and reliable, and he adds to our knowledge of early Bulgarian history on several points. He records the conversion to Christianity of a member of the royal family called Enravotas, a son of the Khan Omurtag. Paganism was still the religion of Bulgaria's ruling classes; and Enravotas, after publicly professing Christianity, was martyred by order of his brother, the Khan Malamir (831–6).

The subject of martyrdom brings Theophylact back to his central theme. He describes in glowing terms the baptism of the Khan Boris in 864 by Byzantine priests and the subsequent spread of Christianity in his realm, and thus prepares the ground for the posthumous history of the Fifteen Martyrs. Their graves, he tells us, had remained abandoned and unknown since the Avars sacked Tiberiopolis. In Boris's reign (852–89) the saints began to manifest themselves by miraculous apparitions and by healings; whereupon Boris, 'ever ardent for divine things', decided to exhume their bodies and give them solemn burial in a church. Theophylact's account of the discovery and translation of the Strumitsa relics is very curious; it bears out once again the precision of his source. The exhumation took place amid a concourse of clergy, nobles, and people, and after digging to some depth 'they chanced upon the saints' sarcophagi; each was covered with a slab of cut marble, inscribed with [the occupant's] name and the outline of his body, his profession, his rank, and the expression on his face'.[194] Instead of burying the relics in Strumitsa, Boris had them

Makedonija od IX–XVIII vek (Skopje, 1983), 127–37. I am indebted for these references to Professor S. Ćurčić.

[193] *Historia Martyrii*, cap. 27, col. 189.

[194] Ἐντυγχάνουσιν ἤδη ταῖς τῶν ἁγίων λάρναξιν, ἐκ λίθου μὲν μαρμαρίνου πριστῆς τὰς

removed to a new church which he had built in honour of the Fifteen Martyrs in nearby Bregalnitsa. Theophylact gives no reason for this decision; no doubt it was done because Bregalnitsa was the seat of a bishopric.[195] In readiness for the translation, the saints' bodies were wrapped in shrouds, and laid in wooden chests; and marble slabs from the sarcophagi were removed to an unspecified sanctuary in the diocese. The exact location of Bregalnitsa is uncertain: recent archaeological work places it in the valley of the eponymous river, probably on or near the site of ancient Bargala, some thirty miles north-west of Strumitsa.[196]

The citizens of Strumitsa, meanwhile, seeing that they were about to lose the relics of their supernatural protectors, rose in revolt. A major riot was averted only by the presence of mind of the governor: a compromise was reached, by the terms of which the relics of only the three senior martyrs who head the list—Timothy, Comasius, and Eusebius—were removed to Bregalnitsa. The people of Strumitsa were allowed to keep the remaining twelve for the time being,[197] and they were presumably buried in the cruciform church there, now recently excavated.

The final scene took place in the new church at Bregalnitsa. It follows fairly closely the standard pattern of the translation-tales which abound in Byzantine hagiography. Amid the usual concourse of clergy and people, the coffined relics of the three martyrs were solemnly deposited on the right-hand side of the nave. Native clergy were appointed to minister to the needs of the church, and 'the Bulgarian language', that is, Old Church Slavonic, was to be used in the liturgy.[198]

σκεπούσας αὐτὰς σανίδας ἐχούσαις, ἄνωθεν δὲ ἐπιγεγραμμένον ἑκάστου τό τε ὄνομα, τό τε σχῆμα τοῦ εἴδους καὶ τὸν τρόπον τοῦ βίου καὶ τὸ ἀξίωμα καὶ τὸν χαρακτῆρα τῆς ὄψεως: (cap. 37). I have followed Gautier's slight emendations (pp. 267–8) to Migne's text (col. 204).

[195] Theophylact states rather vaguely that the church was 'in the bishopric of Bregalnitsa' (ibid., cap. 37, col. 204), but later he makes it clear that the relics were to be interred in the city of that name (ibid., cap. 41, col. 208).

[196] B. Aleksova and C. Mango, 'Bargala: A Preliminary Report', *Dumbarton Oaks Papers*, xxv (1971), 265–81. For Bargala, the site of a bishopric in the fifth and sixth centuries, see Pauly–Wissowa, s.v. For the geography of the area see N. G. L. Hammond, *A History of Macedonia*, i (Oxford, 1972), 200–3.

[197] *Historia Martyrii*, cap. 40, col 205.

[198] Ibid., cap. 41–2, col. 208. In the reign of Boris's son Symeon and by his order, the three martyrs were joined by two more, transferred from the Strumitsa church, Socrates and Theodore: ibid., cap. 47, col. 213.

Despite the conventional mould of Theophylact's story—a classic Roman *martyrion*, followed by an equally standard translation tale—his account as a whole shows two strikingly original features. Firstly, the precision and vividness are proof that he used a written Slavonic source which, directly or indirectly, went back to an eyewitness account of the discovery in Strumitsa of the relics of the Fifteen Martyrs, and of their subsequent transfer to Bregalnitsa. The second, and no less remarkable, feature is his success in giving a local flavour to an earlier and broader hagiographical theme. His story makes it clear that by Boris's reign the cult of the Fifteen Martyrs of Tiberiopolis was solidly entrenched in Macedonia. The recent excavations have tellingly confirmed the accuracy of his account, at least with regard to Strumitsa. It may be supposed that the main reason for writing the *Martyrion* was Theophylact's desire to promote this cult. As the excavations have shown, a major reconstruction of the cruciform Strumitsa church was carried out in his lifetime, probably during his Ohrid episcopate. Strumitsa and Bregalnitsa were part of his archdiocese, and not very far from Ohrid. They are likely to have been part of St Clement's diocese in the late ninth and the early tenth century; and it is hard to avoid the suspicion that Clement as well as Boris had a hand in fostering the cult of the Fifteen Martyrs in Macedonia.

Perhaps this mention of Clement may prove of further relevance in the light of Theophylact's aims and methods as a hagiographer. In the *Martyrion* he tried to connect a local Macedonian cult, centred in the Vardar valley, with the history of Christian martyrs in the Roman Empire and, by claiming that one of the saints of Tiberiopolis had attended the Council of Nicaea, with the most venerable traditions of Eastern Christianity. This could hardly fail to enhance the prestige of Ohrid and of the whole Bulgarian Church. In the *Vita Clementis* he made the same attempt to make a local theme universal, by grafting the cultural attainments of Christian Macedonia, at the end of the ninth century, on to the wider accomplishments of Cyril and Methodius. The result, in both works, has been the same: a panegyric to Bulgarian Christianity and to Boris, its principal architect. The *Martyrion* describes the conversion of the Bulgarians in plainly biblical terms: 'What was previously not a people but a barbarian nation became and was called a people of God, and the inheritance of the Bulgarians, which had not been an object of mercy, was called an object of mercy by God who calls those things which are not as though they were. . . . The Bulgarian people have become, as it is written, a royal priesthood, a holy nation, a peculiar people.'[199]

In using a Pauline quotation to express his belief that through baptism the Bulgarian nation was called from non-existence into being,[200] Theophylact was applying a classic theme of Christian apologetics: conversion of a pagan people to Christianity endowed it with a distinct collective identity. Through its Pauline antecedents, we have seen that this concept of national self-determination formed part of the Cyrillo-Methodian ideology. There is no explicit mention of this ideology in the *Martyrion*; but we must remember Theophylact's manifest approval of the clergy at the church of the Fifteen Martyrs in the late ninth century celebrating the office in Old Church Slavonic.[201]

Perhaps Theophylact's two hagiographic works reveal different aspects of his remarkable capacity for empathy. He looked on Clement, whom he described as 'the first bishop in the Bulgarian language',[202] as his direct predecessor; and the concluding section of his *Martyrion* calls the Fifteen Martyrs of Tiberiopolis 'those saints of ours'.[203]

It is hard to gauge exactly the aims and results of Theophylact's activity in Bulgaria. The view, unpopular in recent years, that he detested his Slavonic flock and that he was committed to the uprooting of their culture and the Hellenization of their Church, is, in my opinion, seriously misleading. We may assume, however, that according to his lights and his resources, both spiritual and material, he loyally performed the task entrusted to him by his imperial master: that of holding the inhabitants of his mainly Slav-speaking archdiocese in subjection to Byzantium. He was certainly a firm believer in the principle of order[204] and the duty of obedience to the emperor— 'the earthly god, so to speak', as one of his letters describes him.[205]

---

[199] *Historia Martyrii*, cap. 35, cols. 200–1. The references are to Deut. 32: 21; Hos. 2: 23; Rom. 4: 17; 1 Pet. 2: 9.

[200] Θεοῦ . . . καλοῦντος τὰ μὴ ὄντα ὡς ὄντα: Rom. 4: 17.

[201] See above, p. 75.

[202] Βουλγάρῳ γλώττῃ πρῶτος ἐπίσκοπος: *Vita*, xx. 62 (Tunitsky, 122; Milev, 128).

[203] τῶν καθ' ἡμᾶς τούτων ἁγίων: *Historia Martyrii*, cap. 54, col. 220.

[204] F 17, PG cxxvi, col. 340 = G 58: 329: τὸν Θεὸν τάξεως ὄντα Θεόν, ἀλλὰ μὴ ἀκαταστασίας καὶ ἀταξίας.

[205] L 8, col. 516 = G 12: 167: τοῦ θεοστεφοῦς καὶ κραταιοῦ βασιλέως καὶ θεοῦ ἐγκοσμίου, ἵνα οὕτως εἴπω.

Another letter stipulates that his suffragan bishops should be experienced in secular as well as ecclesiastical affairs.[206] Though in political matters the archbishop was subordinate to the local military governor, his duties were not confined to the spiritual domain. His war with the imperial tax-collectors provides ample evidence of this. He realized how damaging they were to his own efforts at conciliating the Bulgarians; and it was with these officials in mind that he quoted the words of the Gospel: 'A man's foes shall be they of his own household' (Matt. 10: 36).[207] Like all intelligent colonial administrators, Theophylact knew that gentle methods are usually more effective than violence; so he urged that the people of 'barbarian lands' be treated with kindness rather than the power of the sword.[208] Only by tempering firmness with humanity, he repeatedly stressed, could the Bulgarians be kept from turning disloyal and rebellious; and he exhorted the imperial authorities to treat them with caution and restraint, 'lest the patience of the poor be finally exhausted'.[209]

How successful Theophylact was in applying these principles is hard to say. Except when he wished to invoke the sanction of the law, he probably underplayed, especially in his letters to Constantinople, the degree of disaffection he encountered in Bulgaria. The various monsters that haunt his letters are nearly always tax-collectors. The only well-documented example of something approaching a popular revolt against him was a murky affair, stirred up by a Bulgarian peasant named Lazarus; he gathered a group of malcontents and lodged a complaint about 'the tyranny of the archbishop' with the imperial authorities; but even he, Theophylact maintained, was a creature of the chief tax-collector Iasites.[210] We do not know whether the citizens of Ohrid went on singing provocative patriotic songs, like the one that so enraged Theophylact on his first arrival.

We are better informed on Theophylact's ecclesiastical activity in Bulgaria. Towards his suffragan bishops—presumably all Greeks—he showed real qualities of leadership, exhorting them to stand firm when times were difficult, and stay in their sees and look after their

---

[206] L 13, col. 525 = G 18: 193: Δεῖ γὰρ ἀνδρὸς ταύτῃ [ἐπισκοπῇ] συγκεκροτημένου καὶ πρὸς τὰ πνευματικὰ καὶ τὰ κοσμικά.

[207] L 29, col. 549 = G 37: 255.

[208] M 31, col. 428 = G 86: 453: βαρβαρικῶν χωρῶν καταδουλώσεις χρηστότητι μᾶλλον ἐπαγομένων ἢ δόρατι. The subject of the sentence is Bryennios. Cf. F 15, col. 336 = G 56: 321.

[209] οὐδ' ἀπολεῖται εἰς τέλος ἡ τῶν πενήτων ὑπομονή: M 30, col. 425 = G 85: 451.

[210] M 43, cols. 456–60 = G 98: 499–505.

flocks.[211] We have no direct knowledge of his relations with his parish clergy, most of whom must have been Slav-speaking Bulgarians. Some, we may suppose, after nearly a century of Byzantine rule, had more knowledge of Greek than their predecessors in Clement's day.[212] To this Theophylact may have contributed: one of his letters has the superscription: 'To Bulgarians taught by him'.[213] The addressees have sometimes been taken to be the whole of his Bulgarian flock. But the fact that the letter is in Greek, refers to its recipients as 'you who are mine', and requests them to convey his greeting to a wider group of 'those who are mine and not mine',[214] suggests that it was written to a select group of Bulgarians who were pupils of Theophylact. He was probably training them for the priesthood, and it is hard to believe that he taught them in any other language but Greek.

Greek, the official language of the archdiocese of Bulgaria in Theophylact's time, was undoubtedly used for the liturgy in the diocesan cathedrals. But nearly all the parish clergy must have continued to use Church Slavonic, and there is no evidence that this liturgical situation displeased Theophylact. So fervent an admirer of Clement and his masters Cyril and Methodius could hardly have objected to the use of their Slavonic liturgy. Indeed he seems to imply that hymns translated by Clement were still sung in churches of Bulgaria, and he adds, admittedly from hearsay, that Clement's works in Old Church Slavonic are still 'preserved by industrious folk'.[215] Many other writings in that language must have circulated in Bulgaria in Theophylact's time, and philologists have shown that a fair number of well-known Old Church Slavonic manuscripts of the eleventh and twelfth centuries were copied in Macedonian or East Bulgarian scriptoria.[216] Nor is this surprising: for the role played by Ohrid and its scriptorium in transmitting Byzantine culture to the

---

[211] L 27–8, cols. 544–8 = G 35, 36: 245–7, 249–51.

[212] See above, p. 31.

[213] Τοῖς παιδευθεῖσιν ὑπ' αὐτοῦ Βουλγάροις: M 48, col. 465 = G 103: 517. Gautier mistranslates 'Aux Bulgares qu'il a châtiés': G 103: 516.

[214] Διαγγείλατε οὖν οἱ ἐμοὶ τοῖς ἐμοῖς τε καὶ οὐκ ἐμοῖς: ibid.

[215] Φέρονται γὰρ ταῦτα πάντα παρὰ τοῖς φιλοπόνοις σωζόμενα: Vita, xxii. 66 (Tunitsky, 126; Milev, 132). The wording suggests that Theophylact had not seen these manuscripts himself, perhaps because he was unable to read Old Church Slavonic.

[216] See W. K. Matthews, 'Sources of Old Church Slavonic', *The Slavonic and East European Review*, xxviii (1949–50), 466–85; A. Dostál, 'Les relations entre Byzance et les Slaves (en particulier les Bulgares) aux xie et xiie siècles du point de vue culturel', *Proceedings of the Thirteenth International Congress of Byzantine Studies* (Oxford, 1966), 173–4.

Balkan Slavs could not have been so great had not both literary traditions continued to exist side by side, interacting in a bilingual milieu in the schools and monasteries of Macedonia.[217]

It is in this bilingual and bicultural world of the Balkans at the beginning of the twelfth century that Theophylact, during his Ohrid incumbency, properly belonged. Whether he encouraged or simply tolerated the Slavonic liturgy in his archdiocese is a matter of opinion. Some historians, reacting against the distorted picture painted by some scholars, of Theophylact as a malevolent Hellenizer, have argued that he actively promoted a Bulgarian national consciousness; others have maintained that he was moved above all by an enlightened and humane concern for his flock.[218] This is surely to give him too high marks for good behaviour. Not all his verbal sallies against the Bulgarians were prompted by literary convention; at times, in reacting to his 'barbarian' surroundings, he allowed himself a snobbery and fastidiousness unbecoming in a bishop; and his war with the tax-collectors was not stoked only by altruism.

Geographically and culturally, the two worlds of Theophylact were surely too far from each other for any bridge between them to be solid and enduring. Yet he endeavoured to be such a bridge-builder, and if he failed, it was not for want of trying. In the end the disaffection of the local population proved too great. The comparative ease with which the Bulgarians regained their independence in 1187 demonstrated the bankruptcy of the Empire's efforts to hold down and absorb the Slavs of the northern Balkans.

A modern Greek historian, describing the problems of adaptation encountered by Byzantine provincial bishops in the twelfth century, perceptively described them as 'double-natured and bilingual':[219] they longed for the amenities of civilized life, yet they remained at their uncongenial posts; they came to terms with their provincial

[217] The survival of a vernacular liturgical tradition in Macedonia is shown in the account by the Byzantine historian and scholar Nicephorus Gregoras of a Byzantine embassy to Serbia in 1326, in which he took part. The envoys celebrated Easter in Strumitsa with a local community that was manifestly chanting the offices in Church Slavonic: *Correspondance de Nicéphore Grégoras*, ed. R. Guilland (Paris, 1927), 41–3.

[218] I. Snegarov, *Istoriya na Okhridskata arkhiepiskopiya*, i (Sofia, 1924), 222–4; D. Xanalatos, "Θεοφύλακτος ὁ Βουλγαρίας καὶ ἡ δρᾶσις αὐτοῦ ἐν 'Αχρίδι", *Θεολογία*, xvi (1938), 228–40; Katičić, "Βιογραφικὰ περὶ Θεοφυλάκτου, ἀρχιεπισκόπου 'Αχρίδος" (see n. 19), 364–85.

[219] διφυεῖς καὶ δίγλωσσοι: P. Kalligas, *Μελέται Βυζαντινῆς ἱστορίας ἀπὸ τῆς πρώτης μέχρι τῆς τελευταίας ἁλώσεως, 1205–1453* (Athens, 1894), 148, reviewed by H. Gelzer in *Byzantinische Zeitschrift*, vii (1898), 190–3, and cited by Xanalatos, op. cit. 239.

surroundings, yet their eyes were for ever turned towards Constantinople. Theophylact suffered from the same mental split. There is more than a trace of irony in these words he wrote to his friend and patroness, the *basilissa* Maria: 'So I return to the Bulgarians, I who am a true Constantinopolitan and, strange though it is, a Bulgarian'.[220]

We do not know how long Theophylact remained at his post. The last firm data we can glean from his Ohrid letters is 1108.[221] If we can trust the date on a manuscript of one of his poems, he was still alive in 1125, but whether he was still archbishop of Ohrid at that time is not clear.[222]

Theophylact's posthumous fame was plagued by misunderstanding and error. We have seen that Erasmus, who made much use of his commentaries, believed for a time that his name was Vulgarius. An even more egregious mistake was made by the Bulgarian monk Paisy, of the monastery of Hilandar on Mount Athos. In his 'Slavo-Bulgarian History', that manifesto of modern Bulgarian nationalism written in 1762, he asserted that Theophylact was patriarch of Tŭrnovo (the see of the primate of Bulgaria after 1235) and in the same breath promoted him to the rank of a saint.[223] We may doubt whether Theophylact had deserved this posthumous mystification.

His long and difficult career as archbishop of Ohrid can best perhaps be summed up by two terse quotations from his letters. The first, the epigraph to one of the very first letters he wrote after his arrival in Ohrid, expresses his misgivings and his fear at the aspect of his new abode. The quotation is from his beloved Euripides, and the mouthpiece for these feelings is Teiresias in *The Phoenician Women*: observing Creon's horror at the news that his son must die if Thebes is to be

---

[220] Κάτειμι τοίνυν ἐπὶ Βουλγάρους ἀτεχνῶς Κωνσταντινουπολίτης, τὸ ξένον Βούλγαρος: L 1, col. 504=G 4: 141 (who has Βουλγάροις). The exact meaning of τὸ ξένον is unclear.
[221] *Théophylacte d'Achrida*, 36–7. For other views on the length of Theophylact's tenure of his post, see B. Panov, *Teofilakt Ohridski kako izvor za srednovekovnata istorija na makedonskiot narod* (Skopje, 1971), 41–5.
[222] *Théophylacte d'Achrida*, 37, 121–2, 353.
[223] *Istoriya slavenobolgarskaya*, ed. I. Ivanov (Sofia, 1914), 36–7, 75–6. Cf. I. Snegarov, 'Les sources sur la vie et l'activité de Clément d'Ochrida', *Byzantinobulgarica*, i (1962), 112–14. The belief in the sanctity of Theophylact, held in the 17th c. in Paris (see *Théophylacte d'Achrida*, 48 nn. 1, 2) perhaps goes back to a genuine cult centred on, or confined to, Ohrid. See N. Velimirović, *The Prologue from Ochrid*, i (Birmingham, 1985), 395.

saved, the blind prophet exclaims: 'This is no longer the same man, he
starts back'.[224] The second quotation conveys something of the
indomitable character of the scholarly bishop, for whom his long
provincial episcopate must have seemed a never-ending exile. It is
taken from the *Odyssey*, and records its hero's resolution, despite his
sorrow on seeing his ships, within sight at last of Ithaca his home,
driven back by the winds blowing from Aeolus' bag, to resist the wish
to drown himself in the sea from despair. Like Odysseus, who in the
face of calamity remained steadfast on board his ship, Theophylact
could say: 'But I endured, and stayed.'[225]

---

[224] F 1, col. 308 = G 6: 147; *Phoinissai*, 920: ἀνὴρ ὅδ' οὐκέθ' αὑτός· ἐκνεύει πάλιν.

[225] 'Ἀλλ' ἔτλην καὶ ἔμεινα: M 10, col. 376 = G 71: 383; *Od.* 10. 53. The same two
verbs, also in a heroic context, are brought together in two passages of the *Iliad*: 11.
317, 19, 308.

3

Vladimir Monomakh

IN 1054 Prince Yaroslav, sovereign of Russia, died near his capital, Kiev. His reign (1019–54) had brought Russia a new political stability, cultural achievement, and international prestige. His victory in 1036 over the Turkic Pechenegs, who for more than a century had controlled the steppe-lands north of the Black Sea, removed for a generation the military threat from the Eurasian nomads to Russia's southern border. Kiev became in Yaroslav's reign a major European metropolis, whose buildings excited the wonder of visitors from the west. Medieval chroniclers extol Yaroslav as a patron of learning: he is said to have assembled in Kiev a group of scholars who translated books from Greek into Slavonic, and the first independent works of Russian literature were written in his reign. Russia's international status was assured by the matrimonial ties which bound the princely house of Kiev to some of the greatest dynasties of Europe. Yaroslav's family tree exemplifies these links: his wife was the daughter of the king of Sweden; one of his sons married into the imperial family of Byzantium; his three daughters were wives of the kings of Norway, Hungary, and France. It is no wonder that Yaroslav's reign appeared to later generations as a golden age; alone among Russian rulers, he came to be styled *Mudryi*, 'the Wise'.

The year before Yaroslav died, a grandson was born to him from the marriage of his son Vsevolod to a Byzantine princess. A contemporary Russian chronicler records that she belonged to the imperial house of Byzantium;[1] and her son, known to his contemporaries and to posterity as Vladimir Monomakh, tells us in his autobiography that he inherited his surname from his mother.[2] There is little doubt that she was the daughter of the Byzantine emperor Constantine IX

---

[1] *Povest' vremennykh let*, ed. D. S. Likhachev and V. P. Adrianova-Peretts, (Moscow–Leningrad, 1950), i. 108 (hereafter P); (unreliable English translation by S. H. Cross and O. P. Sherbowitz-Wetzor: *The Russian Primary Chronicle* (Cambridge, Mass., 1953), 142 (hereafter ET)). All translations in the text are my own.

[2] P 153; ET 206, mistranslating the passage.

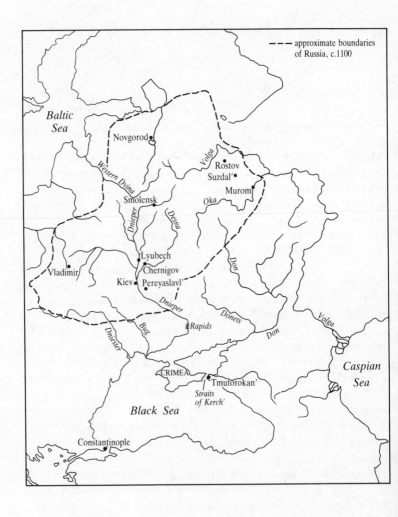

Baltic
Sea

Novgorod

Volga

Rostov

Suzdal'

Murom

Western Dvina

Smolensk

Oka

Dnieper

Desna

Don

Lyubech

Chernigov

Vladimir

Kiev

Pereyaslavl'

Dnieper

Donets

Bug

Rapids

Don

Volga

Dniester

CRIMEA

Tmutorokan'

Caspian
Sea

Straits
of Kerch'

Black Sea

Constantinople

Map 2. Russia, *c.* 1100

Monomachos (1042–55); and it is virtually certain that the name Monomakh was, in a Russian form, that of Vladimir's imperial grandfather. The Monomachoi were a distinguished Byzantine family, whose high standing is attested in the sources of the eleventh and twelfth centuries.[3] Constantine, a wealthy senator who belonged to the Byzantine civil aristocracy, became emperor in 1042, on his marriage to the elderly Empress Zoe. At sixty-four, Zoe was clearly too old to bear children. But Constantine had been married twice before, and, although we lack conclusive evidence, it is likely that Vladimir's mother was a child of the second of these marriages.[4]

The eleventh-century Byzantine scholar Psellos has left us a vivid portrait of Vladimir's putative grandfather. He describes him as handsome, athletic, kindly, pleasure-loving and fickle, and something of a womanizer.[5] He was in no way a remarkable ruler, though his reign witnessed several memorable events: among them the establishment of the imperial Law School and the schism (in 1054) between the Byzantine and the Roman Churches. In 1043 his navy repelled a major attack on Constantinople by the Russians, planned by Yaroslav of Kiev. The Byzantine victory was followed by a peace-treaty and by the marriage between Vsevolod Yaroslavich and the relation (almost certainly the daughter) of the Emperor Constantine IX. The child of this marriage, born in 1053, in whom—as his contemporary, the Byzantine primate of the Russian Church, later put it—God compounded 'imperial and princely blood',[6] is the subject of this chapter. He became one of the leading figures in Russia's medieval history.

Yaroslav's death was followed by a national crisis which threatened the security of the Kievan state and jeopardized the achievements of the preceding age. During the next half-century the rulers of Russia were faced with two intractable problems. The first was political. The princes of Kiev had so far maintained a real, if precarious, ascendancy over most of Russia by appointing their close relatives as rulers over the different principalities and city-states into which the country was then divided. This centralizing policy clashed

[3] A. P. Kazhdan, *Sotsial'nyi sostav gospodstvuyushchego klassa Vizantii XI–XII vv.*, 63, 92, 115–17, 177, 191–2.

[4] See V. L. Yanin, and G. G. Litavrin, 'Novye materialy o proiskhozhdenii Vladimira Monomakha', in D. A. Avdusin and V. L. Yanin (eds.) *Istoriko-arkheologichesky sbornik: A. V. Artsikhovskomu*, (Moscow, 1962), 204–21; V. G. Bryusova, 'K voprosu o proiskhozhdenii Vladimira Monomakha', *Vizantiisky vremennik*, xxviii (1968), 127–35.

[5] *Chonographie*, ed. E. Renauld, i (Paris, 1926), 124–54, ii (Paris, 1928), 1–71.

[6] Cited in A. S. Orlov, *Vladimir Monomakh* (Moscow–Leningrad, 1946), 50.

with another, equally potent, force which worked to secure the right of all members of the princely family to exercize authority in the land and to draw revenues from it. This tension between the efforts of the Kievan princes to secure monarchical hegemony on the one hand, and the principle of shared authority invoked by other members of the ruling clan on the other, was a source of constant political instability during the second half of the eleventh century and the early years of the twelfth. An attempt to restore some balance between these two opposing impulses appears to have been made by Yaroslav before his death. He divided his realm among his five sons, stipulating that the eldest, Izyaslav, was to have authority over his brothers and reign in Kiev. All were urged to avoid feuding and to live in amity with one another. The next two brothers in order of seniority, Svyatoslav and Vsevolod, were given respectively—together with their adjoining lands—Chernigov and Pereyaslavl', the two cities which, after Kiev, ranked highest in importance in south Russia.

The nature and aim of Yaroslav's 'testament' have long been debated by historians; and there is still no agreement whether it inaugurated a new method of succession to Kiev and to the other principalities, or whether its more limited purpose was to reconcile seniority within the princely family with the equally compelling need to partition the common domain.[7] It seems, however, that the dispositions of 1054 were essentially a compromise between Kiev's claim to hegemony and the local interests of other principalities. The compromise, whatever its precise motives, did not work for very long. The 'triumvirate', instituted *de facto* after Yaroslav's death, was disturbed by a popular rising in Kiev in 1068, interrupted for three years in 1073 by a conspiracy hatched by Svyatoslav and Vsevolod against Izyaslav, and came to an end in 1078 when Izyaslav, restored to the Kievan throne in the previous year, was killed in battle in one of the chronic bouts of internecine strife. Civil war was becoming a threat to the very survival of the state.[8]

The second problem facing the Russian rulers was a military one. The Pechenegs had been decisively defeated by the armies of Yaroslav in 1036. Twenty-five years later they were succeeded as overlords of

[7] See the discussion by A. D. Stokes, in R. Auty and D. Obolensky (eds.), *An Introduction to Russian History*, (Cambridge, 1976), 67–70.

[8] The fullest treatment in English of the political history of Kievan Russia is by G. Vernadsky, *Kievan Russia* (New Haven, Conn., 1948). See also the bibliography in Stokes, op. cit. 75–7.

the steppe by another Turkic nomadic people, called Kipchak in their own language, Komanoi by the Byzantines, and Polovtsy by the Russians. They proved to be an even more dangerous and determined foe than the Pechenegs. Their first recorded attack took place in 1061. For the next century and a half they were seldom at peace with the Russians, and even the great southern cities—Kiev, Chernigov, and Pereyaslavl'—which lay in the exposed area of the wooded steppe, at times endured siege conditions. The raids and invasions of the Polovtsy are chronicled in contemporary sources, often with pathetic or gruesome details. One example out of many is the account in the Russian Primary Chronicle, written in the early twelfth century, of the burning in 1093 of a town south of Kiev. Its citizens, 'great numbers of Christian folk', were led into captivity, 'wretched, tormented, numb with cold, tortured by hunger and thirst, with haggard faces and blackened bodies; [prisoners] in an alien land, their tongues swollen, made to walk naked and barefooted, their feet lacerated by thorns; tearfully they replied to one another, saying: "I am from this or that town", others said: "I am from this or that village." Thus they questioned each other with tears, speaking of their origin and sighing, eyes raised to heaven.'[9]

Such pictures of human misery alternate in the contemporary records with another, more optimistic, theme: that of national resistance. War against the pagan Polovtsy was waged, with varying success, by most Russian princes of the time. Its episodes, tragic or victorious, are chronicled in Russian historical and epic works, often with strong emotional overtones, and are seen as a defence of the national heritage and a holy war for the Christian faith. These medieval writings, extolling personal valour and skill in warfare, contributed to the image, which has survived into modern times, of the Kievan period as Russia's heroic age.

Vladimir Monomakh, the subject of this chapter, was to play a leading role in devising and implementing policies designed to achieve the two main tasks facing Russian society of the time: political unity and military defence.

His childhood passed in the relatively peaceful conditions that prevailed in Russia immediately after the death of Yaroslav and during the early years of the 'triumvirate'. His father, Vsevolod, had been given the principality of Pereyaslavl'. There, we may assume,

---

[9] P 147; ET 179.

Vladimir spent his childhood and early teens. He was later to rule for eighteen years in that city, one of the most prestigious in Russia, the centre of an important principality which extended south and east of Kiev, and as far west as the left bank of Dnieper. Of all the Russian lands this was the most exposed to attacks from the steppe. Vladimir was probably in Pereyaslavl' during the first Polovtsian invasions of the 1060s; in 1066, as a boy of thirteen, he must have seen Halley's comet, which the Russian Primary Chronicle describes as an augury of coming disasters. And it was probably in Pereyaslavl', under his father's tutelage, that he learnt the technique of border warfare against the mounted Polovtsian archers, in which he in his later years became so proficient.

The first recorded event of Vladimir's life, after the chronicle's brief reference to his birth, was a journey that took him from Pereyaslavl' to the other end of Russia. He tells us in his autobiography that he 'was sent' by his father to Rostov.[10] This is doubtless a reference to his appointment as prince of this city, probably in 1068. He was then fifteen. The journey, he notes with evident self-satisfaction, took him across the land of the Vyatichi: these were a Slav tribe who lived in the vast and still partly impassable forests of central Russia and along the banks of the Oka. Rostov, a town of venerable age, situated not far from the upper Volga, was then the political centre of a huge territory which stretched northward almost as far as Lake Onega,[11] and was then part of Vsevolod's patrimony. Much of it was occupied by aboriginal Finnic tribes, through Rostov itself, a centre of vigorous Russian colonization, was probably by then a largely Slav city. Two centuries later this area, between the upper Volga and the Oka, became the nucleus of the Muscovite state. In the second half of the eleventh century, however, this north-eastern borderland of Kievan Russia, mostly covered by dense forests, was still a political and cultural backwater. Vladimir's journey from Pereyaslavl' to Rostov was long and no doubt hazardous. The contrast between the two regions could scarcely have been greater: he had left behind a country of open horizons, with close commercial and cultural links with Byzantium, and constant concern with military defence, and exchanged it for a land at once more primitive and more secure,

---

[10] P 158; ET 211.
[11] See A. N. Nasonov, '*Russkaya Zemlya' i obrazovanie territorii drevnerusskogo gosudarstva* (Moscow, 1951), 173–96; M. N. Tikhomirov, *The Towns of Ancient Rus* (Moscow, 1959), 415–20.

enclosed by forests, lakes and swamps, in whose countryside
Christianity was barely beginning to make headway in the teeth of
strong pagan resistance. To strengthen the new faith Vladimir had a
church built in Rostov, modelled on the main church of the
Monastery of the Caves in Kiev.[12]

Vladimir's period of rule in Rostov was brief. By 1070 he was
probably transferred by his father to Smolensk. His reign in Rostov,
and perhaps his transfer to Smolensk as well, coincided with dramatic
events in south Russia. In 1068 the Polovtsians attacked in force: the
Russian army, jointly commanded by the *triumviri*, was routed not far
from Pereyaslavl'. Izyaslav, accused by the Kievans of failing to give
them adequate protection, and faced with a popular revolt, fled to
Poland. Meanwhile the Polovtsians, thrusting northward, had
reached the neighbourhood of Chernigov. Its prince Svyatoslav,
Izyaslav's younger brother, hastily assembled a force of some three
thousand men and defeated a Polovtsian army numbering, according
to the Russian chronicler, twelve thousand. The next year (1069),
with Polish assistance, Izyaslav regained his throne, expelling an
intrusive cousin, who had usurped his authority in Kiev during his
absence abroad.

In Smolensk, his new residence, Vladimir was much closer to the
events of south Russia than he had been in far-away Rostov. Standing
on the Dnieper, at a key point on the water route from Scandinavia to
Byzantium, close to the watershed between the Baltic (down the
Western Dvina), the Black Sea (down the Dnieper) and the Caspian
(down the Volga), Smolensk, one of the oldest cities in Russia, was an
important commercial centre.[13] By 1070 it played a major role in
Russia's relations with Byzantium and with central and western
Europe. Vladimir's connection with the city was to last long: he may
well have ruled there continuously from 1070 to 1078, and he is
recorded as laying the foundation of a stone church in that city as late
as 1101.[14]

Some time before 1076—perhaps in 1074 or 1075—Vladimir
married Gytha, daughter of King Harold of England. The marriage is
recorded in two medieval Scandinavian sources, Snorri Sturluson's

---

[12] *Das Paterikon des Kiever Höhlenklosters*, ed. D. Tschiżewskij (Munich, 1963) 11–
12.

[13] Nasonov, op. cit. 159–72; Tikhomirov, op. cit. 372–81; L. V. Alekseev,
Smolenskaya zemlya v IX–XIII vv. (Moscow, 1980).

[14] *Ipat'evskaya Letopis'* (St Petersburg, 1908), col. 250.

Heimskringla and Saxo Grammaticus' *Gesta Danorum*.[15] After the battle of Hastings, Gytha, together with other members of her family, sought refuge in Exeter; whence, in 1068, shortly before the city fell to William the Conqueror, she escaped to Flanders, and from there moved to Denmark. The Danish King Sweyn, her cousin, is said to have arranged her marriage with Vladimir. In Russian sources Gytha appears curiously insubstantial: she is mentioned only twice, both times casually, on the occasion of her death in 1107.[16] In 1076 she bore her husband a son, Mstislav, who began to play an important role in the affairs of Russia at the turn of the century, and in 1125 succeeded his father as prince of Kiev. In Scandinavian sources he is called Harold:[17] which allows us to assume that, alongside his Russian name, Vladimir's eldest son bore another, in honour of his English grandfather.

In the year of Mstislav's birth Vladimir was sent by his uncle Svyatoslav, the prince of Kiev, on a distant campaign to the west. Its aim, ultimately conditioned, as we shall see, by Russia's internal politics, was to give military assistance to the Poles against the Czechs. King Bolesław II of Poland, an ally of the Russians, supported the cause of Pope Gregory VII. Bolesław's enemy, the duke of Bohemia Vratislav II, was an ally of the Emperor Henry IV. Gregory VII, who sought to encircle and isolate Henry, used his Polish ally in an attempt to coerce the Czechs. In the summer of 1076 the Polish army faced the combined forces of Henry IV and Vratislav of Bohemia near Meissen. The role played in this apparently abortive military encounter by the Russian expeditionary force is not clear: its presence is mentioned neither in Polish nor in Czech documents. All we have by way of evidence are two brief sentences, the one in the Russian Primary Chronicle and the other in Vladimir's autobiography. It seems that the Russians advanced into Silesia, and remained on Polish territory for five months. This episode in Vladimir's career affords us a glimpse

---

[15] Saxo Grammaticus, *Gesta Danorum*, xi. 6.3 (ed. J. Olrik and H. Ræder, i (Copenhagen, 1931, 308); Snorri Sturluson, *Heimskringla*, 'Magnússona saga', 20, 'Magnúss saga Erlingssonar' 2 (ed. Bjarni Aðalbjarnarson (Reykjavik, 1945–51), iii. 258, 375). See also E. A. Freeman, *The History of the Norman Conquest of England*, 2nd ed. (Oxford, 1876), 752–3; and T. N. Dzhakson, 'Islandskie korolevskie sagi o russko-skandinavskikh matrimonial'nykh svyazyakh', *Skandinavsky sbornik*, xxvii (1982), 112.

[16] P 161, 186; ET 203, 14.

[17] M. P. Alekseev, 'Anglo-saksonskaya parallel'' k Poucheniyu Vladimira Monomakha', *TODRL*, ii (1935), 52; Dzhakson, loc. cit.

of the role—admittedly a marginal one—played by the Russians in the great contest between Empire and Papacy.[18] Its first round was fought between Gregory VII and Henry IV in the very year (1076) when Vladimir's troops advanced deep into central Europe to assist the allies of the pope against those of the emperor. While the Russians, apparently without having struck a blow, were returning home from the Polish–Bohemian border, Henry IV was setting out across the Alps on his historic journey to Canossa.

Vladimir's expedition to central Europe in 1076 is of interest to his biographer for another reason. The Russian chronicle tells us that the expedition was commanded jointly by him and his first cousin, Oleg Svyatoslavich.[19] This is the earliest mention in the sources of a man whose life was to become closely involved with Vladimir's own. For the next forty years the two cousins will appear together in contemporary records with growing frequency, in a relationship lacking neither tragedy nor depth, sometimes united by family bonds, more often pitted against each other by dynastic rivalry and conflicting ambitions.

The precarious triumvirate of Yaroslav's sons, it will be recalled, broke up in 1073. In that year Svyatoslav and Vsevolod conspired against their elder brother Izyaslav, who, once again, sought refuge in Poland. From there he appealed for help to the Emperor Henry IV. Svyatoslav, who had taken over the principality of Kiev from his exiled brother, countered this move by an attempt to support the Poles, Henry's enemies. It was for this purpose that he dispatched, in 1076, his son Oleg and his nephew Vladimir on the military expedition to Poland noted above. Izyaslav's diplomatic manœuvres at Henry IV's court in Mainz came to nothing; nor was he more successful in his attempt to switch sides in the Investiture Contest by sending his son to Rome to solicit the help of Pope Gregory VII.[20] Only Svyatoslav's death enabled him, on 15 July 1077, to return to Kiev and reclaim his principality.

---

[18] See A. V. Florovsky, *Chekhi i vostochnye slavyane*, i (Prague, 1935), 50–8; F. Dvornik, *The Slavs, Their Early History and Civilization* (Boston, Mass., 1956), 284–92; V. A. Kuchkin, 'Pouchenie Vladimira Monomakha i russko-pol'sko-nemetskie otnosheniya 60–70 godov XI veka', *Sovetskoe slavyanovedenie* (1971), 2, 21–34.

[19] P 131; ET 164.

[20] Gregory VII, *Register*, ii. 73, 74, ed. E. Caspar: MGH, *Epistolae selectae*, ii/1 (Berlin, 1955), 233–7; *The Correspondence of Pope Gregory VII*, tr. E. Emerton (New York, 1932), 78–9; A. W. Ziegler, 'Gregor VII. und der Kijewer Grossfürst Izjaslav', *Studi gregoriani*, i (1947), 387–411.

Izyaslav's return did not restore stability to Russia. His brothers' plots had raised a political spectre that was to haunt the country for the next twenty years: the question of who was to reign in Chernigov. Since 1054 this city had been Svyatoslav's patrimony. But when in 1073 he became prince of Kiev in the place of the exiled Izyaslav, Chernigov was assigned to Vsevolod, Vladimir's father. This arrangement continued after Izyaslav's return in 1077. There were, however, other powerful claimants to the throne of Chernigov: Svyatoslav's sons considered that, on their father's death in December 1076, they were the legitimate heirs to that principality. Whether or not they were legally entitled to hold this view, it was clear that Izyaslav had no intention of allowing any of them to rule the land which had belonged to the treacherous Svyatoslav. This policy of revenge created a quasi-permanent opposition led by the dispossessed Svyatoslavichi, who were the source of much trouble until the end of the century. The most active and politically successful of them was Oleg.[21]

In April 1078 Oleg was invited by Vladimir to dine with his father Vsevolod in Chernigov.[22] He had recently been expelled (doubtless by Izyaslav) from his west Russian principality; and Vladimir, by arranging this dinner, was probably trying to bring about a reconciliation between his cousin and his father. Their joint expedition to Poland in 1076 had no doubt cemented a friendship between the two kinsmen: a link that was strengthened when Oleg became, probably in the same year, the godfather of Vladimir's first-born, Mstislav.

We do not know what passed between Oleg and Vsevolod at this fateful dinner in Chernigov. Very probably Oleg declared that the city was rightfully his, and his uncle rejected the claim. Whereupon, according to the Russian chronicle, Oleg 'fled from Vsevolod' to Tmutorokan'.[23] This city (whose Greek name was Tamatarcha) was the capital of a small Russian principality facing the Crimea, on the eastern side of the Straits of Kerch'. Though separated from Kievan Russia by three hundred miles of steppe-land, mostly controlled by the Polovtsians, it had close political links with Chernigov which went back at least to the early eleventh century. It was to Tmutorokan' that the dispossessed Svyatoslavichi and other princely malcontents retired to nurse their grievances and hatch their plots to regain

---

[21] On the Svyatoslavichi, see O. M. Rapov, *Knyazheskie vladeniya na Rusi v X-pervoy polovine XIII v.* (Moscow, 1977), 96–103.

[22] P 159; ET 212.

[23] P 132; ET 165.

Chernigov. In the summer of 1078 they very nearly succeeded. Oleg and his cousin Boris, supported by a Polovtsian army, advanced from Tmutorokan', defeated Vsevolod's forces on the borders of Russia, and entered Chernigov. Vsevolod fled from the city, and found refuge with his elder brother in Kiev.

Vladimir was in Smolensk when the news of the invasion reached him. Vsevolod had no doubt urgently called for his help. Vladimir's loyalty to his father seems to have been unbounded, to judge from his readiness at all times to act as his military and political agent, and from the respectful terms in which he refers to him in his autobiography. The price of his loyalty now was a break with Oleg, his friend and former companion-in-arms. Vladimir hastened south at his father's call, cut his way through the Polovtsian army, and—his earliest recorded military success—helped Vsevolod and Izyaslav to recapture Chernigov. A decisive clash between the rival Russian princes could no longer be delayed. It took place on the field of Nezhata, near Chernigov, on 3 October 1078. The armies of Izyaslav and Vsevolod were victorious, and Oleg was forced to return to Tmutorokan'. Izyaslav, however, was killed in battle; the vacant throne of Kiev now passed to Vsevolod, and Vladimir, who took part in the fateful encounter, was given Chernigov.[24]

The city in which Vladimir was to reign for the next sixteen years ranked second in Russia. Situated on the lower Desna, not far from its confluence with the Dnieper, Chernigov was the capital of a principality which stretched from the middle Dnieper to the upper Oka. Drawing its wealth from large landed estates and its share of the Baltic–Black Sea trade, the city had by the second half of the eleventh century become a major cultural centre, with a nascent literary school and a fine stone cathedral.[25] The Svyatoslavichi, its local dynasty, entrenched in far-away Tmutorokan', were licking their wounds and acquiring a taste for local autonomy that grew, later in the century, into a studied indifference to the interests of Kiev. Chief among the protagonists of this *sacro egoismo* was Oleg Svyatoslavich. However, his claims to Chernigov posed no immediate threat to Vladimir. In 1079 he was arrested in Tmutorokan' by the Khazars, and exiled to Constantinople. It is generally believed that this move

[24] P 133; ET 166.
[25] See Nasonov, *Russkaya Zemlya*, 57–68; Tikhomirov, *Towns*, 357–71; A. K. Zaytsev, 'Chernigovskoe knyazhestvo', in L. G. Beskrovnyi (ed.), *Drevnerusskie knyazhestva X–XIII vv.* (Moscow, 1975), 57–117.

was instigated by the Byzantine government, with the aim of aiding
Vsevolod, prince of Kiev and the husband of an imperial princess,
against his troublesome nephew. Oleg remained on Byzantine
territory for four years, two of which he spent on the island of Rhodes,
and did not return to Tmutorokan' before 1083.[26]

The first years of Vladimir's reign in Chernigov were marked by a
series of victories over the steppe nomads. During his first winter
(1078–79) in the city he repelled a Polovtsian invasion, and in 1080,
on his father's orders, defeated the Torki near Pereyaslavl'. These
Turkic nomads who, like the Pechenegs and the Polovtsians, came
from western Asia, had recently devastated imperial lands in the
Balkans, thrusting south as far as the environs of Thessalonica. The
Byzantines knew them as Ouzoi (Uz). Fortunately for the empire, their
horde was decimated by the plague, while some of the survivors
recrossed the Danube and returned to the Pontic steppes. In 1080,
facing Vladimir's army, they must have posed a far lesser threat to the
Russians than they had to the Byzantines.

In 1085–6 the Polovtsians were again active in the region of
Pereyaslavl' and Chernigov. In his autobiography Vladimir tells us
how he repulsed them, 'with the help of God and of Our Lady'.[27]

In 1093 Vsevolod died in Kiev. The handsome panegyric which
Vladimir's father receives in the Russian Primary Chronicle[28] may
well point to an early twelfth-century redactor devoted to him and his
family; we should note, however, that Izyaslav, his elder brother, is
accorded an equally glowing panegyric in the same document:[29] only
Svyatoslav, the usurper, receives no encomium, the chronicle
recording his death without comment.

With the demise of the last surviving son of Yaroslav and the advent
to power of the next princely generation, the problem of the
succession to the thrones of Kiev, Chernigov, and Pereyaslavl' had to
be resolved afresh within the family. If we can believe the chronicle,
Vladimir was tempted to claim his father's throne, but in the interests
of peace decided to stand down in favour of his cousin Svyatopolk
Izyaslavich, his senior.[30] Svyatopolk was duly enthroned in Kiev
while Vladimir, after attending his father's death, returned to

---

[26] P 135; ET 168; cf. D. S. Likhachev, in *Povest' vremennykh let*, ii. 412–13 (hereafter
P ii).

[27] P 160; ET 213.   [28] P 141–2; ET 174.   [29] P 133–5; ET 166–7.

[30] P 143; ET 175.

Chernigov. Oleg, still deprived of his patrimony, remained in Tmuto-rokan'.

Much of Svyatopolk's reign (1093–1113), as described by the Primary Chronicle, was spent in wars with the Polovtsians. In May 1093 the combined forces of Svyatopolk and Vladimir were routed by the river Stugna, south of Kiev. The chronicler hints at serious disagreements of strategy and some personal enmity between the two cousins. In full flight, the forces of Vladimir and his younger brother Rostislav were crossing the river when the latter, despite his brother's efforts to save him, was drowned.[31] The death of the young prince shocked his contemporaries and inspired several popular laments. Nearly a century later, one of these was incorporated into the *Lay of Igor's Campaign*, Russia's greatest heroic poem.

Sadly, we know virtually nothing of Vladimir's reign in Chernigov. There may well have been among the townsfolk and the landed aristocracy residual loyalties to the exiled branch of their princely family, and particularly to its most prominent representative, Oleg Svyatoslavich. These loyalties, if they existed, were soon put to the test. In 1094, escorted by a Polovtsian army, Oleg rode out from Tmutorokan' to claim his patrimony, Chernigov. The events that followed are described by Vladimir in his autobiography:

And then Oleg came against me to Chernigov together with the Polovtsians, and my forces did battle with them for eight days over a small rampart, and refused them entry into the fortress. Having pity on the souls of Christians, and on the burning villages and monasteries, I said: 'The pagans must not be allowed to boast.' And I gave my brother (i.e. cousin) his father's domain, and retired myself to my own father's domain of Pereyaslavl'. And we moved out of Chernigov on St Boris's day, and we rode through the Polovtsian troops in an armed company of some hundred men, and also women and children. The Polovtsians licked their lips as they looked at us, standing like wolves at the river ford and on the hills; but God and St Boris did not deliver us up to them, and we reached Pereyaslavl' safely.[32]

This vivid account deserves a brief comment. It is one of the few passages in Vladimir's autobiography in which the narrative rises above a homely and matter-of-fact style, and patently strives for literary effect: a sign, we may surmise, that the memory of this frightening experience continued to haunt him in the years to come. The repeated references to St Boris, his great-uncle and one of Russia's patron saints, is consistent with the religious outlook that permeates Vladimir's writings. Yet the passage does raise the awkward question—which will be discussed later in broader terms—of the author's truthfulness and reliability. Can we believe that Vladimir yielded Chernigov to his rival solely for the high-minded motives he cites? The length and fierceness of the fighting, and his somewhat inglorious departure from the city, suggest that Oleg imposed a military solution, and that Vladimir in the end bowed to naked force. It would be rash, however, wholly to dismiss his own explanation: and there seems no adequate reason to doubt that, in deciding to evacuate Chernigov in 1094, Vladimir—apart from military reasons—was moved by the sight of the suffering population, and repelled by the thought of the Polovtsians gaining comfort from the sight of Russian princes fighting one another.

In Pereyaslavl', where he had probably spent his childhood and early youth, Vladimir reigned from 1094 to 1113. In his autobiography he complains of the hardship of those years: 'together with my retainers I suffered much from war and hunger'.[33] These difficulties were caused by the Polovtsians and by Oleg. In 1096, in alliance with Svyatopolk, Vladimir repelled an invasion of the Polovtsians provoked, no doubt, by the treacherous murder of their envoys, committed on his orders. So great was the Polovtsian threat in that year that their army, under the redoubtable Khan Bonyak, nearly captured Kiev in a surprise raid, and plundered the Monastery of the Caves on the outskirts of the city.

With Chernigov firmly in his grasp, Oleg was able, in the closing years of the century, to play an active part in Russian politics. His activities are severely condemned by the chronicler. In 1096, as he refused to come to Kiev to discuss a common strategy against the Polovtsians, Svyatopolk and Vladimir declared war on him. Oleg fled from Chernigov to north-east Russia, where he attacked several towns belonging to Vladimir. In a battle outside Murom, Vladimir's second son Izyaslav was killed while defending the city against Oleg's forces. It is a mark of the chronicler's objectivity that, for all the harshness with which he condemns Oleg's actions, he admits that in claiming Murom, which had belonged to his father, he had right on his side.[34]

In the midst of this family tragedy Vladimir's eldest son Mstislav,

---

[33] P 161; ET 213.   [34] P 168; ET 185.

then prince of Novgorod, emerged as a man of peace. He offered—subject to certain conditions—to mediate between Oleg and Vladimir. Oleg, in turn arrogant and deceitful, attacked the town of Suzdal', but was defeated, and forced at last to cooperate with his cousins.

Mstislav's willingness to act as a peacemaker between his father and Oleg is understandable: he was, it will be recalled, Oleg's godson. Vladimir's reaction to the death of his son, for which Oleg was largely responsible, is more remarkable. At Mstislav's request he sent Oleg a letter, offering him the hand of reconciliation. The contents and tone of this letter will be discussed later. For the present we may note that it halted the civil strife in Russia. In 1097, faced with what seems to have been a military stalemate, Svyatopolk, Oleg, Vladimir, and several of their cousins met at Lyubech on the Dnieper to conclude peace. The chronicler, summing up the sense of the meeting by what is doubtless a fictional speech, makes the princes declare: 'Why do we ruin the land of Russia by continual strife against each other? The Polovtsians meanwhile create dissension in our land and rejoice that there is warfare among us. From now on let us be of one heart, and defend our land.'[35]

The conference of Lyubech, at which representatives of all branches of Yaroslav's descendants 'sat on the same carpet' and 'in the same tent' (Russian medieval equivalents of the round-table conferences of today), attempted to bring political stability to the land. The princes decreed that each branch of the family should retain its own 'patrimony': Kiev, Izyaslav's city, would be held by his son Svyatopolk; Oleg and his brothers were to rule in Chernigov, the patrimony of their father Svyatoslav; while Vladimir was to retain Pereyaslavl', his father Vsevolod's domain. To mark the binding nature of this agreement, each of the princes kissed the cross.

It has been observed that the decisions of the Lyubech conference contain no reference to the principle of seniority within the princely family. This principle, which gave a real, if tenuous, sense of unity to the different territories of the realm, was enshrined in Yaroslav's 'testament'. In its place the conference of Lyubech proclaimed the right of each branch of the ruling family to its territorial 'patrimony'. A significant step had been taken towards a new political regime—that of the sovereign existence of virtually independent principalities.

The Lyubech conference was the first of several at which the

[35] P 170; ET 187.

princes met to settle their political differences and plan their war
strategy. Increasingly, as the eleventh century gives way to the
twelfth, the chronicle attributes the initiative for the anti-Polovtsian
campaigns to Vladimir. It is indeed probable that his qualities of
leadership were by then widely recognized by his peers and subjects.
From his capital in Pereyaslavl' he ruled over regions as diverse and
strategically vital as Smolensk, Novgorod, and the upper Volga.

In all the principal events of Svyatopolk's reign Vladimir is
portrayed by the Chronicle as playing a leading role. After the
horrifying blinding of Vasil'ko, a west Russian prince (1097),[36] we
see him—in agreement, this time, with Oleg—avenging the crime; in
1103, in association with Svyatopolk, conducting a campaign deep
into the steppe, and defeating, south of the Dnieper rapids, a
Polovtsian host, vast, the chronicler asserts, as a forest;[37] and in
1107, this time in alliance with Svyatopolk and Oleg, gaining a
further victory, followed by yet another in 1111. These three
campaigns removed the Polovtsian threat from Russia's southern
borders for several decades and established Vladimir's considerable
military reputation.[38]

In 1113 Svyatopolk, prince of Kiev, died. For the second time
Vladimir drew back from the prospect of becoming the ruler of the first
city in Russia. Its citizens, however, sent him a message, inviting him
to mount the throne, an offer Vladimir declined. The motive ascribed
to him by the chronicle—the fact that he was in mourning for his late
cousin—is unconvincing. It is more likely that he felt reluctant to
accept the Kievan throne without being empowered to do so by an
inter-princely conference, and that he was aware that there were
other, senior, candidates, one of whom was Oleg. But riots broke out
in Kiev against the city authorities and the Jews, who seem to have
enjoyed Svyatopolk's favour. The Kievans then sent a second, and
more urgent, message to Vladimir warning him of an impending
attack on local nobles and monasteries, and stating that he would
bear the responsibility for further violence. To avert what seems to
have been an incipient social revolution, Vladimir accepted the
throne. He was met at the gates of Kiev by the primate of All Russia,

[36] P 171–3; ET 188–91.   [37] P 184; ET 201.
[38] S. A. Pletneva, *Kochevniki srednevekov'ya* (Moscow, 1982), 58, suggests that a
major cause of the victory of the Russians in 1103 was the fact that they attacked in
early spring, when the Polovtsians were still scattered in their winter encampments by
the Sea of Azov, and not ready to fight.

the Metropolitan Nicephorus, and a deputation of bishops and citizens.[39]

De jure as well as in fact, Vladimir was now the leading prince in Russia. Partly due to the growth of local separatism, Kiev since Yaroslav's death had gradually lost some of its former commanding status in the land. But it still possessed great wealth and prestige. Its geographical position, astride the main commercial routes of eastern Europe, made it an emporium for the products of Byzantium, Germany, and central Europe. The renown it still enjoyed, at home and abroad, as 'the mother of the Russian cities'[40] was enhanced by the presence within its walls of the primate of the Russian Church, the 'metropolitan of Kiev and All Russia'. The city's appearance owed much to Yaroslav's building activity.[41] The five major buildings erected in his capital at his behest included a new citadel with a monumental entrance (the Golden Gate) and the churches of the Annunciation, St George, and St Irene. Among them the cathedral of St Sophia held pride of place. Its very name, and its triple status of court church, the main cathedral of the land, and seat of the Russian primate, show that Yaroslav intended it to be, in function if not in appearance, a copy of the great church of St Sophia in Constantinople. Its mosaics, which date from the 1040s, were almost certainly executed by Constantinopolitan artists; while a group of frescoes on the tower staircases leading to the galleries of the church have been dated authoritatively to Vladimir's reign in Kiev. No less remarkable was the mosaic decoration in the church of the Archangel Michael, built by Svyatopolk between 1108 and 1113. Two famous monasteries stood on the outskirts of the city: the Monastery of the Caves, the leading monastic house of early medieval Russia, and the Monastery of St Michael at Vydubichi, the latter founded by Vladimir's own father. Both monasteries, especially the former, were closely associated with the compilation of successive versions of the Primary Chronicle. Kiev, the cradle of the Russian nation, thus became the mother of Russian letters. Its outward appearance made a powerful impression on foreign visitors: the Saxon chronicler Thietmar of Merseburg, writing in the early eleventh century, described Kiev as a city of over four hundred (!) churches and eight public squares[42]; and another eleventh-century chronicler, Adam of Bremen, called it

---

[39] P 196–7.   [40] P 20; ET 61.   [41] P 102; ET 137.
[42] *Chronicon*, viii. 32: MGH, *Scriptores rerum Germanicarum*, NS ix (Berlin, 1935), 530.

Constantinople's rival and 'the most brilliant ornament of Greece'.[43] There is manifest exaggeration in these western accounts, yet twelfth-century Kiev, with its numerous stone buildings which stood on a hill overlooking the Dnieper, spanned by the bridge built by Vladimir in 1115, must have been an imposing sight.

If we can believe the Primary Chronicle, Vladimir's enthronement in Kiev brought the city immediate peace: 'all the people were glad, and the rioting stopped'. One of his first measures was to summon a meeting of town officials from south Russia (including a representative of Oleg of Chernigov) to deal with the causes of the riots. The result was a new statute concerning loans at interest, which was included in the *Pravda russkaya*, the earliest known Russian legal code, originally promulgated by Prince Yaroslav. The precise nature and purpose of this 'Statute of Vladimir Vsevolodovich' are debatable. It seems that its principal aims were to prevent abuses connected with loans and safeguard the interests of the ruling classes, threatened by a recurrence of the disorders of 1113.[44]

The chronicles do not tell us much about Vladimir's reign in Kiev. His authority over Russia was unchallenged, except in the western regions, where he repeatedly intervened in order to bring rebellious cousins to heel; he ruled partly through his sons, who represented him in the principal cities of Russia: Pereyaslavl', Smolensk, Novgorod, Suzdal', and Vladimir in Volhynia. The Polovtsians caused no trouble during his reign, except for a brief attack in 1113 which Vladimir repelled with the help of Oleg. The two princes now lived at peace with each other. In the world of twelfth-century Russia, Oleg's patrimony, the principality of Chernigov, was politically going its own way; and it was there, in the city he had fought so long and so fiercely to regain and to hold for his house, that Oleg died in 1115.

In the year of his death Oleg took part, together with Vladimir, in a religious ceremony of national importance. In Vyshgorod, a town on the Dnieper twenty kilometres upstream from Kiev, amid a large concourse of clergy and people, the relics of Boris and Gleb, the first Russian saints to be canonized, were transferred from the wooden church where they had lain since 1072 into a stone one, built for the purpose by Vladimir and Oleg. Boris and Gleb were the sons of St

---

[43] *Gesta Hammaburgensis ecclesiae pontificum*, 3rd edn. (Hanover–Leipzig, 1917), ii. 22 (p. 80): 'Aemula sceptri Constantinopolitani, clarissimum decus Graeciae'.
[44] *Pravda russkaya*, ed. B. D. Grekov, ii (Moscow–Leningrad, 1947), 425–8; *Medieval Russian Laws*, tr. G. Vernadsky (New York, 1947), 43–8.

Vladimir and the brothers of Yaroslav, and in 1015 had been assassinated by order of an elder brother. The manner of their death, and especially their acceptance of it in a spirit of Christian resignation, made a powerful impression upon their compatriots. Russians of all classes and stations in life became convinced that the two murdered princes were numbered among the saints of God. This popular cult, centred on Vyshgorod, the place of their burial, was encouraged by the ruling dynasty, which led to a formal recognition of the brothers' sanctity, first by the Russian Church and then, in 1072, by the Byzantines. The three accounts of their death written in Russia during the hundred years that followed show that Boris and Gleb were regarded as martyrs, not in the sense that they were killed for the Christian faith, but because by their act of non-resistance they chose to die as innocent and voluntary victims, in imitation of Christ's sacrificial death.[45] These holy princes became their country's earliest patron saints; and, by a curious paradox, the devotees of meekness and non-resistance came to be seen as military champions and supernatural defenders of the Russian land. Vladimir Monomakh on many occasions showed his veneration for the memory of his two great-uncles. Their cult could still act as a force for unity in the land. And it is significant that the long and bitter enmity between Vladimir and Oleg, which not even the spiritual bond created at the baptism of Vladimir's son had been able to exorcize, was in the end soothed in the common act of homage which they paid at the grave of their sainted kinsmen. Describing this ceremony, the Russian chronicle admits, however, that there was still some rivalry between them: Vladimir wished the tomb containing the bodies of Boris and Gleb to be placed in the centre of the church, while Oleg and his brother had chosen as the relics' repository their own family vault to the right of the nave. The issue was decided by lot: and Oleg won. The consecration of the new church was followed by a banquet, at which Oleg acted as host, and by festivities lasting three days. The crowds, the chronicler tells us, were huge; and, on Vladimir's orders silken fabrics, woollen garments, and squirrel-skins were distributed to the people. This last recorded meeting between Vladimir and Oleg breathes an air of peace and reconciliation.[46]

[45] See D. Obolensky, 'Early Russian Literature', in R. Auty and D. Obolensky (eds.), *An Introduction to Russian Language and Literature* (Cambridge, 1977), 65–8, and the bibliography on p. 86.

[46] P 199–200.

Vladimir died on 19 May 1125, at the age of seventy-two. In one manuscript of the Primary Chronicle he is called 'a good champion of the Russian land', and praised for 'wiping away much sweat for the land of Russia'.[47] Another version of the Chronicle gives him a more extended obituary, with religious overtones:

He had great faith in God and in his kinsmen, the holy martyrs Boris and Gleb . . . He was very compassionate and had received a special gift from God: whenever he entered a church and heard the singing, he would begin to weep . . . He died on the L'ta [or Al'ta, a river near Pereyaslavl'] close to his beloved church [of SS Boris and Gleb] which he had founded with much care. His sons and boyars carried his body to Kiev, and he was laid to rest in St Sophia, beside his father.[48]

It was probably in 1117 that Vladimir wrote his autobiography, entitled in the only manuscript in which it has survived—the so-called Laurentian text of the Primary Chronicle, copied in 1377—*Pouchenie*, literally 'Instruction'.[49] The work, incomplete in its extant form, consists of three loosely connected parts: firstly, a didactic passage concerned with man's religious and social duties, and addressed in the first place to his sons, but aimed too at a wider circle of readers; secondly, an autobiographical section—mostly a list, with occasional comments, of Vladimir's journeys and campaigns; and thirdly, the text of his letter to Oleg, written in 1096. In all three sections the author speaks of himself and reveals something of his character, life-style, and beliefs. It thus seems right to describe the *Pouchenie* as an autobiography,[50] a form of writing perhaps familiar to Vladimir from his mother's world: self-portraiture at the time was becoming increasingly common in Byzantine literature.[51]

[47] *Ipat'evskaya letopis'*, s.aa. 1125 (col. 289), 1140 (col. 303). The expression seems to have been traditional in Kievan Russia. According to the Primary Chronicle, Yaroslav after his capture of Kiev in 1019 'wiped away his sweat, in the company of his retainers' (P 98; ET 134). This recalls the sweat ($i\delta\rho\hat{\omega}\tau\epsilon\varsigma$) poured forth for his subjects in war by the Emperor Basil I (Theophanes Continuatus, v, ch. 89, Bonn, 332), and the 'sweat and toil' of battle shared with his soldiers by the Emperor Alexius I (*Alexiad*, xiii. 8). For the 'imperial sweat' as a *topos* of imperial panegyrics see Kazhdan–Epstein, *Change in Byzantine Culture*, 214.

[48] *Lavrent'evskaya Letopis'*, s.a. 1125 (Leningrad, 1926), cols. 294–5.

[49] P 153–63; ET 206–15 (s.a. 1096). The text is reprinted in *A Historical Russian Reader*, ed. J. Fennell and D. Obolensky (Oxford, 1969), 52–62 (hereafter *Reader*). For commentaries and modern works on the *Pouchenie*, see Obolensky, Early Russian Literature', 87.

[50] See T. N. Kopreeva, 'K voprosu o zhanrovoy prirode "Poucheniya" Vladimira Monomakha', *TODRL* xxvii (1972), 94–108.

[51] See Kazhdan–Epstein, *Change in Byzantine Culture*, 220–30.

The opening passage contains several clues both to Vladimir's state of mind and to the circumstances which led him to write it. On two occasions he refers to his advanced age,[52] although if he wrote in 1117 he would have been only sixty-four. Because of his age, he fears, his readers may be tempted to make fun of him. This remark is perhaps more than mere literary convention, and we may suspect that Vladimir's anxiety stemmed less from an awareness of his age than from a feeling that the moral precepts he was about to offer would be more appropriate coming from a cleric than from a layman.

In the same opening section Vladimir relates an episode from what seems to have been a fairly distant past. It probably occurred in 1099, and its importance lies in the fact that it inspired Vladimir to look up, and copy, a number of scriptural passages which he later incorporated into his Autobiography. This is how he recalled it.

Envoys from my brothers [i.e. first cousins] met me on the Volga, and said: 'Hasten to join us, that we may drive out the two sons of Rostislav and take their land; if you do not come with us, we will go our way, and you yours.' And I said: 'Even if you are angry with me, I cannot go with you, nor break my oath.'[53]

The sons of Rostislav were relatives of Vladimir, and ruled in western Russia. One of them was the hapless Vasil'ko who was blinded in 1097. Vladimir's cousins, who were plotting against them, almost certainly included the prince of Kiev, Svyatopolk. Their message to Vladimir contained an open threat. He seems to have been in no position to risk an armed conflict with his powerful cousins; yet their proposal for joint action against the Rostislavichi was a direct challenge to the policy of inter-princely co-operation, recently defined at the conference of Lyubech, and to which Vladimir was personally committed. He too on that occasion had sworn an oath on the cross.

The moral predicament which provides the overture to the Autobiography was not unfamiliar to Vladimir. In 1094, when Oleg challenged him for the possession of Chernigov, and again in 1096, when his son was killed in battle against Oleg's forces, he had been faced with a similar choice between personal and national interests.

---

[52] P 153; ET 206; *Reader*, 52. Vladimir tells us that he wrote his work 'seated on a sleigh'. As Likhachev has pointed out (P ii. 433–4), the metaphorical meaning of this expression ('in my declining years') finds support in the medieval Russian custom of conveying the body of a dead person to its resting-place on a sleigh. 'With one foot in the grave' is a possible English translation.

[53] P 153; ET 206; *Reader*, 52.

This time too the dilemma was a painful one. 'In sorrow' he sought solace in Holy Writ. He opened the Book of Psalms at random and read these words: 'Why art thou cast down, O my soul? and why art thou disquieted within me? Hope in God: for I shall yet praise him' (Ps. 43: 5 AV).

Vladimir found these words well suited to his mood. He later decided, he tells us, to commit them to writing, together with a number of other passages from the Psalms which sustained his belief that man's surest refuge is trust in God who will protect him in the hour of trial, when danger threatens or his principles are put to the test. These quotations, no doubt chosen to echo the predicament in which he found himself in 1099, provided the stimulus for the writing of his Autobiography.

A string of further quotations from scriptural, patristic, and liturgical texts—all no doubt available to him in Old Church Slavonic translations, and some perhaps dredged up from his memory, serve as an introduction to the first of Vladimir's moral precepts. It draws its force from the belief in God's merciful nature and his fatherly concern for man. To attain salvation his sons need not engage in severe ascetic training: 'repentance, tears, and works of mercy' are sufficient to gain the kingdom of heaven. Vladimir is obviously thinking here of those members of the ruling class who have neither the time, nor perhaps the inclination, for elaborate religious practices: if you are on horseback, he says, and have nothing else to do, better than harbour idle thoughts, repeat in your mind the prayer 'Lord, have mercy', if you know no other.

This injunction is followed by more quotations from the Psalms, leading to a passage of lyrical description, which provides a contrast to the rather stark prelude of the *Pouchenie*.

Who would not praise and glorify thy power and thy great wonders and bounty, arranged in this world? How the sky is ordered, how the moon and the stars, darkness and light, and the earth laid upon the waters, O Lord, by thy providence! Diverse animals and birds and fishes all adorned by thy providence, O Lord! And we marvel at this wonder: how thou createdst man out of the dust of the ground, and how diverse are the images in human faces—if one were to gather together the whole world they would not be of the same image, but each by God's wisdom would have its own image. And we marvel at how the birds of the skies come from the land of spring, and fly first of all into our hands, and stay not in one land but, whether strong or weak, fly over all lands, by God's command, that the forests and fields may be filled. And all this God has given for the good of man, for his food and joy . . . and those birds of the skies are taught by thee, O Lord; when thou commandest they begin to sing, and make men glad in thee; and when thou dost not they fall silent, though they have tongues.[54]

Many attempts have been made to discover the source of this remarkable passage. The idea that the variety in human faces is one of God's most wonderful works was not unknown in western medieval literature.[55] But Vladimir's almost ecstatic contemplation of the manifold marvels of the created world finds its closest parallel in the *Shestodnev* ('Six Days of Creation') by the Bulgarian churchman John the Exarch. This work, written in Old Church Slavonic during the reign of the Bulgarian Tsar Symeon (893–927), was a part-translation, part-adaptation—with additional material—of St Basil's *Hexaemeron*, a Greek commentary on the account of the creation of the world in the first chapter of the Book of Genesis.[56] The *Shestodnev* seems to have been much read in early medieval Russia, and it is probable that, in the passage cited, Vladimir modelled himself, at least partially, on the work of John the Exarch.[57] However, the similarities of form and content are not all that close, and hardly amount to direct paraphrase; so that, in default of any other persuasive textual parallel, we may assume that at least the wording of the passage is Vladimir's own. But even if a more convincing prototype of this passage were to be found one day in Byzantine or Old Church Slavonic literature, the value of this lyrical excursus as a guide to its author's mind would scarcely be diminished. When all has been said about the textual pedigree of this 'nature' passage, it still provides first-hand evidence of Vladimir's ability, in a life filled with strenuous activity, to pause in wonder before the beauty and variety of the natural world.

Following the 'Mirror for Princes' tradition, the didactic section of the *Pouchenie* is concerned with man's duties to God, his fellow men, and himself.[58] His social obligations, if he belongs to the ruling class, are to dispense justice, protect the weak, co-operate with the church,

---

[54] P 156; *Reader*, 55.

[55] See R. Köhler, 'Die Ungleichheit der menschlichen Gesichter', *Germania. Vierteljahrsschrift für deutsche Alterthumskunde*, viii (1863), 304–5.

[56] *Das Hexaemeron des Exarchen Johannes*, ed. R. Aitzetmüller, 7 vols. (Graz, 1958–75).

[57] See D. S. Likhachev, *Velikoe nasledie* (Moscow, 1975), 123–6; ET, *The Great Heritage* (Moscow, 1981), 148–9.

[58] For the Byzantine 'Mirror for Princes' tradition, see Hunger, *Hochsprachliche profane Literatur*, i. 157–65.

be efficient in the conduct of war, control his troops, preside with love and authority over his family, and seek good repute abroad by hospitality shown to strangers. Towards himself the ruler is urged to be strict, counting his public actions as 'labour', requiring discipline and training. Some of this certainly reflects Vladimir's own leanings: thus he writes with manifest admiration of his father who, without leaving Russia, learned five languages—clearly an unusual achievement, even in the cosmopolitan society of eleventh-century Kiev; and he advises his sons to follow a regular daily routine, dividing their time between consulting their retainers, dispensing justice, hunting, riding and, somewhere in this busy round of occupations, lapsing into the 'God-appointed' midday siesta.

The autobiographical section which follows, and forms about one-third of the *Pouchenie*, is mostly an artless catalogue of Vladimir's 'travels' (*puti*)—military campaigns and politically motivated journeys—from *c.* 1068 to *c.* 1117. He recalled eighty-three major ones, 'and the lesser ones I cannot remember'. Some of the more important have already been mentioned. The overall impression is one of frequent movement and strenuous activity. With manifest pride he records that during the sixteen years of his reign in Chernigov he travelled some hundred times to Kiev to see his father: and he covered the distance—about eighty-five miles—on horseback in a day, before the beginning of vespers. His very language echoes this restless activity. Verbs of action abound: 'I went', 'I came', my father 'sent me', 'I campaigned', 'We vanquished' (a common variant is 'God helped us'), 'We pursued', 'We scattered them'.

Vladimir's zest for strenuous activity can also be seen in his account of his hunting exploits; here too he seems to have followed the new conventions of Byzantine literature which, in the twelfth century especially, began to extol hunting as part of the imperial image.[59] As elsewhere in his autobiography, his pride in his physical attainment is tempered by the belief that his exploits in the chase were due to divine aid:

This is what I did in Chernigov: I captured ten and twenty wild horses with my own hands ... Two bisons tossed me and my horse on their horns, a stag gored me, an elk trampled me underfoot, another gored me with his horns, a wild boar tore my sword from my thigh, a bear bit my saddle-cloth next to my knee, and another wild beast jumped on to my flank and threw my horse with

[59] Kazhdan–Epstein, *Change in Byzantine Culture*, 110, 243–4.

me. And God preserved me unharmed. I often fell from my horse, fractured my skull twice, and in my youth injured my arms and legs, not sparing my head or my life.

The existing text of the *Pouchenie* ends with Vladimir's letter to Oleg, written in all probability in 1096, as a peace-offering at the end of the civil war in which Vladimir's son was killed, fighting Oleg's forces. It was probably the presence of this letter in some collection of Vladimir's writings that led the medieval copyist to group them together in the Chronicle under the year 1096, although the didactic and autobiographical sections of the *Pouchenie* were probably written some twenty years later. The letter draws its quiet dignity from the sincerity of Christian forgiveness, from Vladimir's awareness of his spiritual bond with Oleg, the godfather of his dead son, and from his acceptance of the need to subordinate personal feelings to the overriding cause of national unity:

Oh, long-suffering and wretched man that I am . . . Look, brother, at our fathers. What did they carry away with them [into the grave] . . . except what they did to their souls? You, my brother, should first have written these words to me. When my child—and yours—was killed before your eyes, and when you saw his blood and his body, as he lay like a newly blossomed and withered flower or as a slaughtered lamb, you should have said, standing over him and reading the thoughts of your soul: 'Alas, what have I done?' . . . You should have repented before God, sent me a letter of consolation, and let my daughter-in-law come to me . . . that I might embrace her and mourn her husband and their marriage, in the place of wedding-songs: for I did not witness her joy of former times, nor their wedding, because of my sins. For God's sake send her to me with your first envoy that I might weep with her, and give her a home, and she might sit like a turtle-dove upon a dried-up tree, and I may be comforted in God . . . Is it strange that a man should have perished in war? The best of our forefathers died in this way . . . Send me your envoy, or a bishop, and write me a letter in truth . . . Then you will turn our heart towards you, and we shall live better than before.[60]

Several critics have tried—not very successfully—to show that some of the imagery of this letter was borrowed, from written sources or from oral laments. The overall effect remains powerful and moving: a testimony to its author's command of language, personal sincerity,

---

[60] P 163–5. For a literary study of this letter see G. Bercoff, 'Plädoyer für eine "literarische" Würdigung von Vladimir Monomachs Brief an Oleg', *Zeitschrift für slavische Philologie*, xli/2 (1980), 289–305.

and generosity of spirit; a witness, too, to the strength and maturity of his Christian faith.

The question of Vladimir's sincerity raises a problem of great importance to his modern biographer. How far can we trust the picture of his character and achievements that emerges from his writings? It should be clear at the start that, despite a manifest intention to cut a figure in the eyes of his sons and perhaps of posterity as well, Vladimir does not conceal several actions which, even by the standards of his contemporaries, could be judged discreditable. Thus he mentions the treacherous murder, which he sanctioned, of two Polovtsian chieftains who had come to Pereyaslavl' in 1095 to offer peace;[61] and the massacre of the inhabitants of Minsk, for which he admitted responsibility.[62] And he confesses to a sense of guilt for having attacked Oleg in Chernigov in 1096. His Autobiography, to be sure, lacks any hagiographical features; nor did his contemporaries regard Vladimir as a saint, as his son Mstislav was later regarded. Nevertheless, the impression of his personality which we gain from his writings is a highly favourable one. Is it credible?

For many years this question has been bound up with the complex problems of Russian chronicle-writing in the second decade of the twelfth century. Most present-day scholars accept the general conclusions of A. A. Shakhmatov (d. 1920), the foremost authority on medieval Russian chronicles.[63] He argued that the Primary Chronicle (*Povest' vremennykh let*) acquired its present form in three successive stages. Its first redaction was compiled in 1112 by the monk Nestor in the Kiev Monastery of the Caves, during the reign of Svyatopolk. Early in his own reign Vladimir Monomakh commissioned Sylvester, abbot of the Monastery of St Michael at Vydubichi on the outskirts of Kiev, to prepare a revised version. Sylvester, who completed his work in 1116, introduced important changes into Nestor's account of Svyatopolk's reign. Nestor's version has not come down to us: Shakhmatov believed that it might have been lost or hidden at that time. Finally, in 1118 the rivalry between the Monastery of the Caves and that of St Michael was resolved in favour of the former, and an unknown monk of this community was given by Vladimir the task of preparing a third version. He based it on Sylvester's text of 1116, adding some new material, concerned particularly with Vladimir Monomakh and his family.

---

[61] P 161; *Reader*, 60. [62] P 160; ET 212; *Reader*, 59.
[63] See in particular his study *Povest' vremennykh let*, i (Petrograd, 1916), i–lxxvii.

Each of these successive versions of the Chronicle, according to Shakhmatov, was politically biased. In Nestor's version the events of the late eleventh and early twelfth centuries were described in a manner flattering to Svyatopolk. Sylvester, at the behest of his patron Vladimir, whose father had founded the monastery of which he was abbot, edited the end-section of Nestor's text, presenting Vladimir in a more favourable light, and stressing his double role in fighting the Polovtsians and working for national unity. In the third and final version Vladimir's achievements are extolled even higher, and the author, who seems to have greatly admired him and his family, inserted the Autobiography into the text of the Chronicle.

This is no place to discuss Shakhmatov's reconstruction of the intricate genealogy of the Russian Primary Chronicle. Two general points should be made, however. Firstly, for all his unparalleled knowledge of Russian chronicles and sophisticated technique of textual criticism, his conclusions remain hypothetical. Secondly, the partiality and at times deliberate falsification which his theory assumes in the compilers of the Primary Chronicle, and the monasteries to which they belonged, sometimes taxes one's credulity. To be sure, these compilers did at times show some personal bias in the selection and presentation of their material, a bias which often stemmed from loyalty to a particular person or institution. Nevertheless it seems hazardous to regard them as wholesale forgers, playing an elaborate game of hide-and-seek with their medieval readers (and with modern scholars as well). In fairness to Shakhmatov, it should be said that he stopped short of such extreme conclusions, though unfortunately not all his disciples were to show the same restraint.

It is likely enough that the Chronicle has exaggerated Vladimir's wisdom and achievements. This, one suspects, is particularly true of its somewhat disparaging account of Svyatopolk's reign in Kiev, in which Vladimir clearly overshadows him: for Vladimir's immediate predecessor seems to have been a distinguished soldier, and probably played a larger role in planning and leading the anti-Polovtsian campaigns than the Chronicle gives him credit for. Yet it is hard to believe that in depicting Vladimir's character the chronicler (whether Nestor, Sylvester, or the anonymous author of the 1118 version) could have allowed himself seriously to diverge from the truth. He was, after all, writing in the first place for his contemporaries, who had some knowledge of the facts, derived from memory, experience, or hearsay. To distort Vladimir's true image would have been

pointless, and perhaps counter-productive. Rather than imagine that
this image was falsified by an elaborate conspiracy to suppress the
truth, is it not better to accept the evidence at its face value and to
recognize that his contemporaries admired Vladimir for his qualities
of heart, body, and mind?[64]

Few of these were better placed to assess Vladimir's character than
Nicephorus, metropolitan of Kiev from 1104 to 1121, the head of the
Russian Church. Two letters written by this Byzantine prelate to
Vladimir have survived in a Church Slavonic translation. In one of
them, whose ostensible subject is the importance of fasting as a means
of mastering human passions,[65] Nicephorus warns Vladimir against
listening too readily to informers, and urges him to show leniency to
those he has banished or otherwise punished. We do not know why
the metropolitan thought it necessary to utter these mild rebukes; but
the importance of his letter lies in the brief though vivid sketch of the
addressee. Vladimir is described as a man seldom to be found at home,
content to sleep on the ground, who dislikes fine raiment, wears a
poor man's clothes while travelling through the forest, and dons his
princely apparel only when about to make his entry into a town. His
entertainment is lavish, yet at table he likes to serve his guests himself.
This does not sound like a conventional eulogy; and it is easy to
imagine the surprise of this prelate from Constantinople at finding
such rustic manners in a ruler, who, through his mother, was
descended from an emperor of Byzantium; the details he gives of
Vladimir's simple tastes and out-of-doors activity sound the more
authentic for the parallels they offer to several passages of the
Pouchenie. Nicephorus' letter is an independent testimony of great
value to Vladimir's character and life-style: it corroborates the
positive picture painted of him by the Russian sources; and, by
suggesting that the relations between the prince of Kiev and his Greek
metropolitan were friendly and close, it adds to our knowledge of
Vladimir's affinity with the society and thought-world of Byzantium.

Of Vladimir Monomakh's political relations with Byzantium we
know surprisingly little. The Russian Primary Chronicle states
obscurely that in 1116 a conflict broke out between him and the
Emperor Alexius Comnenus over the control of several cities on the

---

[64] On this point see Orlov, *Vladimir Monomakh*, 34–58.
[65] Published in *Russkie dostopamyatnosti*, i (Moscow, 1815), 60–75. Cf. Orlov, op. cit.
49–53.

lower Danube.[66] Its outcome is unknown, but its effects are unlikely to have been lasting: by 1122 at the latest peaceful relations were restored between Russia and Byzantium, and Vladimir's grand-daughter Irene married a son of the Emperor John II Comnenus.[67]

Besides the *Pouchenie*, which, we have seen, was probably written in part under Greek literary influence,[68] there is another field—the visual arts—in which a direct connection between Vladimir and his mother's Byzantine homeland can be traced, with some likelihood if not perhaps always with complete certainty. Three instances are worth citing.

The first comes from the study of Vladimir's lead seals, some twenty-five of which have been found. The early ones, dating from the eleventh century, follow the conventions of Byzantine sphragistics: the legends are Greek, Vladimir's Christian name Basil is dignified by a high-sounding imperial court title, and is followed by his Byzantine family name.[69] Only gradually, at the end of the century, were the Greek inscriptions on Monomakh's seals replaced by Slavonic ones.[70]

The second example is particularly curious and, in several respects, mysterious. In 1821 a gold medallion was discovered near Chernigov (Plate 3). It is an amulet, presumably intended to be worn round the neck.[71] On the obverse side is a representation of the Archangel Michael, holding the labarum in his right hand and the orb in his left,

[66] P 201. The identity of the 'Tsarevich Leon', described by the Chronicle as the son-in-law (or brother-in-law) of Vladimir and said to have captured several Byzantine cities on the Danube, is unclear. See M. Mathieu, 'Les faux Diogènes', *Byzantion*, xxii (1952), 133–48; Vernadsky, *Kievan Russia*, 351, n. 91; V. T. Pashuto, *Vneshnyaya politika drevney Rusi* (Moscow, 1968), 186–7; G. Litavrin, 'Rus'i Vizantiya v XII veke', *Voprosy Istorii*, 1972, no. 7, p. 43.

[67] *Ipat'evskaya letopis'*, col. 286; see S. Papadimitriou, 'Brak russkoy knyazhny Mstislavny Dobrodei s grecheskim tsarevichem Alekseem Komninom', *Vizantiisky vremennik*, xi/1–2 (1904), 73–98.

[68] See also A. Vaillant, 'Une source grecque de Vladimir Monomaque', *Byzantinoslavica*, x (1949), 11–15, and the two articles by L. Müller in *Russia Mediaevalis*, i (1973), 30–48, iv (1979), 16–24.

[69] Σφραγ[ὶς] Βασιλ[ε]ίο[υ] τοῦ πανευγενεστάτου ἄρχοντος Ῥωσίας τοῦ Μονομάχ[ου]: V. L. Yanin, *Aktovye pechati drevney Rusi X–XV vv.* i (Moscow, 1970), 16–17.

[70] See Yu. Morgunov, 'Novyi variant pechati Vladimira Monomakha', *Kratkie Soobshcheniya Instituta Arkheologii*, cxliv (1975), 104–5.

[71] See I. I. Tolstoy, 'O russkikh amuletakh, nazyvaemykh zmeevikami', *Zapiski Imperatorskogo Russkogo Arkheologischeskogo Obshchestva*, iii (1888), 363–77, 394–413, and pl. xv; M. Sokolov, 'Apokrificheskiy material dlya ob'yasneniya amuletov, nazyvaemykh zmeevikami', *Zhurnal Ministerstva Narodnogo Prosveshcheniya*, cclxiii (May 1889), 339–68; N. N. Voronin and M. K. Karger (eds.), *Istoriya kul'tury drevney Rusi*, ii (Moscow–Leningrad, 1951), 444–5.

and a circular inscription in Greek, with the words: 'Holy, holy, holy
Lord of Sabaoth. Heaven and earth are full [of Thy glory].' On the
reverse side is depicted the naked bust of a woman, from which ten
serpents radiate in all directions. This Medusa-like design is surrounded by two concentric inscriptions, one in Church Slavonic, the
other in Greek. The Slavonic one reads: 'Lord, help thy servant Basil.
Amen.' The Greek one, incomplete, has been tentatively reconstructed as follows: 'O womb, dark and black, you have coiled like a
serpent, hissed like a dragon, roared like a lion: [now] sleep like a
lamb'.[72]

Both the female bust with the snakes, and the Greek invocatory
inscription, are far from unique. They are found fairly commonly on
similar objects of late antique or Byzantine workmanship. They are
uterine amulets, whose purpose was to relieve pains of the womb and
diseases affecting it, to bring about conception, and to ensure that the
baby was carried to full term. The design of the female bust with
radiating serpents is believed to derive from the figure of the Graeco-
Egyptian god Chnoubis, whose gem-amulets were used in late
antiquity as a remedy for pains and diseases of the stomach; as for the
inscription, it is a magical charm addressed to the womb (ὑστέρα),
which is admonished to cease its restless movements, compared to
those of noisy wild beasts, and to resume a quiet and motionless
position.[73] The belief that pains of the womb are caused by disorderly
movements of that organ is ancient: we find it already in Plato[74] and
in Hippocratic treatises.

The Slavonic inscription on the reverse side of the amulet follows
the conventional wording of the Byzantine invocatory formula Κύριε

---

[72] Ὑστέρα μελάνη μελανωμένη ὡς ὄφις εἰλύεσαι καὶ ὡς δράκων συρίζησε καὶ ὡς λέων
βρύχησε καὶ ὡς ἀρνίον κοιμήθητι. I am grateful to Nigel Wilson and Ihor Ševčenko for
help in deciphering the last word of the inscription.

[73] See G. Schlumberger, 'Amulettes byzantines anciennes destinées à combattre les
maléfices et maladies', *Revue des études grecques*, v (1892), 89–92; W. Drexler, 'Alte
Beschwörungsformeln', *Philologus: Zeitschrift für das classische Alterthum*, lviii (NF xii)
(1889), 594–616; V. Laurent, 'Amulettes byzantines et formulaires magiques',
Byzantinische Zeitschrift, xxxvi (1936), 300–15; C. Bonner, *Studies in Magical Amulets,
Chiefly Graeco-Egyptian* (Ann Arbor, Mich., 1950), 90–1; A. A. Barb, 'Diva Matrix',
Journal of the Warburg and Courtauld Institutes, xvi (1953), 193–238; V. N. Zalesskaja,
'Amulettes byzantines magiques et leurs liens avec la littérature apocryphe', *Actes du
XIVe Congrès international des études byzantines*, iii (Bucharest, 1976), 243–7; M. R.
Lefkowitz, *Heroines and Hysterics* (London, 1981), 13, 15; G. Vikan, 'Art, Medicine, and
Magic in Early Byzantium, *Dumbarton Oaks Papers*, xxxviii (1984), 65–86.

[74] *Timaeus*, 91 B–D.

βοήθει τῷ σῷ δούλῳ, of which the equally common Slavonic equivalent is 'Gospodi pomozi rabu svoemu'.

There has been some speculation about the identity of the Basil on whose behalf this Christian prayer was offered, and who must be presumed to have owned and worn this medallion. A number of clues point to Vladimir Monomakh. Firstly, Basil was his baptismal name.[75] Secondly, Chernigov, near which the medallion was discovered, was his residence for sixteen years, from 1078 to 1094. Thirdly, the size (7.2 cm in diameter) and the value of this solid gold object—gold is a material almost unique in these amulets—suggest that its owner was wealthy and high-ranking. Fourthly, Vladimir, with his Byzantine family connections, could more easily than anyone else in Russia have obtained it, perhaps from Constantinople. Finally, the Slavonic inscription on the medallion has been dated on palaeographical grounds to the eleventh or twelfth century. Iconographically, too, the association of these amulets with the Gorgon-like figure is typical of this period.[76] All these arguments are circumstantial; yet they point in the same direction, and some have already been used to support the prevalent view that Vladimir was the owner of this talisman,[77] which provides a curious example of Christian–pagan syncretism and of Graeco-Slav bilingualism in Russia in the late eleventh and early twelfth centuries.

The third piece of evidence pointing to a direct link between Vladimir and Byzantium comes from the field of monumental painting. It was probably during his reign in Kiev (1113–25) that a cycle of paintings was executed on the walls and vaults of two tower staircases in the Church of St Sophia. These staircases lead to the galleries where the prince, his family, and his courtiers attended divine service. Several of these paintings represent scenes enacted in the hippodrome of Constantinople. Acrobats, jugglers, and jousters disport themselves in the arena, while charioteers are poised to begin the race. The emperor, who appears in three of the paintings, is shown wearing the crown and the *chlamys*, seated in the imperial box and presiding over the games (Plate 4). The setting is the Kathisma Palace,

---

[75] P 153; ET 206; *Reader*, 52.   [76] Zalesskaja, op. cit. 244.

[77] B. A. Rybakov, *Russkie datirovannye nadpisi XI–XIV vekov* (Moscow, 1964), 19–20 strongly supports this view, argues that the medallion was made in Russia between 1078 and 1094, when Vladimir reigned in Chernigov, and provides drawings of both its faces (pl. 34, 1 and 2). See also V. G. Putsko, 'Kievskaya skul'ptura XI veka', *Byzantinoslavica*, xliii (1982), 60.

on the eastern side of the hippodrome, facing the arena; the palace is depicted here as a three-storeyed building, with open galleries occupied by courtiers and other spectators. In another fresco the emperor is seated on his throne, flanked by two officials, while a third shows him, wearing the crown and mounted on a white horse, riding in triumph. In all three portraits the emperor's head is haloed, in accordance with the conventions of Byzantine imperial iconography.[78]

The depiction of these ceremonies of the Byzantine court on the walls of Russia's principal cathedral church is a striking illustration of the political links between Kiev and Constantinople. For the games of the Byzantine hippodrome, and the ceremonies of the palace generally, were regarded as a symbolic exaltation of the emperor's sovereignty and part of the 'imperial liturgy' which visibly expressed it. The frescoes in the tower staircase of St Sophia not only illustrate the spell cast on the imagination of the Russians by the distant glories of Constantinople; they remain as visible evidence of the attempt made by the princely patron of the church—most probably Vladimir Monomakh—to bring home to his subjects the basic principle of Byzantine political philosophy: the belief that, at least in an ideal and 'metapolitical' sense, the emperor's authority extends over the whole of Orthodox Christendom. A distinguished art historian has suggested that the details of the hippodrome and of the Kathisma Palace in Constantinople may have been described to the painters of those frescoes—if they were Russians—by Vladimir's mother.[79] She was, as we have seen, very probably the daughter of the Emperor Constantine IX. Her son, sovereign ruler of Russia and the new patron of the cathedral church built by his paternal grandfather, may well have taken this initiative, in the realm of the visual arts, to bring Constantinople closer to Kiev.

[78] See A. Grabar, *L'Empereur dans l'art byzantin* (Paris, 1936), 62–74; V. N. Lazarev, *Old Russian Murals and Mosaics* (London, 1966), 20–9, 47–67, 236–41; id., *Drevnerusskie mozaiki i freski XI–XV vv.* (Moscow, 1973), 107–21; D. Obolensky, *The Byzantine Commonwealth* (London, 1971), 346.

[79] Lazarev, *Drevnerusskie mozaiki i freski*, 107.

4

Sava of Serbia

In 1172, deep in the mountains of Serbia, a dramatic encounter took place between the local ruler, Stephen Nemanja, and the Byzantine emperor Manuel I Comnenus. For the past hundred years, under their native princes, the Serbs of the interior[1] had been increasingly rebellious subjects of their imperial overlord. Stephen, who styled himself the grand *župan* of Raška (the country known to west Europeans of the time as Rascia), was a sore trial to the Byzantines. His contemporary, the historian Nicetas Choniates, referred to him contemptuously as 'the satrap of the Serbs', describing him as 'inordinately insolent' and as 'a mischievous fellow who deemed meddlesomeness to be shrewdness'.[2] Soon after his accession, *c.* 1166, Nemanja attacked Byzantine garrison-forces along the road between Belgrade and Niš. The Emperor Manuel decided to teach him a lesson. At the head of a small army he advanced through Sofia into the Serbian interior. Deserted by his allies, the Venetians and the Hungarians, Nemanja lost his nerve. In the words of Nicetas Choniates,

when he saw that the emperor was in pursuit, he showed himself in battle but briefly and then hid in the cover of mountain caves which he sealed with stones. At last his pride was shattered, and he prostrated himself at Manuel's feet. Lying outstretched, mighty in his mightiness,[3] he pleaded that he be not made to suffer cruelly; he was filled with anguish lest he be removed as sovereign over the Serbs and the political power be transferred to those who were more fit to rule, those whom he had thrown down so that he might seize power.[4]

Another contemporary Byzantine historian, John Kinnamos, adds a few vivid details to this scene of imperial triumph:

---

[1] The Serbs on the Adriatic coast had their own separate history in the 11 c. Reference to their territory, Diocleia or Zeta, will be made below.

[2] *Historia*, ed. I. van Dieten (Berlin, 1975), 158; ET, *O City of Byzantium: Annals of Niketas Choniates*, H. J. Magoulias (Detroit, 1984), 90. I have slightly changed his translation, and C. M. Brand's version of Cinnamus (see n. 5 nd 7).

[3] μέγας μεγαλωστί: *Iliad* 16. 776; *Odyssey* 24. 40.   [4] *Historia*, 159; ET p. 90.

[Nemanja] asked that he might gain an audience with him [Manuel] without personal risk. So when the emperor asssented, he came and approached the tribunal, with head uncovered and arms bare to the elbow, and feet unshod; a halter was about his neck, and a sword in his hand. He offered himself to the emperor for whatever treatment the emperor willed. Having mercy on him for this, he [Manuel] set the accusation aside. After this success the emperor departed from Serbia, and the grand *župan* went with him.[5]

It is not without interest that thirteen years earlier Manuel had imposed the same public humiliation, followed by a similar gracious pardon, on another rebel. This previous offender was Reginald of Châtillon, a French knight who had taken part in the Second Crusade and established himself as Prince of Antioch without the emperor's permission; he had so far forgotten his fealty that he plundered Cyprus.[6] Manuel made his way into Antioch with a considerable force. The delinquent Frank was brought before him with head uncovered, arms bared to the elbows, barefoot, a rope round his neck and a sword in his hand.[7] The subsequent treatment of the two rebels was characteristically different. Reginald, a well-connected French aristocrat, was reinstated in Antioch, though Manuel imposed stringent conditions. Nemanja, too, was restored to his position as grand *župan* of Raška; but not before he was forced, in 1172, to accompany the emperor to Constantinople and take part in his triumphal entry as a defeated barbarian, insulted and derided by the populace.[8] An eyewitness, the well-known scholar and writer Eustathius, metropolitan of Thessalonica, supplies a few curious details of Nemanja's enforced sojourn in Constantinople. On 6 December 1174, in a rhetorical address to the Emperor Manuel, Eustathius spoke with admiration of the stature and bearing of Nemanja and described how the Serbian ruler inspected with some complacency, in the imperial palace at Blachernae, the paintings of the different phases of his rebellion, where he himself was identified by name.[9]

Nemanja seems to have remained a loyal subject of the emperor

---

[5] Joannes Cinnamus, *Historiae*, bk. 6, ed. A. Meineke (Bonn, 1836), 287–8; ET, *Deeds of John and Manuel Comnenus by John Kinnamos*, tr. C. M. Brand (New York, 1976), 215.

[6] See S. Runciman, *A History of the Crusades*, ii (Cambridge, 1952), 345–52.

[7] Cinnamus, bk. 4 (Meineke, 182–3; ET 139).

[8] Constantine Manasses, in *Vizantiisky vremennik*, xii (1906), 89–91.

[9] *Oratio ad Manuelem imperatorem*, ed. V. Regel in *Fontes Rerum Byzantinarum*, i 1 (St Petersburg, 1892), 43–4; German tr. G. L. F. Tafel, *Komnenen und Normannen* (Ulm, 1852), 221–2. For the date of this speech see Kazhdan–Franklin, *Studies on Byzantine Literature*, 123.

1, St Clement of Ohrid: late fourteenth- or early fifteenth-century icon. Icon collection in St Clement, Ohrid. Photograph: S. Ćurčić

(a)

(b)

2. Lake Ohrid: (a) general view. Photograph: Yugoslav National Tourist Office, London; (b) with the monastery church of Sv. Jovan Kaneo (late thirteenth century). Photograph: B. Drnkov

3. Replica of gold amulet probably owned by Vladimir Monomakh: (*a*) obverse; (*b*) reverse. Collection of V. M. and N. V. Teteryatnikov

(*a*)

(*b*)

4. Byzantine emperor watching the games from the imperial box in the hippodrome of Constantinople: early twelfth-century painting, St Sophia, Kiev. Photograph: V. N. Lazarev

5. Monastery of Hilandar, Mount Athos: (*a*) aerial view. Photograph: V.J. Djurić; (*b*) main courtyard. Photograph: R. K. Kindersley

(Virtually all buildings, including the fourteenth-century church, post-date Sava)

6. St Sava: painting of 1220s in the narthex of the monastery church, Mileševa. Photograph: Institute for the Protection of Monuments, Belgrade

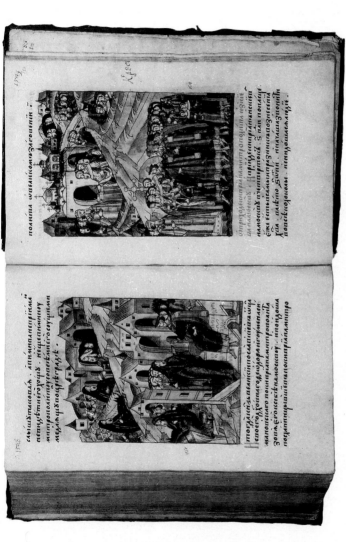

7. Left, Prince Dimitri of Moscow sends for Cyprian; right, Prince Dimitri's meeting with Cyprian. Miniatures from a sixteenth-century illuminated manuscript (*Litsevoy svod*) of the *Nikon Chronicle*. Photograph: Library of the Academy of Sciences of the USSR, Leningrad

(a)

(b)

8. Maximos the Greek: (a) from a colophon in a sixteenth-century Russian manuscript; (b) seventeenth-century Russian icon

until Manuel's death in 1180, but soon afterwards he repudiated Byzantine rule. By 1190 the territory of the Serbian state extended from the lower reaches of the Rivers Morava and Drina in the north to the Šar Planina in the south, while in the south-west it included the coasts of Southern Dalmatia and Montenegro. In the first half of the eleventh century this stretch of the Adriatic coast and its interior had formed the heartland of the earliest Serbian state to achieve international status. It was known first as Diocleia and later as Zeta. Centred in the areas round Lake Scutari and the Gulf of Kotor, Diocleia, both culturally and economically, looked out across the Adriatic and Ionian Seas to Italy and Byzantium.

The annexation by Stephen Nemanja, in the 1180s, of this predominantly maritime land was of great moment in the history of the medieval Serbian state. In the first place it added to Raška a sizeable minority which owed allegiance, through the Latin bishoprics on the southern Adriatic, to the Church of Rome: in terms of religion and culture, this established medieval Serbia on the crossroads of Byzantium and the West. In the second place, Raška inherited some of Diocleia's political traditions, and chief among these was the internationally recognized royal prerogative of its sovereign. In revolt against Byzantium some time before 1077, the Diocleian ruler received a royal crown from Rome,[10] acknowledging, then or earlier, spiritual allegiance to the pope.

This twofold Diocleian inheritance determined Serbia's religious orientation and political traditions during the lifetimes of Nemanja and his son Sava. The Latin presence in the coastal provinces was balanced by the Greek jurisdiction over the interior, in the person of the bishop of Ras, the capital of Raška, near Novi Pazar, who was a suffragan of the autocephalous archbishop of Ohrid. This ecclesiastical dualism was mirrored in Nemanja's baptism by a Latin priest in his native Diocleia, followed, still in his infancy, by chrismation, or sacramental anointing, performed by the Greek bishop of Ras.[11] As

---

[10] We do not know when the rulers of Diocleia acquired the royal title. In early 1077 Pope Gregory VII sent a letter to 'Michael, King of the Slavs': Gregory VII, *Register*, v. 12, ed. E. Caspar: MGH, Epistolae selectae, ii 2 (Berlin, 1955), 365. Michael reigned from *c.* 1052 to 1081. His son and successor, Constantine Bodin, was referred to in 1089 by the anti-Pope Clement III as 'rex Sclavorum gloriosissimus': *Acta et diplomata res Albaniae mediae aetatis illustrantia*, ed. L. Thallóczy *et al.*, i (Vienna, 1913), 21–2. Cf. S. Ćirković (ed.), *Istorija Srpskog Naroda*, i (Belgrade, 1981), 189–91 (hereafter *ISN*).

[11] Relying on a statement by Nemanja's son Stephen (see below, p. 122), most modern historians assert that Nemanja was baptized twice, the first time by a Latin

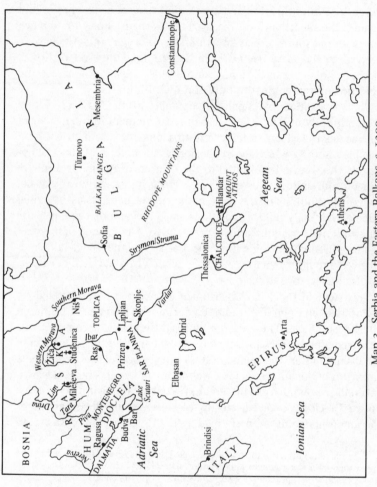

Map 3. Serbia and the Eastern Balkans, c. 1200

for the political traditions of the Diocleian kingdom, they were taken over, as we shall see, in the early thirteenth century by Nemanja's son Stephen, who sought and obtained a royal crown from Rome.

During the remaining years of his reign Nemanja continued to combine political hostility to Byzantium with an eagerness to absorb, by close co-operation with the local Orthodox Church, the fruits of Byzantine culture.

Nowhere was his political enmity towards Byzantium more apparent than in his dealings with the German emperor, Frederick Barbarossa, during the Third Crusade. In July 1189, at a friendly reception in Niš, Nemanja offered Frederick his allegiance and military help against Byzantium on condition that the emperor recognized his sovereignty over the lands he had conquered from the Greeks. However, Frederick's unwillingness to be side-tracked from the Crusade made all these overtures vain.

Nemanja's last military encounter with the Byzantines occurred in the autumn of 1190, when the army of the Emperor Isaac II defeated his troops on the River Morava. The ensuing peace-terms were surprisingly favourable to Nemanja: he was allowed to keep a considerable part of the Byzantine lands he had annexed, and the emperor implicitly recognized Serbia's autonomy. For the first time in history a marriage-alliance was concluded between the ruling families of Byzantium and Serbia: Nemanja's second son, Stephen, married Eudoxia, the niece of the Emperor Isaac II,[12] and received the title of Sebastocrator, one of the highest in the Byzantine hierarchy. The title, no less than the marriage, denoted Serbia's incorporation, as an autonomous state, into the Byzantine cultural commonwealth.

Nemanja's collaboration with the Orthodox Church was deeply rooted in Serbia's past. The country had been converted between 867 and 874 on the initiative of the Emperor Basil I, probably through the missionary work of Latin clerics from Dalmatian cities under Byzantine sovereignty.[13] Two decades later some of the two hundred disciples of St Methodius, exiled from Moravia after their master's

cleric, the second time by the Orthodox bishop of Ras. However, such a practice would have been unthinkable in the 12th or 13th c. Nemanja's son Sava, in his own biography of his father (see below, p. 122) plainly states that his 'second baptism' was in fact chrismation (anointing with holy oil).

[12] For the date of the marriage, see J. Kalić, *Vizantijski izvori za istoriju naroda Jugoslavije*, iv (Belgrade, 1971), 164 n. 194.

[13] *ISN* 212.

death in 885, probably joined in this work of evangelization, bringing to the Serbs the Slavonic liturgy and scriptures. The subsequent religious history of Raška is shrouded in mist until the early eleventh century, when several bishoprics in the Serbian interior were placed by the Emperor Basil II under the archbishop of Ohrid; one of them was the diocese of Ras.

Nemanja's growing devotion to eastern Christianity is shown by the monasteries he founded in Raška. The two earliest were in the Toplica region, in the east of the country; the third, dedicated to St George—Djurdjove Stupove—was built on a hilltop not far from Ras in 1170–1, and soon after Nemanja became grand *župan*; the fourth, Studenica, was his crowning achievement. Built after 1183 in the wooded valley of a tributary of the Ibar, its church of white polished marble combined architectural features of the Byzantine and the Romanesque traditions, and became Serbia's leading monastery.[14] Nemanja's monasteries, Studenica above all, became the models for the great royal foundations—*zadužbine*—which did much to create that close partnership of Church and state so characteristic of medieval Serbia. Richly endowed with land and property, renowned for the paintings in their churches, they were often built, like the Cistercian abbeys of western and central Europe, in remote valleys, and their architecture in part, and their paintings almost wholly, followed the Byzantine tradition. So did the monastic rule of their communities.

Serbian monasticism, essentially Byzantine in character, owes a great debt to Sava, Nemanja's youngest son. More generally speaking, it was he who played the principal role in setting a Byzantine stamp on the culture of medieval Serbia.

The historian who attempts to write the life of this central figure in Serbia's medieval history may well feel apprehensive at the sheer range of Sava's activities. He will be discouraged by his many guises: successively a provincial governor, an Athonite monk, and an archbishop; a diplomat entrusted with delicate missions by his brother the king; a founder of several monasteries and the organizer of their liturgical life and discipline; a legislator in the field of canon law; the first primate of Serbia's autonomous Church; a voyager on the pilgrim-routes of the eastern Mediterranean; his country's earliest articulate writer; the focus of a posthumous cult that spread

---

[14] On Studenica, see M. Kašanin *et al.*, *Studenica* (Belgrade, 1968) (in English).

throughout the Balkan peninsula and even captured some of its Muslim population later on; Serbia's unrivalled patron saint; a semilegendary figure right down to the present day, celebrated in folklore, poetry, and song; his mythopoeic sway must be unique in eastern Europe;[15] and all this, and a wider compass still, are there to daunt his biographer.

A further difficulty lies in the nature of the sources. These are predominantly hagiographic. Their authors' professed aim is to extol the deeds of Sava and his father, and to provide edifying reading. Historical accuracy and comprehensiveness, though by no means alien to their purpose, are not their principal concern. Until recently even professional historians, when writing about Sava, had difficulty in freeing themselves from the insidious pressure of hagiographical conventions and clichés. Given the nature of the evidence, to do so completely is no doubt impossible. However, recent Yugoslav scholarship has done much to lay the foundation for a critical biography of Sava. The following pages claim to be no more than an exploratory essay.[16]

Sava—Rastko was his original name—is believed to have been born in 1175. One of his medieval biographers tells us that when he reached fifteen his father gave him a province to govern. A recently discovered document[17] has shown that it lay near the western borders of the state. It comprised the area between Ragusa (Dubrovnik)[18] and the middle course of the River Neretva and included a sizeable stretch of the Adriatic coastline. The Serbs called it Hum (or Hlm); in the late Middle Ages it came to be known as Hercegovina, or Duchy of St Sava.[19] Rastko's experience as a provincial governor was

[15] With the exception, perhaps, of Alexander the Great.
[16] The bibliography on St Sava, nearly all of it in the Serbo-Croat language, is immense. An example of the best modern scholarship on the subject is the collection of papers read at a colloquium to commemorate the 800th anniversary of Sava's birth, organized by the Serbian Academy of Sciences and Arts: *Sava Nemanjić—Sveti Sava: Istorija i predanje*, ed. V. Djurić (Belgrade, 1979) (hereafter *SNSS*). A landmark in the history of Sava studies was V. Ćorović's critical edition of his works, *Spisi sv. Save* (Belgrade–Sremski Karlovci, 1928) (hereafter *SSS*).
[17] See R. Novaković, in *Sveti Sava: Spomenica povodom osamstogodišnjice rodjenja 1175–1975* (Episcopal Synod of the Serbian Orthodox Church, Belgrade, 1977), 25–32 (hereafter *Sveti Sava* (1977)).
[18] Ragusa was then under Byzantine sovereignty.
[19] See C. Jireček, *Geschichte der Serben* (Gotha, 1911–17; repr. Amsterdam, 1967), ii. 189–90. See below, p. 170.

brief: it probably lasted less than two years (1090–1). But it may well have given him a direct knowledge of the centres of Latin Christianity on the Dalmatian coast and of the wider Mediterranean horizons to which this maritime region had access.

The next well-attested event of his life was his escape from his father's court to Mount Athos, where he became a monk. The story of his flight is told, with some discrepancies, in four medieval Church Slavonic documents. As these documents are the principal source of our knowledge of Sava's biography, here is a brief account of them.

First comes the Life of Stephen Nemanja by his son, Rastko-Sava. It was planned as the introductory chapter to Sava's *typicon*, or constitution, of the monastery of Studenica, and was probably written about 1208. The historical and literary importance of this work will be discussed later. For the present we may note that it is an eyewitness account of the last years of Nemanja's life, which he spent in the company of Sava, also an Athonite monk. It follows only partly the rhetoric and conventions of contemporary Byzantine hagiography, and it lacks the formal structure of a medieval Greek *Vita*. Its simple and unaffected style, as well as its author's willingness to transgress the humble and reticent formulae and speak about himself, are among the qualities which appeal to a modern reader.[20]

The need for a fully fledged *Vita* of Nemanja on the Byzantine model was met by another biography, written in 1216 by his second son, Stephen, his father's successor as grand *župan* of Serbia. By this time Nemanja was a canonized saint, widely revered both in his own country and on Mount Athos. Though written later than Sava's biography, Stephen's *Vita* shows no signs of direct borrowing.[21] It is a longer, more formal and sophisticated work, and it conforms more closely to the prevailing Byzantine hagiographical pattern: a rhetorical prologue, an account of the saint's deeds on earth, a panegyric, and a description of posthumous miracles.[22] It includes some details

---

[20] The text of Sava's Life of his father is printed in *SSS*, 151–75. There is a good German translation by S. Hafner in *Serbisches Mittelalter: Altserbische Herrscherbiographien* (Graz, 1962), i. 35–61. Cf. R. Marinković, *SNSS* 201–13. For the sources and the literary style of the work, see H. Birnbaum, 'Byzantine Tradition Transformed: the Old Serbian *Vita*', in H. Birnbaum and S. Vryonis (eds.), *Aspects of the Balkans: Continuity and Change* (The Hague–Paris, 1972), 247, 249, 272–3, 277–80.

[21] See V. Ćorović, 'Medjusobni odnošaj biografija Stevana Nemanje', *Svetosavski zbornik* (hereafter *SZ*), i (Belgrade, 1936).

[22] The text is printed in *SZ* ii (Belgrade, 1939). The German translation, by S. Hafner, is found in *Serbisches Mittelalter*, 73–129. On the conventions of Byzantine hagiogra-

about Sava's early life on Mount Athos, and, because of its more hagiographical character, in the Middle Ages it was a good deal more popular than Sava's own Life of Nemanja.

The third of our sources is a full-length Life of Sava himself, written in the mid-thirteenth century by Domentijan, an Athonite monk who had probably been Sava's disciple. It was completed, at the latest, nineteen years after Sava's death, and perhaps ten years earlier.[23] It was dedicated by its author to King Stephen Uroš I, who perhaps commissioned it. Containing lengthy quotations from the Scriptures, it stresses the providential and other-worldly aspects of Sava's life. Domentijan was an early practitioner of a new style of hagiographical and panegyrical writing which was to enjoy a great vogue in Eastern Europe during the late Middle Ages: an ornate and rhetorical style with a tendency to interweave the narrative with theological reflections and to reduce the factual material to a minimum, with the aim of raising the story to a timeless and transcendental plane.[24]

The last is another full-length biography of Sava. Its author, Teodosije, like Domentijan, was a monk of Athos, but he belonged to a later generation and wrote in the late thirteenth or the early fourteenth century. Though he clearly depends on Domentijan for much of his material,[25] his style and outlook are significantly different. Compared with his predecessor's sobriety of content and monumental style, Teodosije appears vivid and entertaining, and

---

phy, see H. Delehaye, *Les légendes hagiographiques* (Brussels, 1927); ET, *The Legends of the Saints*, tr. D. Attwater (London, 1962).

[23] Domentijan, *Život svetoga Simeuna i svetoga Save*, ed. Dj. Daničić (Belgrade, 1865). Domentijan's Life of Sava has been variously dated to 1242/3 and to 1253/4. These different dates are given by the Vienna and Leningrad manuscripts respectively: see *Sveti Sava* (1977), 13.

[24] On Domentijan as a writer, see Ćorović, *SSS* 6–19; A. Schmaus, 'Die literarhistorische Problematik von Domentijans Sava-Vita', in M. Braun and E. Koschmieder (eds.), *Slawistische Studien zum V. Internationalen Slawistenkongress in Sofia 1963: Opera Slavica*, iv (Göttingen, 1963), 121–42; S. Radojčić, *SNSS* 215–21; *ISN* 337–9. On this hagiographical style see D. S. Likhachev, *Razvitie russkoy literatury X–XVII vekov* (Leningrad, 1973), 83–93.

[25] Some scholars have sought to reverse the relationship between Sava's two biographers, and argued that Teodosije's work was the earlier. Among them were N. Radojčić and A. Schmaus: see *Südost-Forschungen*, xv (1956), 196. This view is increasingly discounted today: see M. Dinić, 'Domentijan i Teodosije', *Prilozi za književnost, jezik, istoriju i folklor*, xxv 1–2 (1959), 5–12; see S. Ćirković, *SNSS* 11. In his excellent introduction to L. Mirković's Serbian translation of Teodosije's Life of St Sava (Belgrade, 1984, pp. vii–xi), D. Bogdanović argues that it was written in the early decades of the 14th c.

more concerned with psychological motivation. He frequently expands Domentijan's laconic accounts; among possible reasons for these amplifications are a desire to bring greater consistency into his stories, the literary influence, perhaps, of the late antique romance, and at times his own lively imagination. Unlike Domentijan, Teodosije, as we shall see, was hostile to the Latin Church, and his outlook appears to be typical of Athonite monks of his time. To judge from the number of surviving manuscripts of his work, his was by far the more popular of Sava's two medieval biographies.[26]

The story of Rastko's flight to Mount Athos, as one passes from each of these accounts to the next, becomes increasingly circumstantial and dramatic. Sava's own story, written in the third person singular, is a model of modesty and sobriety. Teodosije, the furthest removed in time from the event, is the most prolix and lavish in detail and graphic in description: Rastko, still a layman and pursued by an armed escort, is discovered on Athos, in the Russian monastery of St Panteleimon: there he plays an elaborate game of hide-and-seek with his pursuers, at the end of which (while they sleep after too lavish a monastic banquet) he escapes to the top of the monastery tower, where he triumphantly appears in full monastic garb and flings down his secular clothes, his shorn hair, and a letter addressed to his father. The search-party, seeing that Sava as a monk is beyond their jurisdiction, set off for home; whereupon Sava, his aim achieved, descends from his eyrie.[27] When due account has been taken of hagiographical commonplaces or imaginative reconstructions, we are probably left with the following kernel of solid fact: in or about 1191, Rastko, then about sixteen, travelled from his father's court in Ras to Mount Athos in secret. There he was befriended in the Russian monastery, which then stood about two miles north-east of the present St Panteleimon.[28] His father, suspecting where he had gone, sent a military escort to bring him back. However, by the time it found him, Rastko was already the monk Sava, either in St Panteleimon or in the Greek

---

[26] Teodosije Hilandarac, *Život svetoga Save*, ed. Dj. Daničić (Belgrade, 1860; repr. Belgrade, 1973). Cf. C. Müller-Landau, *Studien zum Stil der Sava-Vita Teodosijes* (Slavistische Beiträge, 57, Munich, 1972).

[27] Teodosije, op. cit. 12–21.

[28] See P. Lemerle, 'Chronologie de Saint-Pantéléèmôn des origines à 1500', in *Actes de Saint-Pantéléèmôn*, ed. G. Dagron, P. Lemerle, and S. Ćirković (Paris, 1982), 3–10.

monastery of Vatopedi whose community he later joined. The escort returned to report failure to their sovereign.[29]

The Greek monastery of Vatopedi was to be Sava's home for the next seven years. One of the earliest and most influential communities of the Holy Mountain—its foundation dates back to 985—Vatopedi, with its rich library and close contacts with Thessalonica and Constantinople, played an important role in Byzantine society. By the twelfth century Mount Athos, a narrow and mountainous peninsula jutting out from Chalcidice into the Aegean, had become the leading centre of East Christian monasticism, and a meeting-place for monks of many nationalities. Apart from the Greeks, who were the most numerous, Georgians, Russians, Bulgarians, and Italians had their own monasteries there, and they were about to be joined by the Serbs. National antagonisms were not unknown; yet the sense of solidarity rooted in a common tradition of ascetic endeavour and spirituality seems to have been more important. The Byzantines, aware of the reality of this supranational bond, called these different ethnic communities of Athos not 'nations' (ἔθνη) but 'tongues' (γλῶσσαι).[30] This cosmopolitan outlook, which became stronger still during the later Middle Ages, made of Mount Athos an important source of Byzantine culture for the different lands of Orthodox Eastern Europe: in the scriptoria of its principal monasteries monks read, copied, and translated works of Byzantine religious and secular literature, which were then transmitted to their various home countries. Learning in those times was a frequent, though not a necessary, adjunct of the spiritual life: organized monasticism had existed on Athos since the

[29] The sources, and the modern authorities, disagree on whether Rastko was made a monk in St Panteleimon or Vatopedi. Stephen Nemanjić (*SZ* ii, 37–8) states that it was in Vatopedi. Domentijan, rather confusingly, writes of two separate tonsures, the first one in St Panteleimon, the second in Vatopedi (op. cit. 124–8). These may be two successive monastic professions, corresponding to two different grades of the monastic life: that of ῥασοφόρος ('wearer of the habit') and the more advanced rank of σταυροφόρος or μικρόσχημος ('wearer of the cross' or of the 'Lesser Habit'). Most of the mature monks wear the 'Lesser Habit'. The 'Greater Habit' is worn only by those who have pledged themselves to the strictest life of asceticism and prayer. See P. Sherrard, *Athos: The Mountain of Silence* (London, 1960), 63–4; id., *Athos. The Holy Mountain* (London, 1982), 122–7; E. Amand de Mendieta, *Mount Athos: The Garden of the Panaghia* (Berlin–Amsterdam, 1972), 220–5. On the other hand, according to Sava (*SSS* 160–1) his father received 'the holy angelic and apostolic habit, the little habit and the great one'. A sensible attempt to explain and reconcile the discrepancies in the sources regarding the whole episode of Sava's flight from Serbia to Mount Athos was made by S. Stanojević, 'O odlasku sv. Save u manastir', *SZ* i. 43–64.

[30] D. Zakythinos, in *Hilandarski zbornik*, i (1966), 34.

tenth century at least, and, following the tradition of Eastern
Christian asceticism, it had assumed three different forms: the
eremitical life, practised by anchorities who then, as they do today,
lived mainly in crags and caves on the southern tip of the Athonite
peninsula; then there were the *lavrai* (*skity* in Slavonic), groups of
hermits living separately under the direction of an abbot and meeting
periodically for the common celebration of the Eucharist; and lastly,
the highly organized and centralized coenobitic communities, whose
members shared the same building and were subject, under the
authority of an abbot, to the identical discipline of prayer and work.
The first coenobitic monastery on Athos was founded in 963 under
the patronage of the Emperor Nicephorus Phokas, and Vatopedi
followed the same pattern. In the isolated hermitages the contemplative tradition often burnt with a brighter flame, and a contemporary
of St Sava, a Russian abbot who visited Mount Athos about 1219,
described the monastic rule followed by these hermits: every day they
read half the Psalter and made from three hundred to five hundred
prostrations. Physical work was prescribed; and at all times they were
encouraged to recite, both orally and in their heart, the 'Jesus prayer',
which for many centuries has been central to the 'hesychast' tradition
of Orthodox spirituality: 'Lord Jesus Christ, Son of God, have mercy
upon me.'[31]

This manifold tradition of Athonite monasticism was to leave a
deep mark on Sava's life. It was the nursery of his spiritual life and his
religious outlook. It provided models which helped him later to build
up and organize the monasteries of Serbia; and amidst his administrative burdens and his frequent journeys at home and abroad, he
returned to the Holy Mountain again and again. Probably as much as
his native land, Athos remained a spiritual home for him all his life.

In March 1196 the aged Nemanja, after a reign of thirty-six years,
abdicated in favour of Stephen, his second son. Perhaps his abdication
had been hastened, if not caused, by Byzantine pressure. Nemanja
had fought Byzantium for most of his life; his son Stephen, the son-in-
law of the new Emperor Alexius III (who on 8 April 1195 deposed his
younger brother, Isaac II), could be expected to keep Serbia firmly in

---

[31] See A.-E. Tachiaos, 'Le monachisme serbe de Saint Sava et la tradition hésychaste
athonite', *Hilandarski zbornik*, i (1966), 85. On the 'Jesus prayer' see I. Hausherr, 'La
méthode d'oraison hésychaste', *Orientalia Christiana*, ix/36 (1927), 97–210; see also 'A
Monk of the Eastern Church', *The Prayer of Jesus* (New York–Rome–Tournai–Paris,
1967).

the Byzantine orbit.[32] However, other and more personal motives must have weighed heavily in Nemanja's decision. Soon after abdicating he entered a monastery,[33] and the sincerity of his vocation is beyond question. Both Domentijan and Teodosije attribute his double decision to abandon his throne and become a monk to the example and the promptings of Sava, and they may well be right.

With Stephen Nemanjić installed as grand *župan*, Raška's continued membership of the Byzantine cultural commonwealth seemed assured. Yet Serbia's Adriatic provinces still looked out, just as they did in the eleventh century, towards Rome and the West. Vukan, Nemanja's eldest son, ruled them as king 'of Dalmatia and Diocleia'. Nominally, he was a subject of his younger brother, the grand *župan*; but increasingly his desire for independence caused him to look to the papacy for ecclesiastical, and to the Hungarian crown for political, support.

Nemanja, henceforth known as the monk Symeon, joined the community of Studenica, his own foundation. Eighteen months later he set out, on what was to be his last journey, to join his son on Mount Athos.[34] The meeting between father and son in Vatopedi is described with quiet dignity by Sava and Stephen, with religious warmth by Domentijan, and with lyrical emotion by Teodosije. The arrival of the powerful and renowned Serbian ruler as a humble postulant seems to have created a sensation; and, if we can believe the last three of these writers, monks from monasteries and hermitages all over Athos flocked to Vatopedi to witness the unusual sight. Domentijan and Teodosije were clearly impressed by the lavish presents brought by Nemanja for distribution among the Athonite cloisters; they write of horses and mules, and of buckets of gold and silver and precious liturgical vessels: earlier he had sent similar gifts from Serbia to Sava in Vatopedi.[35] Earlier still, Stephen Nemanjić tells us, his father the grand *župan* used to send presents to some of the principal churches in Jerusalem and Bari, and Rome.[36] There is something puzzling about the largesses so frequently bestowed upon churches and monasteries by the monks Symeon and Sava. Their medieval biographers may well have exaggerated their value. Even so, the impression remains

---

[32] For the date of Nemanja's abdication, and attempts to connect it with the Byzantine *coup d'état* of 8 April 1195, see Ostrogosky, *History*, 409 n. 1.

[33] Sava (*SSS* 161) states that his father remained in Studenica for two years.

[34] Domentijan, 153–4; Teodosije, 41.   [35] Teodosije, 28, 33.

[36] Stephen Nemanjić, 34.

that Nemanja's family were unusually munificent, at least towards the Athonite monasteries. Where did all this wealth come from? A century later the answer would have been clear: Serbia's foreign trade with Dalmatia, Venice, and South Italy, in which the merchants of Ragusa and Kotor were the middlemen, was reaching its peak; so was the country's mining industry, organized and manned by 'Saxon' settlers from Hungary: they worked the rich mines of silver, lead, copper, and iron which made Serbia's fortune. But in the days of Nemanja and Sava most of this lay in the future: Serbia's economic boom did not begin until the mid-thirteenth century.[37] Unless these buckets of gold and silver were the invention of hagiographers, Serbia by the turn of the twelfth century must already have been a richer country than historians have generally supposed.

The idea of founding a Serbian monastery on Athos probably took root in Sava's mind soon after he came to Vatopedi, and it must have reached the planning stage during the weeks after his father's arrival. Financial assistance was requested from their son and brother, the grand *župan* Stephen, and readily granted.[38] After visiting a number of the monasteries—in each of them they left generous gifts[39]—father and son chose the site of a half-ruined Greek monastery in an area about twelve miles north-west of Vatopedi called τῶν Μηλεῶν, not far from the north coast of the peninsula. The name of this monastery was Helandarion (μονὴ τοῦ Χελανταρίου),[40] and to achieve their aim they needed permission from the abbot of Vatopedi, the governing body of Athos, and the Byzantine emperor, who exercised supreme jurisdiction over the Holy Mountain. The abbot of Vatopedi was only too pleased at the prospect of gaining control over a monastery which, under prevailing Byzantine law, fell under the authority of the *prōtos*, or president of the Athonite governing body; and so, at the end of 1197, he sent Sava to Constantinople to seek the emperor's agreement. His journey to the Byzantine capital was successful: the Emperor Alexius III, Sava's relation by marriage, removed Helandarion and its surroundings from the jurisdiction of the *prōtos* by special edict and placed them under the abbot of Vatopedi.[41] Sava returned to

---

[37] See *ISN* 357–71.

[38] As Stephen himself tells us at some length (pp. 43–50).

[39] Domentijan, 157–60; Teodosije, 36–44.

[40] *Actes de Chilandar*, ed. L. Petit, *Vizantiisky vremennik*, Appendix to xvii (1911; repr. 1975), no. 4, pp. 8–11.

[41] *Actes de Chilandar*, no. 4, p. 10. The edict issued by the emperor was a χρυσόβουλλον σιγίλλιον. The document is not extant. It is possible that during his first

Athos early in 1198, with the first stage in their plan accomplished. It was probably then and under Sava's supervision that they began the restoration of Hilandar, as the Serbs were henceforth to call it (Plate 5). The work was far enough advanced by July 1198 for Symeon Nemanja to move there from Vatopedi.

Meanwhile conflict had broken out between Vatopedi and the Athonite governing body. The latter, unwilling to accept the loss of jurisdiction over Hilandar, met under the chairmanship of the *prōtos*, probably in the spring of 1198. Presumably they had already reached agreement with Symeon and Sava over their future course of action. This was to petition the emperor to grant Hilandar to the two Serbian monks in full 'legal possession', and enable them 'to found a monastery there according to their will'.[42] The specious grounds for this request were that Hilandar and its dependencies, left in the possession of Vatopedi, would fall into complete ruin!

In June 1198 the Emperor Alexius III answered with another document—χρυσόβουλλος λόγος—addressed to Symeon Nemanja and Sava.[43] Pointing out that the monastery was being restored at their expense, and that it was destined for Serbian monks, the emperor cancelled his earlier *sigillion* giving Hilandar with its surroundings to

---

visit to Constantinople in 1197–8, Sava met Constantine Mesopotamites, the recently deposed metropolitan of Thessalonica. Constantine, promoted λογοθέτης τῶν σεκρέτων by the Emperor Isaac II (1185–95), had, as a very young man, wielded great political power in his reign and at the beginning of the reign of his successor Alexius III. Nicetas Choniates, who painted a vivid and unflattering portrait of Mesopotamites (pp. 439–41; ET 241–2), alleged that 'he led the emperor about in the manner of a leader-whale' (ὡς τὸ κῆτος ὁ λεγόμενος προπομπός). Mesopotamites, who had a passion for politics, was never far from Constantinople in those days, even during his tenure of the see of Thessalonica. After his deposition he retained powerful friends in the Byzantine capital, including the empress Euphrosyne. It is not impossible that he helped Sava to acquire useful contacts in the city. According to Domentijan, 226, Sava and Mesopotamites became close friends 'in their youth'. Mesopotamites, reinstated as metropolitan of Thessalonica, later ordained Sava archimandrite. See below pp. 133–4. He was clearly a man of principle: during his second tenure of the see of Thessalonica he refused, owing to his Nicaean loyalties, to crown Theodore Angelos of Epirus emperor: George Acropolites, *Opera*, i, ed. A. Heisenberg (Stuttgart, 1978), 33–4. On this curious personage, see V. Laurent, 'La succession épiscopale de la métropole de Thessalonique dans la première moitié du XIIIème siècle', *Byzantinische Zeitschrift*, lvi (1963), 285–6, 288–92; Kazhdan–Franklin, *Studies on Byzantine Literature*, 137, 226–8, 233–5, 252. Cf. A. D. Karpozilos, *The Ecclesiastical Controversy between the Kingdom of Nicaea and the Principality of Epiros (1217–1233)* (Thessalonica, 1973), 72.

[42] Ibid., no. 3, p. 6: αἰτούμενοι αὐτοὺς ἀναδέξασθαι τὰς τοιαύτας μονὰς δικαίῳ οἰκείῳ καὶ μοναστήριον ἐν αὐταῖς συστῆσαι κατὰ τὸ αὐτῶν βουλητόν.
[43] Ibid., no. 4, pp. 8–11.

Vatopedi, and placed it under 'the authority and management' of
Symeon and Sava. The Serbian monastery was to enjoy 'total
freedom',[44] 'subject to no one'—neither to the *prōtos* of Athos, nor to
the abbot of Vatopedi. The emperor declared Hilandar 'independent
and self-governing',[45] with the same privileges as other non-Greek
Athonite monasteries such as Iviron—the Georgian foundation—and
the Italian monastery of Amalfitans. Only the emperor exercised pre-
eminent rights of patronage over these 'imperial monasteries'.[46]

The 'authority' and powers of 'management' over Hilandar were
vested jointly in Symeon and Sava by the imperial chrysobull (July
1198), and devolved on them, as the monastery's founders. The role
of 'founder'—*ktitor*—was an important one in Byzantine monasticism. He was not necessarily the monastery's actual founder: the title,
and its attendant privileges (which sometimes included the right to
draft its *typicon*, or constitution), were also accorded to distinguished
benefactors.[47] Symeon and Sava invited the grand *župan* Stephen,
probably after the issue of the chrysobull, to become Hilandar's chief
ktitor,[48] thus bringing the new foundation under the patronage of
three members of Serbia's ruling family.

Hilandar was still a small community with an abbot and ten to
fifteen monks,[49] but the original church, largely intact, was greatly
enlarged. On 13 February 1199 Symeon Nemanja died there, aged
eighty-six.[50] Sava, who was with him to the end, has left a moving
account of his father's last hours,[51] on which Domentijan and
especially Teodosije were later to embroider. Sava now became

---

[44] ἐλευθερίας . . . πάσης: Actes de Chilandar, no. 4, p. 10.

[45] αὐτοδέσποτον καὶ αὐτεξούσιον . . . καὶ καθ' ἑαυτὴν διεξαγομένην: ibid.

[46] See E. Herman, 'Ricerche sulle istituzioni monastiche bizantine. Typika ktetorika,
caristicari e monasteri "liberi"', *Orientalia Christiana Periodica*, vi (1940), 348–53,
361–72; H.-G. Beck, *Kirche und theologische Literatur im byzantinischen Reich* (Munich,
1959), 130.

[47] Beck, op. cit. 135.   [48] Stephen Nemanjić, 43.

[49] Sava gives two different figures: ten in the *typicon* of Hilandar (SSS 28); fifteen in
the Life of Symeon Nemanja (SSS 171).

[50] The lengthy debate whether Symeon Nemanja died in 1199 or 1200 has been
convincingly resolved in favour of 1199 by F. Barišić, 'Hronološki problemi oko godine
Nemanjine smrti', *Hilandarski zbornik*, ii (1971), 31–40. This excellent study has at last
dispelled the fog generated by the contradictions between the Greek and the Slavonic
sources, and has enabled us to see the different stages in the history of Hilandar's
foundation in a clearer light. Barišić's conclusions have been accepted by M.
Živojinović, SNSS 16–18, and by V. Mošin, ibid. 108–14. For his age at the time of his
death, see Sava, 174.

[51] See below, pp. 138–9.

Hilandar's effective *ktitor*,[52] and with the aim, it seems, of increasing its revenues, he made a second journey to Constantinople in the spring of 1199. The Emperor Alexius, in response to his request, issued another chrysobull in June, confirming the rights of *ktitor* to Sava and of full autonomy to the monastery. In addition, Hilandar was given land and buildings of the derelict monastery of Zygon on the western edge of Athos and, to help the transport of supplies, permission to own a boat free of taxes.[53] By August, Sava was back,[54] and the monastery, under Methodius, Symeon Nemanja's nominee[55] and the first abbot, grew fast. In a few years it housed ninety monks; it had become, in Sava's own words, 'magnificent'.[56]

It would be hard to overstate the role of Hilandar in the religious and cultural history of the Serbian people. It soon achieved prominence in the cosmopolitan world of Athos. Greek writings on the ascetic and spiritual life were translated into Slavonic there, and monks from many Eastern European countries learned the theory and practice of contemplative or 'hesychast' prayer at the feet of the same masters. A glimpse of the international character of Athos at the end of the twelfth century can be caught in Sava's description of his father's funeral service: it was chanted by Greek, Georgian, Russian, and Bulgarian, as well as Serbian monks.[57] The fact that Hilandar was the joint creation of the two most revered saints of their nation gave the monastery a unique position in the hearts of the Serbs; and for centuries to come it ensured its role as their main channel for Byzantine culture and spirituality. Sava, who frequently journeyed between Hilandar and Serbia, stands with his father at the very beginning of the history of this cultural transmission. It was almost certainly on Athos that he wrote the *typicon* of Hilandar; and he is believed to have had a hand in the drafting of the monastery's earliest foundation-charter, which his father issued in 1198;[58] this suggests

---

[52] Sava, *Typicon of Chilandar*, SSS 28; Life of Symeon Nemanja, 171.

[53] *Actes de Chilandar*, no. 5, pp. 11–15.　　　　　　　　　　[54] Barišić, op. cit. 47.

[55] The appointment of a monastery's abbot by its *ktitor* was contrary to canon law. This was allowed only in exceptional circumstances, and to distinguished *ktitores*: see M. Živojinović, *SNSS*, 18.

[56] SSS 28, 171.　　　　　　　　　　　　　　　　　　　[57] SSS 171.

[58] This document is not to be confused with the *typicon* of Hilandar. The text is printed in Ćorović, SSS 1–4. For its relationship to the *typicon*, see F. Granić, SZ i. 70. For the charter's legal significance, see Mošin, SNSS 111–12. For an ideological analysis of Nemanja's foundation-charter, see S. Hafner, *Studien zur altserbischen dynastischen Historiographie* (Munich, 1964), 54–63.

that Sava had assembled a team of translators from Greek into Church Slavonic, who worked in the scriptorium under his supervision.[59]

Domentijan tells us that, in Constantinople, Sava stayed in the monastery of the Evergetis ($\Theta\epsilon o\tau\acute{o}\kappa ov$ $\tau\hat{\eta}s$ $E\dot{v}\epsilon\rho\gamma\acute{\epsilon}\tau\iota\delta os$).[60] He and his father were among this monastery's greatest benefactors, and were regarded by the monks as its *ktitores*.[61] Its precise whereabouts is uncertain, but we know that it stood outside the city walls, probably two miles or so. Sava doubtless lived in the monastery's *metochion*, or dependency, between the church of St Andrew in Krisei and the Pēgē gate, in the south-western part of the city.[62] Founded in the eleventh century, the monastery of the Evergetis was famous for its influential and often-imitated *typicon*. It was probably in its city *metochion*[63] that Sava got his first-hand knowledge of Constantinople's monastic life. While he had his quarters there, perhaps in the summer of 1199, he got hold of a copy of the *typicon* of the Evergetis monastery and had it translated into Church Slavonic.[64] In a slightly adapted form, it became the constitution of Hilandar.[65] Its detailed rulings on liturgy, confession, communion, fasting, clothes, conduct in church and in the refectory, the appointment of abbots and other functionaries, and the monastery's autonomy,[66] shaped Hilandar's character as an 'imperial' and coenobitic foundation. The same *typicon*, with slight adaptations, was later set up—also by Sava—as the constitution of Studenica, and became the model for the *typica* of other medieval Serbian monasteries.

---

[59] See A.-E. Tachiaos, *SNSS* 86–9. [60] Domentijan, 180.

[61] Domentijan, ibid.; Teodosije, 51–2.

[62] See R. Janin, *La Géographie ecclésiastique de l'Empire byzantin*, I: *Le siège de Constantinople et le Patriarcat Œcuménique*, iii. *Les églises et les monastères* (Paris, 1969), 178–84.

[63] The fact that Sava stayed in the monastery's *metochion* is confirmed by the evidence of Antony, the future archbishop of Novgorod, who visited Constantinople in 1200: 'Kniga palomnik: Skazanie mest svyatykh vo Tsaregrade', ed. Kh. M. Loparev, *Pravoslavnyi Palestinsky Sbornik*, xvii/3 (St Petersburg, 1899), 26.

[64] See V. Mošin, *SNSS* 115.

[65] The degree to which Sava took an active part in the translation of the Evergetis *typicon* is debatable. He cannot have been the sole translator, but he may have dictated parts of it. See A. Belić, *SZ* i. 231–2. The Hilandar *typicon* contains several passages in which he writes directly of himself: see Ćorović, *SSS*, xii–xiii. The poor quality of the translation has raised the question of how well Sava knew Greek at the time: See V. Jagić, 'Tipik Hilandarski i njegov grčki izvor', *Spomenik Srpske Kraljevske Akademije*, xxxiv (1898), 1–66. Sava himself tells us that he found it difficult to read (or translate?) the Greek Psalter: *SSS* 201. Cf. B. St. Angelov, *Iz starata bŭlgarska, ruska i srŭbska literatura*, iii (Sofia, 1978), 58.

[66] The text is printed in Ćorović, *SSS* 14–150. For a useful discussion of the monastic rules of this *typicon*, see F. Granić, *SZ* i. 67–128.

By the year 1200 Sava had become a dominating figure on Mount Athos. With his late father, he was not only the founder of the new 'imperial' monastery for the Serbs; thanks to his princely munificence on the Holy Mountain, he was also regarded as the *ktitor* of half a dozen Athonite foundations.[67] In these years he seems to have been chiefly drawn to the life of solitary prayer. He had purchased a hermitage in Karyes, the administrative centre of Athos, which Domentijan calls a *hēsychastērion*, and there, in the company of one or two other monks, he retired for periods of rigorous asceticism and prayer.[68] This hermitage, Teodosije tells us, was charmingly adorned by its fruit trees and its springs of fresh water.[69] The church used by the miniature community there was dedicated to his patron, Saint Sava—or Sabas—of Palestine. Here, too, Sava wrote a *typicon* for the life of its residents, ensuring their autonomy.[70]

Despite his spiritual and moral authority in Athos and even in Constantinople, Sava was still a simple monk. He was not in holy orders. This was common in the Eastern Church, where the great majority of monks were—and still are—unordained. The same had once been true in the West, but was now growing less common. By then Sava's ecclesiastical superiors must have recognized his flair for leadership and his administrative gifts. Domentijan—writing, it is true, with the help of hindsight—states that he was being prepared for the episcopate.[71] Probably during the first half of 1200, Sava was ordained deacon and then priest by the bishop of Hierissos. Though the bishop had no jurisdiction over Mount Athos, he was authorized, if requested, to ordain its monks to the diaconate and priesthood. After the ceremony, Sava returned to his hermitage at Karyes.

The next stage in Sava's ascent called for the intervention of the bishop's immediate superior, the metropolitan of Thessalonica. Some time between 1200 and 1204[72]—but before the autumn of the latter year—Sava journeyed to Thessalonica, where he was ordained

---

[67] Symeon's and Sava's benefactions caused them to be regarded as joint *ktitores* of The Great Lavra, Iviron, and the main church at Karyes; Sava alone was the *ktitor* of Karakallou, Xēropotamou, and Philotheou. He also rebuilt a church belonging to Vatopedi in Prosfori (the modern Ouranoupolis) outside Athos, and flanked it with a high tower: Domentijan, 156–9, 183–4; M. Živojinović, *SNSS* 16, 19.

[68] Domentijan, 170–1.   [69] Teodosije, 61.

[70] The text is in *SSS* 5–13.   [71] Domentijan, 192.

[72] There is some difference of opinion over the date of Sava's first visit to Thessalonica. V. Mošin, *SNSS* 118, dates it to 1203, S. Stanojević, *Sveti Sava* (Belgrade, 1935), 28, probably to 1204, while M. Živojinović, 'O boravcima svetog Sava u Solunu', *Istorijski Časopis*, xxiv (1977), 64, pushes the event back to 1200 or 1201.

archimandrite in the Church of St Sophia by three bishops, presided over by the metropolitan, Constantine Mesopotamites.[73]

Perhaps Sava's position on Athos was becoming a delicate one; his new ecclesiastical dignity outranked every monk on the Holy Mountain except the *prōtos*. An archimandrite, though inferior to a bishop, was a kind of super-abbot, charged with the duty of supervising a group of monasteries;[74] and there was clearly no place on Athos for a second *prōtos*. Both Domentijan and Teodosije seem to have sensed the anomaly of Sava's position: perhaps this is why they slide rather rapidly over his last years in Hilandar and pass on to the next important event in his life, his return to Serbia at the beginning of 1206.

Whatever the niceties of Sava's status on Athos during those years, he must have been deeply shaken by the tragic events of 1204. On 13 April of that year the armies of the Fourth Crusade captured Constantinople. In the ensuing partition of the Empire among Frankish barons and Venetians, southern Macedonia, which included the Chalcidice peninsula and Athos, was allotted to Boniface, marquis of Montferrat and now king of Thessalonica.

Boniface must have begun to wield his authority over the Athonite monasteries by the first half of 1205,[75] and their position soon became precarious. Relying on the Crusaders' support, the Italian clergy put heavy pressure on the monks to accept the pope's authority and the practices of the Latin Church.[76] Except for Iviron, whose community submitted to Rome in 1206, the monasteries for a while successfully resisted these attempts. In the summer of that year, however, the pressure was stepped up and Cardinal Benedict, Innocent III's legate at Constantinople, placed the Athonite monasteries under the jurisdiction of the Latin bishop of Sebasteia. This villainous prelate built himself a castle—known today as Frangokastro—on Athos territory, and from here, with the help of Frankish barons, he pillaged the monasteries and put the monks to the torture,

---

[73] Domentijan, pp. 191–2. On Constantine Mesopotamites, see above, n. 41.

[74] See the article 'Archimandrite' by J. Pargoire, in *Dictionnaire d'Archéologie chrétienne et de liturgie* (1924); P. de Meester, 'L'archimandritat dans les Églises de rite byzantin', *Miscellanea liturgica in honorem L. C. Mohlberg*, ii (Rome, 1949), 115–37.

[75] See M. Živojinović, 'Sveta Gora u doba latinskog carstva', *Zbornik Radova Vizantološkog Instituta*, xvii (1976), 77–92 (with a French summary), to which the following paragraphs are much indebted. Cf. G. Hofmann, 'Rom und Athosklöster', *Orientalia Christiana*, viii. 28 (1926), 3–40.

[76] See the first-hand evidence of an Athonite monk, cited in J. B. Pitra, *Analecta sacra et classica Spicilegio Solesmensi parata*, vi (Paris–Rome, 1891), cols. 245–50.

in the hope of discovering concealed hoards. The defenceless monks had to endure his savage depredations for four years. They were saved at last by the joint action of Innocent III[77] and Henry of Flanders, the Latin emperor of Constantinople, who deposed and exiled their tormentor.

The disappearance of the bishop of Sebasteia does not seem to have greatly improved the situation of the monasteries, and in 1213 they decided to appeal for protection to the pope. Innocent sent them a reassuring letter. Drawing a neatly phrased contrast between the arid soil and the spiritual fertility of the Holy Mountain, and expressing sympathy for their recent misfortunes, the pope confirmed their earlier liberties and immunities and formally placed them under the protection of St Peter and himself.[78] There can thus be no doubt that by 1213 the monasteries of Athos, like Iviron seven years earlier, had recognized the pope's jurisdiction.[79] This reorganization probably amounted to no more than an administrative formality; nor is it likely to have extended beyond the year 1216, when the sovereign protectors of Mount Athos, Inocent III and the Emperor Henry, both died. Thereafter the Athonite monks showed a growing willingness to recognize the emperor of Nicaea, who claimed to be the legitimate successor of the Byzantine emperors, as their overlord; and in 1223, Pope Honorius III angrily described the monks of Athos as disobedient rebels.[80]

Sava recorded the Latin incursion into Mount Athos with characteristic restraint: 'A great turmoil arose in that region [i.e. Mount Athos]', he wrote in the Life of his father, 'for the Latins came and took Constantinople, the former Greek land, and even invaded us and that holy place; and there was great turmoil.'[81] The deep misgivings with which Sava beheld the coming of the Latins to Athos spread to his family in Serbia: it was then, he tells us, that a letter came from his brothers, Stephen and Vukan, begging him to bring their father's body home.[82] This letter, apparently quoted by Stephen in his life of

[77] Innocent III condemned the bishop of Sebasteia for committing 'enormitates, quae non sunt dignae relatu': PL ccxvi, col. 229.

[78] PL ccxvi, cols. 956–8. The letter was addressed to the abbot of the Great Lavra, and to the other abbots and monks: 'Sancti Athanasii caeterisque abbatibus et monacis Montis-Sancti'.

[79] See Živojinović, op. cit. 84–85.

[80] Hofmann, 'Rom und Athosklöster, 8. Cf. A. Pertusi, 'Monasteri e monaci italiani all'Athos nell'alto medioevo', *Le Millénaire du Mont Athos*, 963–1963, i (Chevetogne, n.d.), 230: 'monachos Montis Sancti inobedientes Sedi Apostolicae ac rebelles'.

[81] Sava, 171.   [82] Ibid. 172.

his father, suggests that the request was prompted by moral and national considerations: the country needed Nemanja's posthumous presence and supernatural protection to ward off the results of internecine strife and foreign invasion.[83] Indeed Serbia was sorely in need of peace and tranquillity. During Sava's eight years on Athos, his brothers had quarrelled violently. Vukan, the eldest, and local ruler of Diocleia and southern Dalmatia, had allied himself with the king of Hungary, and in 1202 the Hungarians invaded Serbia, drove out Stephen, and appointed Vukan as their king's puppet and grand *župan* over the whole country. Peace and normal conditions were only restored about 1205 when, thanks to an invasion by his Bulgarian allies, Stephen regained the throne, and Vukan returned to his coastal provinces, there to cultivate cordial relations with Pope Innocent III.

Accompanying his father's body and escorted by a group of monks from Hilandar, Sava started on the long journey to Serbia probably during the winter of 1206–7. He seems to have run close to some danger from the Latin invaders, for he tells us that, despite the 'great turmoil' he encountered on the way, he passed through fire and water unscathed. He ascribed his salvation to God's help and to the prayers of the Mother of God, and of his father.[84] He was not to see Mount Athos again for ten years.

Early in 1207, Symeon Nemanja's remains were solemnly deposited by his three sons in a tomb he had prepared for himself in Studenica. It was probably here, soon after the translation of his relics, that he was proclaimed a saint, and Sava was entrusted with the duty of composing an order of service in his honour.[85] By encouraging the cult of his father Sava fostered the belief, deeply felt in medieval Serbia, that the peace and security of the realm depended on the presence of the miraculous relics of its holy founder.

Soon after his return Sava was appointed abbot of Studenica. His

[83] Stephen Nemanjić, 55.

[84] Sava, 172. On three occasions (pp. 171–2), to describe the 'turmoil' caused by the Latin invaders, he confines himself to the single word *metež*. He presumably travelled by sea to Thessalonica. For an attempt to trace his subsequent itinerary, see D. Kostić, *SZ* i. 156.

[85] The office was published by Ćorović, *SSS* 176–86. Domentijan, 186–30, and Teodosije, 71–3 state that Symeon was canonized soon after his death in Hilandar, when miraculous oil was reported flowing from his relics. Sava himself, who was best placed to know, says nothing of this; and it seems more likely that the canonization took place in Studenica, after his body had been translated there. See D. Kostić, *SZ* i. 131–67; and Hafner, *Studien zur altserbischen dynastischen Historiographie*, 74–5 n. 120. *Pace* Domentijan, it seems probable that it was in Studenica that Sava composed the liturgical office for his father. For the date of Nemanja's posthumous translation to

rank of archimandrite made him the senior non-Greek churchman in Serbia; since he was the grand *župan*'s brother, his authority was unrivalled. As the head of the leading monastery in the land, he exerted a nation-wide influence throughout the next eight years. The administrative talents he had shown on Mount Athos were now at the service of his country. For his own monastery of Studenica he introduced, with minor changes, the *typicon* of Hilandar he had adapted from the Evergetis monastery in Constantinople.[86] Not the least of his advantages was his experience as a founder of monasteries. Domentijan tells us that 'he brought in to his fatherland every model [of monastic life] from the Holy Mountain', and was soon founding coenobitic houses, *lavrai*, and hermitages.[87] The greatest of Sava's foundations—for the building of which he shared the initiative with his brother, the grand *župan* Stephen—was Žiča, near the confluence of the Ibar and the Morava. Later, as the first seat of the archbishop of Serbia, it became the country's most hallowed shrine. The great stone church, with its tall belfry, took about ten years (1209–19) to build. Teodosije tells us that Sava brought architects and marble workers 'from the Greek land', and when he was archbishop (presumably in 1220), he brought painters 'from Constantinople' to decorate Žiča.[88] Whatever the precise meaning of these statements, and the origin of these artists—they might have come from Nicaea or Thessalonica, if not from Constantinople[89]—the Byzantine origin of Sava's artistic programme for Žiča is beyond question. Nor is there any doubt of his personal share in the building and decoration of its church, and Žiča became the model for the other great thirteenth-century churches of the Raška school.[90]

Literature was another field in which Sava left his mark in Studenica. Here he proved a true pioneer in the history of his people. It was probably there that he composed the liturgical office in honour of

Studenica, see Lj. Maksimović, in *Zbornik Radova Vizantološkog Instituta*, xxiv/xxv (1986), 437–44.

[86] See above, p. 132.   [87] Domentijan, 205.   [88] Teodosije, 97–8, 141.

[89] As Constantinople and Thessalonica were then in Latin hands, they were not likely to abound in local artistic workshops. However, we know from Domentijan, 328, that 'imperial [i.e. Byzantine] masters' had some (unspecified) business with Sava during his brief stay in Constantinople in 1235, shortly before his death. This is probably too late for the wall-paintings in Žiča. It is possible, on the other hand, that Teodosije was using language loosely, and that Sava on his way back from Nicaea in 1219–20 brought, to decorate Žiča, some painters who had been trained in Constantinople before 1204. See V. Djurić, *SNSS* 249, 255–8. See also M. Kašanin, Dj. Bošković, and P. Mijović, *Žiča* (Belgrade, 1969), 8.

[90] See V. Koradj, *SNSS* 231–44; Dj. Bošković, in Kašanin *et al.*, *Žiča*, 53–103.

the newly proclaimed saint, his father Stephen-Symeon Nemanja. This service, which conforms to the rules of Byzantine liturgical *akolouthiai* and was indeed modelled on the one to his namesake St Symeon Stylites, is the earliest known example of Serbian Church Slavonic hymnography.[91] Soon, thanks to the sweet-smelling oil said miraculously to suffuse from his relics, St Symeon Nemanja was to be likened to the most famous similarly gifted eastern saint, Demetrios the *myroblētēs*, patron saint of Thessalonica.[92] But the chief literary work produced by Sava at this time was the Life of his father. As we have seen, it is the introductory section of the Studenica *typicon*. It is modelled in part on the second foundation charter of Hilandar, issued by Sava's brother Stephen between 1200 and 1202.[93] It is also a work of considerable literary skill, whose controlled emotion is the more impressive for its being an eyewitness account. The sobriety of Sava's description of his father's death in Hilandar is particularly moving:

He said: 'My child, bring me [the icon of] the most holy Mother of God, for I have made a vow to yield up the ghost [Matt. 27: 50] in front of her.' And when his command had been carried out, towards the evening, he said: 'My child, do me a service of love, clothe me in the *rason*[94] appointed for my funeral and place me in the same sacred position in which I shall lie in my coffin. Spread a matting on the ground and lay me on it and place a stone under my head, that I may lie here until the Lord comes to visit me and take me hence.' And I did all this and carried out his commands. And all of us who looked on wept bitterly . . . For in truth, my beloved brothers and fathers, it was a wondrous sight: he whom all men in his country feared, and before whom all trembled, was now seen as a stranger and beggar, clothed in a *rason*, lying on the ground on a mat with a stone under his head, receiving the salutations of all the brethren and asking everyone's forgiveness and blessing with love in his heart. When night had fallen they all took their leave of him, and, after receiving his blessing, returned to their cells to do what they had to

[91] Published by Ćorović, *SSS* 176–86.

[92] The comparison was made by Stephen Nemanjić, 63. The cult of St Demetrios was widespread among the Slavs, including the Serbs: see Obolensky, 'the Cult of St Demetrius of Thessaloniki' (cit. Ch. 1, n. 73). For other Balkan saints who exuded holy oil, see Hafner, op. cit. 34–7.

[93] See the sensitive treatment of Sava's Life of his father by D. Bogdanović, in *ISN*, 334–5. For Hilandar's first foundation charter, issued by Stephen-Symeon Nemanja, see above, p. 131 and n. 58.

[94] The *rason* (here more precisely the Outer Rason) is a black, loose over-garment with wide sleeves, reaching to the ankles. The *megaloschemoi* of the Orthodox Church— of whom Symeon Nemanja was one—are buried in the full monastic habit. See Sherrard, *Athos: The Mountain of Silence*, 68–70.

do and rest a little. I and a priest whom I had kept with me remained by his side all that night. At midnight the blessed father fell silent and spoke to me no longer. But when morning came and the singing of matins began in the church, the blessed father's face was suddenly illumined, and he looked up to heaven and said: 'Praise God in his sanctuary: praise him in the firmament of his power.' I said to him: 'Father, whom do you see as you speak these words?' He looked at me and said to me: 'Praise him for his mighty acts: praise him according to his excellent greatness'.[95] And when he had said this he straightaway yielded up his godly spirit and died in the Lord.[96]

On the ideological plane, too, Sava's Life of his father stands at the beginning of a long tradition. Two principal themes were closely combined in this *Vita*: the glorification of the house of Nemanja, and reverence for Serbian monasticism. The first was expressed in the devotion which Nemanja's family inspired in the Serbian people; until the late fourteenth century, every ruler of the country belonged to it. The origins of this ruler-cult may lie partly in the persistence of ancient tribal tradition with its worship of dead ancestors; but it was chiefly the influence of the Church that shed round the Nemanjids a sacred aura and brought them a veneration greater perhaps than that paid to any other royal family in Eastern Europe. The medieval Serbian idea of royal sovereignty rested on a triple foundation: the concept of national 'inheritance' which the dynasty's leading representatives, beginning with Nemanja himself, were held to have 'restored', 'gathered', or 'enlarged'; Old Testament models, which Sava used to liken his father both to Isaac, who blessed his son Jacob, and to Jacob himself, whose body was brought out of Egypt and carried to the promised land by his son Joseph;[97] and, finally, the Byzantine connection: marriage-links with the imperial house and high-sounding titles bestowed by Constantinople gave special prestige to the Serbian ruler and placed him among the emperor's friends and subject-allies.[98] Reverence for the monastic life was the other strand in the literary tradition of medieval Serbia, personified by the fact that the founder of the dynasty and his son became monks; and it fostered close and lasting links between medieval Serbian monasteries and the

[95] These verses (Ps. 150: 1–2) are sung in the Byzantine office of matins, shortly before the 'great doxology', which was intended to coincide with daybreak.

[96] Sava, 169–70. [97] Sava, 157, 173. Cf. Gen. 28: 1; 50: 1–13.

[98] In the opening section of his biography of Nemanja, Sava emphasizes the importance of Serbia's 'Byzantine connection': Nemanja, he states, became a relation (*svat*) of the Emperor Alexius through the marriage of his son and successor Stephen to the emperor's daughter (Sava, 153).

'imperial' house of Hilandar. Athos wove medieval Serbian monasticism into the fabric of Serbian society; it was Sava again who laid the foundations on which his countrymen were to build. His Life of his father, with its peculiar blend of family chronicle, hagiography, and 'translation' tale, with political concepts derived from monastic foundation-charters, provided the model for future writers who continued, until the fall of the medieval Serbian realm, to record the exploits, secular and religious, of a virtually unbroken line of holy kings. Together with the *Vitae* of the archbishops of Serbia, starting with St Sava, these royal biographies—the best were written in the thirteenth and fourteenth centuries—are the main contribution made by the Serbs to the literature of medieval Europe.[99]

As the abbot of the premier monastery in Serbia, Sava could hardly avoid some involvement in affairs of state. His relations with his brother, the grand *župan*, during the next ten years (1207–17) have given rise to much controversy among historians. He is surely not likely to have approved of Stephen's matrimonial affairs. In 1200 or 1201, when Sava was still in Hilandar, Stephen repudiated his Byzantine wife Eudoxia, daughter of the Emperor Alexius III. The circumstances, as told by Nicetas Choniates, were lurid in the extreme. Both parties having accused each other of infidelity, Eudoxia was turned out of the house, virtually naked, by her husband, who 'dismissed her in disgrace to go forth as a wanton'. Stephen's brother Vukan provided her with clothes and an escort to Dyrrachium, whence she travelled to Constantinople with a splendid retinue dispatched by her father, the emperor.[100] Stephen's choice of a second wife, probably in 1207, like his first, was prompted by *raison d'État*. She was Anna, the granddaughter of the formidable (and now defunct) Enrico Dandolo, the Doge of Venice, who had been the true leader and largest beneficiary of the Fourth Crusade.[101]

Stephen's matrimonial vicissitudes were a reflection of the chang-

[99] See the perceptive remarks on this subject by Hafner, op. cit., *passim*. See also H. Birnbaum (n. 20), 243–84.

[100] Nicetas Choniates, 531–2; ET 291–2. Cf. C. M. Brand, *Byzantium Confronts the West* (Cambridge, Mass., 1968), 120. Eudoxia later married Alexius V Doukas Mourtzouphlos, the last Byzantine emperor before the Latin conquest, and, after his death, Leo Sgouros, the Greek lord of Corinth. See K. M. Setton (ed.), *A History of the Crusades*, ii (Madison, 1969), 182 n. 62.

[101] Andrea Dandolo, *Chronica per extensum descripta*, ed. L. A. Muratori (*Rerum Italicarum scriptores*, xii/1, repr. Bologna, 1938), 287. For the probable date of Stephen's marriage with Anna Dandolo, see B. Ferjančić, *ISN* 299. Anna probably died before 1217 (ibid.).

ing political and military situation in the Balkans in the opening years of the thirteenth century. In the closing years of the twelfth the breakdown of the Empire's policy and standing had become glaringly clear, and Stephen's outrageous, and unavenged, treatment of Eudoxia shows how low by 1200 Byzantium had sunk in the eyes of the emperor's son-in-law. The emergence in 1204, on the ruins of Byzantium, of a Latin empire ruled by Franks and Venetians confronted the Slav states of Serbia and Bulgaria with a totally new situation; and the fresh alignment of power, for which centuries of Byzantine presence or hegemony had left them unprepared, steered their rulers into perilous waters. The new power structure in south-eastern Europe made them reassess their foreign policy, and this in turn called for considerable diplomatic skill.

The Bulgarians were the first, by a slender margin, to begin this realignment of their foreign relations. In 1199, their ruler Kalojan approached Pope Innocent III; by next year the pope was congratulating him on his devotion to the Roman church and announcing that he would be sending a legate to Bulgaria.[102] In 1204, after lengthy negotiations, a Roman cardinal crowned Kalojan in his capital, Tŭrnovo; in exchange the king pledged his loyalty to the pope, and that of the Church. Stephen Nemanjić was not slow to follow him. About 1199, answering a letter from Innocent III, he declared that, like his father before him, he had always followed 'in the footsteps' of the Roman Church.[103] This equivocal announcement led to positive action: shortly afterwards Stephen sent an embassy to Rome, with a request for a royal crown and the promise, as a *quid pro quo*, of his country's submission to the pope.[104]

For some years to come Stephen's relations with Rome were obstructed by the Hungarian king, who sought, through Prince

---

[102] PL ccxiv, col. 825.

[103] 'Nos autem semper consideramus in vestigia sanctae Romanae ecclesiae, sicut bonae memoriae pater meus': *Vetera Monumenta Slavorum Meridionalium*, ed. A. Theiner, i (Rome, 1863), 6, no. 11. The statement that Stephen Nemanja followed 'in the footsteps' of the Roman Church may refer to his baptism by a Roman priest. See above, p. 117. However, he may well have had relations with the papacy during his reign: we know that he sent gifts to the church of St Peter's in Rome: Stephen Nemanjić, 34.

[104] *Vetera Monumenta*, i. 36, no. 57; C. Jireček, *Geschichte der Serben*, i (Gotha, 1911), 275–6, 288; M. L. Burian, 'Die Krönung des Stephan Prvovenčani und die Beziehungen Serbiens zum römischen Stuhl', *Archiv für Kulturgeschichte*, xxiii (1933), 149; F. Dvornik, *The Slavs in European History and Civilization* (New Brunswick, NJ, 1962), 97.

Vukan, to rule over Serbia. Stephen's chance came in 1217, when King Andrew II of Hungary sailed to Palestine on a crusade. A thirteenth-century Latin historian—Thomas, archdeacon of Spalatum (or Split)—tells us that when King Andrew set sail from Spalatum in September 1217, Stephen sent his envoys to Rome to ask for the royal crown; Pope Honorius III sent a legate to Serbia and Stephen was crowned. This made the grand *župan* of Serbia the first ruler of Raška to bear the title of king.[105] Thomas's evidence is confirmed by Andrea Dandolo, a fourteenth-century Venetian chronicler, who adds that a Roman cardinal performed the coronation.[106]

Rome and Serbia both benefited from Stephen's coronation. There can be no doubt that Stephen now accepted the pope's spiritual suzerainty and pledged his subjects to the Church of Rome.[107] Papal expansionist aims in the Balkans, revived by Innocent III's agreement with the Bulgarians, were now reinforced by Honorius III's contract with Stephen of Serbia. The world had been shaken and imperilled by the Fourth Crusade; but, by accepting a royal crown from the pope, Stephen ensured a measure of legitimacy and independence for his country. To his countrymen he is known as *Prvovenčani*, or 'The First Crowned'.

What role, if any, did Sava play in all this? We must turn to the Serbian sources for an answer. Writing about 1208, Sava himself could obviously refer neither to his brother's overtures to Rome, nor to his coronation. Nor does Stephen, whose biography of his father was completed, at the latest, in June 1216,[108] a year or so before his embassy to the pope. But Domentijan and Teodosije describe the coronation at some length, and the difference between their accounts and those of the Latin sources are instructive and significant.

On his return from Nicaea, where he had been consecrated archbishop—i.e. in 1220 at the earliest—Sava, according to Domentijan, dispatched bishop Methodius, one of his disciples, to Rome, asking the pope to send him a royal crown so that he, Sava, might

[105] 'Eodem tempore Stephanus dominus Serviae sive Rasiae, qui mega iupanus appellabatur, missis apochrisariis ad romanam sedem, impetravit ab Honorio summo pontifice coronam regni. Direxit namque legatum a latere suo, qui veniens coronavit eum primumque regem constituit terrae suae': Thomas Archidiaconus, *Historia Salonitana*, ed. F. Rački (Monumenta spectantia historiam Slavorum Meridionalium, xxvi, Zagreb, 1894), 90–1.

[106] Dandolo, *Chronica*, loc. cit. We do not know where this coronation took place.

[107] Serbia's maritime provinces, it will be recalled, had at least since Vukan's time acknowledged papal jurisdiction.

[108] V. Ćorović, *SZ* ii. 11.

then crown his brother. The request was backed by the following argument: Nemanja, Stephen's father, had been born in Diocleia—a kingdom 'from the beginning'. The envoy was to inform the pope of Sava's earlier consecration, and to request from him a blessing on the land of Serbia and for Sava himself. The pope duly obliged, and at a solemn ceremony in Žiča Sava crowned his brother with the crown sent from Rome.[109]

Teodosije, who follows Domentijan's dating, leaves out all reference to Rome or to the pope. According to him, Sava crowned his brother in Žiča with a crown of unknown provenance: he describes in detail the gathering of nobles and clergy, the coronation ceremony, and Sava's sermon to the people.[110]

It is clear that the Serbian and the Latin sources are in total disagreement on every essential point. How can we explain this contradiction?

Two basic issues are at stake: who crowned Stephen? And when was he crowned? The Latin documents place the coronation in 1217, or 1218 at the latest; according to the Serbian sources it took place at the earliest in 1220. The principal Latin source, the *Historia Salonitana* of the Archdeacon Thomas, is chronologically precise: Stephen's embassy to Rome and his coronation by the papal legate coincide with King Andrew II's departure from Spalatum in September 1217,[111] on the Fifth Crusade. Domentijan and Teodosije, on the other hand, vaguely state that the coronation took place after Sava's return from Nicaea.

If the coronation took place in 1217 or 1218, Sava is unlikely to have performed it. He was almost certainly out of Serbia at the time: he resigned his post as abbot of Studenica in 1216 or 1217 and departed for Mount Athos.[112] It is hard to avoid the suspicion that Domentijan and Teodosije postdated Stephen's coronation by several years; and that they did so because they could not believe, or did not

---

[109] Domentijan, pp. 245–8.   [110] Teodosije, pp. 141–52.
[111] See Setton (ed.), *A History of the Crusades*, ii, 387–8.
[112] The exact date of Sava's departure is uncertain. Both Domentijan, 214, and Teodosije, 117, state that after his return to Athos he stayed there for 'a long time', (Domentijan), or 'a fairly long time' (Teodosije). By the summer of 1219 he was already in Nicaea: see M. Živojinović, 'O boravcima Svetog Save u Solunu', 69. Most historians today date Sava's departure from Serbia to 1217 (Dj. Slijepčević, *Istorija Srpske pravoslavne crkve*, i [Munich, 1962], 73; D. Bogdanović, *ISN* 317) or to 1216–17 (M. Živojinović, *SNSS* 21). B. Ferjančić, *ISN* 301, asserts that Sava left Serbia in 1217, *after* Stephen's coronation; this seems improbable.

wish their readers to believe, that he had been crowned by anyone but Sava. They knew that Sava had left Serbia by 1217–18; or, if they did not, they surmised that an archbishop—he became one in 1219—was more likely to have performed a royal coronation than the mere archimandrite which he still was in 1217–18. Moreover, both Domentijan and Teodosije must have known of the coronation in Thessalonica as emperor of the Romans of Theodore Angelos—c.1227—by Demetrios Chomatianos, archbishop of Ohrid.[113] Their elaborate story of the ceremony of Stephen's crowning is unlikely to have been invented: it was probably based on what they knew of the coronation of King Radoslav, Stephen's son and successor, which was performed by Sava in Žiča in 1228.[114]

A further piece of evidence strongly reinforces the view that Stephen was crowned in 1217 or 1218, and not in the 1220s. The Register of Honorius III has preserved a letter written to this pope by Stephen Nemanjić in 1220, which contains the following passage: 'Just as all Christians love and honour you and look to you as their father and lord, so we also wish to be considered a loyal son of the holy Roman Church, and of yourself, confident that God's blessing and sanction as well as yours will be visibly granted to our crown and country.' The letter is signed 'Stephanus Dei gratia totius Serviae, Diocliae, Tribuniae, Dalmatiae . . . *rex coronatus*.'[115] It is clear from this document that by 1220 by the latest Stephen was a legally crowned king in the eyes of the pope, and that he had previously recognized his spiritual dominion.[116]

With Stephen's coronation dated to 1217–18, it becomes virtually impossible for Sava to have performed it. All the evidence points to the cardinal-legate of Honorius III. The testimony of the Latin sources is all the more conclusive as, some twelve years earlier, the Bulgarian ruler Kalojan, who had similarly requested a royal crown from the pope, was crowned in Bulgaria by a cardinal from Rome.[117]

Thus on the two crucial points at issue—the date of Stephen's

---

[113] For the date of Theodore's coronation see D. M. Nicol, *The Despotate of Epiros, 1267–1479* (Cambridge, 1984), 4–5 n. 6.

[114] Domentijan, 261; Teodosije, 165–6. Cf. Ferjančić, in *ISN* 308.

[115] C. Baronius, *Annales Ecclesiastici*, xx (Bar-le-Duc, 1870), 432–3. Cf. F. Rački, *Starine*, vii (1875), 53–6. The translation (slightly adapted) is from F. Dvornik, *The Slavs in European History*, 117, n. 4. My italics.

[116] See Jireček, *Geschichte der Serben*, i. 297; Burian, 'Die Krönung des Stephan Prvovenčani', 144.

[117] See Dvornik, *The Slavs in European History*, 94–6; Obolensky, *The Byzantine Commonwealth*, 239; and above, p. 141.

coronation and the identity of the person who crowned him—the Serbian sources can be shown to be unreliable. Domentijan's account is a particularly curious mixture of facts and fiction.[118] Bishop Methodius, whom he names as the envoy sent to Rome with a request for the crown, was a real person: he was Sava's pupil, and between 1198 and 1220 repeatedly travelled between Hilandar, Serbia, and Rome on important matters of Church and state.[119] However, Domentijan's statement that he was sent to Rome by Sava, and that Sava requested the pope's blessing, is unlikely to be true; it is far more probable that the embassy and the request originated with Stephen Nemanjić. In one respect, however, Domentijan's story mirrors faithfully the intellectual climate of mid-thirteenth-century Serbia. His Life of Sava was written at the behest of Stephen Uroš I, king of Serbia from 1243 to 1276, and dedicated to him.[120] His account of Stephen's coronation is strikingly respectful of the Church of Rome. Not only does he make Sava (improbably, as we have seen) apply to the pope for a personal blessing; but he refers to him repeatedly as 'the great thronefellow of the holy apostles Peter and Paul', and calls him 'Pope of the great Roman realm'.[121] He seems to have no difficulty in admitting that Stephen's crown came from Rome. Domentijan's respect for Rome and its bishop may have been stimulated by the Latin sympathies of his patron, Uroš I, and by the Catholic loyalties of his queen, Helen of Anjou.[122] Even so, it is remarkable that an Athonite monk, writing in surroundings which had suffered greatly from Latin

---

[118] The improbabilities in Domentijan's account are exposed in the sensible study by I. Ruvarac, 'O glavnim momentima u životu sv. Save, prvog srpskog arhiepiskopa', *Letopis Matice Srpske*, ccviii (1901), 9, 17–18, 42.

[119] He is mentioned by Sava, as the first abbot of Hilandar (p. 165); by Stephen Nemanjić, as the envoy sent by Symeon from Athos to Serbia, to ask for material help for the building of Hilandar, and again later to thank Stephen for agreeing to become one of the monastery's *ktitores* and to bring him a fragment of the True Cross (pp. 45, 47, 49–50); by Domentijan, as the envoy sent by Sava to Rome (p. 245); and in the Register of Honorius III, as the envoy entrusted by King Stephen in 1220 with a message of loyalty to the pope (see above, p. 144). There can hardly be any doubt that Symeon's envoy to Serbia was the abbot of Hilandar (V. Mošin, *SNSS* 114). We cannot be certain, however, that he was also the bishop Methodius who was sent to Rome in 1217 and 1220; but the identification is tempting.

[120] See p. 123 above.

[121] Domentijan, 245–6. 'Thronefellow' is an attempt to render the original *süprestolnik*, which is a calque of the Greek σύνθρονος.

[122] About 1250 Uroš I married the French princess Helen, who as queen of Serbia remained a devout Catholic. If Domentijan wrote his Life of Sava in 1253–4, he could have had her in mind.

intolerance and brutality, found words to express his veneration for the see of Rome. It is not unreasonable to see in this broadmindedness a sign that, despite doctrinal disputes and jurisdictional rivalry in the mid-thirteenth century, the belief in Christendom as a single body was still alive, even on Mount Athos.

Teodosije wrote half a century later, in another world and in a very different climate of opinion. The Byzantines had regained Constantinople in 1261, and the parasitical Latin empire had ceased to exist. The decades of subjection to the Latin Church, and the anti-Western feelings aroused in Byzantine society by the 1274 proclamation of ecclesiastical union at the Council of Lyons,[123] had caused many Athonite monks to turn against Rome, and Teodosije was one of them. Domentijan was his principal source, but he deleted all references to Rome and to the pope from the account of Stephen's coronation, and presented the ceremony as due entirely to Sava's initiative. In the section dealing with the coronation he characteristically refers to 'the Latin heresy'.[124]

If we may now accept that Stephen was crowned by a papal legate in 1217 or 1218,[125] a further question arises: what was Sava's attitude to this coronation and, more generally, to his brother's Roman policy? We now face one of the most controversial problems of medieval Serbian history.

Most historians have concluded that Sava was wholly out of

---

[123] See D. J. Geanakoplos, *Emperor Michael Palaeologus and the West* (Cambridge, Mass., 1959), 277–304. The stories, still current on Athos, about a violent persecution allegedly carried out by the Emperor Michael VIII against the Athonite monks who resisted his unionist policy are fictional. See Amand de Mendieta, *Mount Athos: The Garden of the Panaghia*, 89. For these stories see R. M. Dawkins, *The Monks of Athos* (London, 1936), 297–307.

[124] Teodosije, 151.

[125] Some historians have attempted to reconcile the evidence of the Latin and the Serbian sources by imagining two coronations, the first performed in 1217 by a papal legate with a crown sent by the pope, the second in 1220 or 1221 by Sava. The main advocate of this view is D. Anastasijević, 'Je li sv. Sava krunisao Prvovenčanog?', *Bogoslovlje*, x (1935), 211–312. His arguments, developed at excessive length, suffer from an anachronistic reading back into the 13th c. of the modern clear-cut distinction between Catholic and Orthodox. In fact, no evidence to support this theory can be found in the contemporary sources. It is rightly rejected by Dvornik, *The Slavs in European History*, 99, by Ostrogorsky, *History*, 431 n. 2 and by B. Ferjančić, *ISN* 300 n. 15. One may cite as a curiosity the attempt by M. Ćorović-Ljubinković to argue that, after Stephen's first coronation by a papal legate, he was crowned a second time by Sava with the reliquary supposed to contain the right hand of St John the Baptist: 'Pretečina desnica i drugo krunisanje Prvovenčanog', *Starinar*, v–vi (1953–4), 105–14. Her arguments do not convince me.

sympathy with Stephen's pro-Roman policy, and that this was the cause of his leaving Serbia in about 1217 and of his return to Athos.[126] In so far as this opinion is not based on an a priori view that Sava was hostile to the Roman Church—in which case the argument is in danger of becoming circular—it seems to rest on two main grounds: firstly, Sava left Serbia at the very time of a Roman cardinal's expected or actual arrival to crown his brother; and secondly, two years later Sava travelled to Nicaea, where he was consecrated archbishop by the Greek patriarch and given permission by the emperor to set up an autonomous Serbian Church. The second of these arguments will be considered later, when it will be argued that Sava's journey to Nicaea in 1219 was undertaken with the full knowledge and approval of the king, his brother. The first argument—the virtual coincidence in time between the arrival of the Roman legate and Sava's departure—should not be dismissed too lightly; but it is certainly not strong enough to support the view that Sava left Serbia in anger at his brother's behaviour.[127]

Several arguments, indeed, can be advanced in favour of the contrary view. Any idea that Sava left for Athos in a fit of pique can probably be ruled out by observing that before his departure from Studenica he took steps to regulate the life of the community and oversaw the appointment of a new abbot.[128] He appears to have been on excellent terms with his brother at the time of his departure; Domentijan tells us that he left Serbia against Stephen's will; and Teodosije adds that Stephen, accompanied by a group of nobles, escorted his brother to the Byzantine frontier.[129] Stephen himself, writing in 1216, called Sava his 'teacher and mentor'.[130] Finally, it is hard to believe that Sava's journey to Nicaea, about two years after he left Serbia, could have been undertaken without consulting with his brother. The two did not meet again before 1220, when Sava returned home from his consecration. These are certainly not conclusive arguments in favour of the view that Sava approved of, or

---

[126] They include such prominent Serbian historians as S. Stanojević, V. Corović, and J. Radonić. See the references in Dj. Slijepčević, *Istorija*, i. 73–4. An early instance of this belief is Ruvarac, op. cit. 16–17, and a recent one B. Ferjančić, in *ISN* 301.

[127] Ruvarac, 'O glavnim momentima', 16; Stanojević, *Sveti Sava*, 42: 'Sava je ljut otišao iz Srbije'.

[128] Domentijan, 213; Teodosije, 116.

[129] Domentijan, 213; Teodosije, 117.

[130] Stephen Nemanjić, 72: 'učitelju i nastav'niku mojemu'.

at least was led to accept, Stephen's coronation by a Roman cardinal; but perhaps they make the contrary opinion appear less likely.[131]

On the more general question of Sava's attitude to Rome and its bishop, reliable evidence is hard to come by. In default of such evidence, partisan viewpoints have often prevailed. Several Serbian and Russian authors, reading back into the Balkan world of the early thirteenth century the sense of a divided Christendom which came to the fore at a much later period, have tried to safeguard Sava's Orthodoxy by portraying him as an enemy of Rome.[132] Some Roman Catholic writers, impelled by the opposite prejudice, have tried to prove that Sava was devoted to the Roman Church.[133] His whole-hearted devotion to the Eastern Church is beyond question; yet there are reasons for believing that he was no enemy of the papacy. It will be recalled that Domentijan asserts that Sava sent an envoy to Rome to ask the pope for a royal crown for his brother Stephen. As we have seen, Stephen, rather than Sava, was likelier to have dispatched the Serbian embassy of 1217. Yet Domentijan is unlikely to have invented the story of Sava's own connection with the embassy—and hence his approval of it. What is important is that in ascribing the initiative for its dispatch to Sava, he intended to praise him, and if we remember that Domentijan was probably Sava's personal disciple, we may well conclude that his view of Rome and its bishop faithfully mirrored that of his master.

Furthermore, Sava's attitude to Rome must have been influenced by the fact that Serbia's maritime provinces contained a large Catholic population. This Latin minority was chiefly concentrated in the cities and monasteries, sometimes under the ecclesiastical jurisdiction of Ragusa (Dubrovnik) and sometimes of Antibari (Bar).[134] The seat of

[131] Those who believe that Sava and Stephen were in full agreement on their ecclesiastical policy include Dvornik, *The Slavs in European History*, 98–100, Slijepčević, *Istorija*, 73–8, and S. Hafner, *SNSS* 384. D. Bogdanović, *ISN* 317, is undecided.

[132] This is true even of so enlightened and authoritative a representative of the Serbian Orthodox Church as Bishop Nikolai Velimirović. His book, *The Life of St Sava* (Libertyville, Ill., 1951), though written with intimate knowledge of Serbian hagiography, is quite unreliable as a work of history. Of greater historical value, though marred by an unduly credulous attitude to the sources, is the brief survey by M. Matejić, *Biography of Saint Sava* (Columbus, Ohio, 1976).

[133] An early example is the 17th-c. titular bishop of Bosnia, Ivan Tomko Marnavić (Marnavitius): *Vita S. Sabbae episcopi*, in *SZ* ii. 118–45. See N. Radojčić, *SZ* i, 319–82.

[134] The sees of Ragusa and Antibari fought for centuries for ecclesiastical primacy on the Dalmatian coast. See *ISN* 188, 195, 346–8; J. Kalić, *SNSS* 34–52. At the Lateran Council of 1215 Antibari gained victory and was given jurisdiction over all the Latin churches within the Serbian state (*ISN* 304).

the archbishop of Bar was on Serbian territory. This region, governed during Sava's lifetime by his brother Vukan, had long-standing connections with Rome, and King Stephen's policy, both at home and abroad, had perforce to take account of the fact that an important number of his subjects, often the wealthiest and most cultured, had belonged to the Roman Church for generations. There is no reason to doubt that Sava shared his brother's concern for the Catholic citizens of the Serbian kingdom.[135]

Serbia, meanwhile, astride the territorial dividing lines between Greek and Latin Christendom, remained in a confused and ambiguous position. With its coastal provinces under the Latin archbishopric of Bar,[136] its interior, including the bishoprics of Ras, Prizren, Lipljan, and Niš, belonged to the archdiocese of Ohrid.[137] Ohrid, the centre of the autocephalous archbishop, lay inside the Greek principality of Epirus, which was founded after 1204 by the Byzantine nobleman, Michael Angelos Comnenus. His realm, with its capital at Arta, included by the time of his death in 1215 the whole of western Greece and a large part of Albania. Michael owed a token allegiance to the emperor of Nicaea, who had 'restored' the defunct Byzantine Empire in western Asia Minor, but his half-brother and successor Theodore Angelos was made of different stuff. Hoping to make Epirus a base for the reconquest of Constantinople, he vied with the Nicaean emperor for leadership of the Greek world; in December 1224, he seized Thessalonica from the Latins; and soon after he was crowned emperor of the Romans by Demetrios Chomatianos, the autocephalous archbishop of Ohrid. 'A second Byzantine Empire in exile had been created.'[138]

Sava's visit to Nicaea should be seen in the light of these great doings. It was probably planned well in advance and, as suggested earlier, on consultation with Stephen.[139] After his return to Hilandar, Sava stayed in contact with his brother by letter; and once he sent one of his own monks to Serbia, with a written message for the king.[140]

---

[135] See the perceptive study 'Svetosavska crkva i Rim u XIII i XIV veku' by S. Hafner, *SNSS* 381–8.

[136] Except for Kotor, which was then under the jurisdiction of the archbishop of Bari in Italy: see M. Janković, *SNSS* 73.

[137] See J. Kalić, *SNSS* 49.

[138] Nicol, *The Despotate of Epiros*, 4; cf. M. Petrović, 'Istorijsko-pravna strana Homatijanovog pisma "Najprečasnijem medju monasima i sinu velikog župana Srbije kir Savi" ' *Zbornik Radova Vizantološkog Instituta*, xix (1980), 187, n. 99.

[139] See B. Kovačević, *Sveti Sava* (1977), 323.

[140] Domentijan, 214–17; Teodosije, 117–25.

Perhaps it is significant that Domentijan and Teodosije, both of whom mention this mission, place it immediately before Sava's journey to Nicaea.

Most historians agree that the journey was undertaken in 1219.[141] Domentijan and Teodosije differ in some particulars, but not in essentials.[142] Their version of the event, partly because of their manifest desire to avoid the impression that Sava's achievements in Nicaea were the result of a prearranged deal, leaves many questions unanswered. Hence this episode of Sava's life has been the subject of much learned conflict.

Domentijan and Teodosije both state, rather improbably, that Sava was travelling on some unspecified business to do with Hilandar. Curiously, neither of them mentions Nicaea: Domentijan states that Sava travelled 'to the east', to visit 'the emperor of Carigrad',[143] while Teodosije claims that he went to Constantinople.[144] Both must have known the real name of the city where the emperor and patriarch resided in 1219. The words used by Domentijan show that for him the Nicaean ruler was the legitimate emperor of Byzantium (for where the emperor dwells, there is the true capital), while Teodosije, who wrote after the recapture of Constantinople by Michael VIII in 1261, ignored the short-lived Latin empire, and doubtless used the anachronism to emphasize the continuity of Byzantine history.

The Nicaean Emperor Theodore I Lascaris was Sava's relation by marriage: he and Stephen Nemanjić had been married to two sisters.[145] Sava, who had twice visited Constantinople before the

---

[141] The date of 1220, preferred by some historians, is not much in favour today. See S. Stanojević, 'Sveti Sava i nezavisnost srpske crkve', *Glas Srpske Kraljevske Akademije*, clix/81 (1933), 235–42; N. Radojčić, 'Sveti Sava i avtokefalnost srpske i bugarske crkve', ibid. clxxix/91 (1939), 179–258; Slijepčević, *Istorija*, 78; Ostrogorsky, *History*, 431. B. Ferjančić, who opted for 1220 in 1979 (*SNSS* 65 n. 3), later changed his mind and in 1981 dated the visit to 1219 (*ISN* 305). 1220 was proposed by F. Dölger, *Regesten der Kaiserurkunden des Oströmischen Reiches*, iii (Munich–Berlin, 1932), 7, and V. Laurent, *Les Regestes des Actes du patriarcat de Constantinople*, i/4 (Paris, 1971), 31–2. Both Dölger and Laurent erroneously state that Sava was appointed in Nicaea 'archbishop of Peć'.

[142] See Stanojević, art. cit., 211–15, 226–35; Dinić, 'Domentijan i Teodosije' (n. 25), 5–7; Slijepčević, *Istorija*, 80.

[143] Domentijan, 217. Carigrad (Tsarigrad), literally 'the imperial city', was the name by which the Southern Slavs called Constantinople.

[144] Teodosije, 126–32.

[145] It is not apparent that the outrageous manner in which Stephen repudiated his Byzantine wife adversely affected Sava's reception by the emperor Theodore. To describe Sava's relationship to Theodore, Domentijan used the term *svat* (p. 217), a

Latin conquest, must have been well known in Nicaea, both personally and by reputation. His warm reception by Theodore, vouched for by both his biographers, may also have been due to the fact that the agreement about to be concluded between the Serbian and Nicaean governments had already been negotiated by the two parties.[146]

This agreement, which was to determine the future of the Serbian Orthodox Church, was ratified in Nicaea in 1219, and was embodied in two decisions. Sava was consecrated archbishop by the Patriarch Manuel,[147] and, by a decree of the Nicaean synod issued with the emperor's authority, the Serbian Church was granted an 'autocephalous' status: this allowed all future archbishop-primates of Serbia to be elected and consecrated without recourse to the patriarch by their own suffragans. Only one condition was imposed: in Serbian churches the Byzantine patriarch was to be given precedence over all other bishops in liturgical commemoration.[148]

The legal implications of these decisions will be discussed later; meanwhile, two preliminary conclusions offer themselves: firstly, although the duty of commemorating the patriarch curtailed *de jure* the autocephaly of the Serbian Church, it did not in practice reduce it very much: the Serbian Church was granted full administrative and judicial sovereignty, as well as the unrestricted right to elect and consecrate its archbishop-primate and its other bishops.[149] Secondly, the method of Sava's appointment and consecration must have raised an awkward canonical problem: Byzantine canon law deprecates the

---

vague term for a relation by marriage. Teodosije, who uses the same word (p. 126), says nothing about King Stephen's marriage to the sister of Theodore's wife, but states (erroneously) that Theodore Lascaris' daughter was then engaged to Sava's nephew Radoslav. Teodosije confused two different Theodores: Radoslav married (probably in 1219 or 1220) the daughter of Theodore I Angelos of Epirus (*ISN* 306–7).

[146] As Slijepčević, *Istorija*, 87, plausibly surmises.

[147] Perhaps on 15 Aug: see Janković, *SNSS* 73.

[148] For this stipulation see Domentijan, 221.

[149] See B. Gardašević, in *Sveti Sava* (1977), 36–37, 63. Stanojević, art. cit. 233–4, has suggested that the obligation incurred by the Serbian church to commemorate the patriarch lapsed c. 1272, when the Emperor Michael VIII disclosed his intention to abolish the autonomy of the Serbian and Bulgarian churches and to subject both to the archbishop of Ohrid. Cf. Geanakoplos, *Emperor Michael Palaeologus*, 278 n. 3. The Serbian church may indeed have shaken off this last trace of formal dependence on the Byzantine patriarchate at the time of the Council of Lyons. This dependence was probably restored by 1375. See D. Obolensky, 'Late Byzantine culture and the Slavs: A Study in Acculturation', *XVᵉ Congrès International d'Études Byzantines. Rapports et co-rapports* (Athens, 1976), 13–15; repr. in id., *The Byzantine Inheritance of Eastern Europe*.

recommendation of a particular person to a specific see.[150] Domentijan and Teodosije were obviously aware of this difficulty and both
assert—implausibly—that Sava put forward one of his clerical
companions for election as archbishop.[151] It seems clear that, in the
teeth of local opposition to the granting of autonomy to the Serbian
church, the emperor had his way in the end. By ratifying the imperial
verdict, the patriarch and his synod gave canonical sanction both to
Sava's election and to the autocephalous rights of the Serbian
Church.[152]

Both sides gained much from the decision of 1219.[153] The Nicaean
authorities, anxious to vindicate their claim to the heritage of
Byzantium, regarded the Slav nations of Eastern Europe as natural,
indeed indispensable allies. In the first half of the thirteenth century,
by diplomatic concessions to the Serbs, the Bulgarians, and the
Russians—mainly through privileges granted to their Churches—the
Nicaean emperors achieved two aims: they buttressed the loyalty of
the Slav Churches to the patriarchate at a time when the combined
pressure of the papacy and of the Latin crusading states threatened
the entire fabric of Orthodox Christendom; and, by appearing to the
Slav rulers of the Balkans as legitimate leaders of the Orthodox
Church, they gained precious support against the challenge of the
rulers of Epirus.[154] The acute phase of the struggle between Nicaea
and Epirus was still to come. But Theodore Angelos, Epirote ruler
since 1215, was already emerging as the most effective Greek
champion against the Latins: in 1217, in a battle near Elbasan in

[150] See D. Obolensky, 'Byzantium, Kiev and Moscow: A Study in Ecclesiastical
Relations', *Dumbarton Oaks Papers*, xi (1957), 40–2; repr. in id., *Byzantium and the Slavs:
Collected Studies* (London, 1971).
[151] Domentijan, 217–18; Teodosije, 126–7.
[152] Gardašević, in *Sveti Sava* (1977), 69; Ferjančić, *SNSS* 66–7.
[153] Stanojević, art. cit. 211–51, has argued that the Nicaean concessions to Serbia
were given in two stages: in 1219 Sava was appointed and consecrated archbishop; but
the autonomy of the Serbian church was only conceded in 1229 or 1230, by John III
Doukas Vatatzes and the Patriarch Germanos II, on the occasion of Sava's second visit
to Nicaea. His thesis is argued with ingenuity and learning, but is difficult to support
against the explicit evidence of both Domentijan and Teodosije that Sava's consecration
and the granting of autonomy took place on the same occasion, during his first visit to
Nicaea. Moreover, M. Petrović, 'Istorijsko-pravna strana', 196, has acutely observed
that in his letter to Sava, written in 1220, Chomatianos accused him of consecrating
'many bishops' in Serbia; Sava would hardly have been able to do this had his church
not been granted autonomy. Most Serbian historians part company with Stanojević on
this issue. They include N. Radojčić (art. cit. 235), B. Ferjančić, *SNSS* 65–7, and D.
Bogdanović, *ISN* 317.
[154] See Obolensky, *The Byzantine Commonwealth*, 241–2.

Albania, he defeated the Latin emperor of Constantinople, Peter of Courtenay, and took him prisoner. More ominous still, from Nicaea's standpoint, was the growing independence of the Epirot Church. The rulers of Arta were encouraging the appointment of bishops in their realm without consulting the patriarch;[155] and with the nomination, at Theodore's suggestion, of Demetrios Chomatianos as autocephalous archbishop of Ohrid (*c.* 1217),[156] a vigorous and assertive churchman was now in a position to challenge the patriarch himself.

The Serbs, too, had every reason to be pleased with the results of Sava's journey to Nicaea. They now had a Church which was independent administratively and, in practice if not quite *de jure*, autocephalous. The international status and prestige of their country were thus greatly enhanced. King Stephen, moreover, had strengthened his links with the Nicaean ruler, who was recognized by most Greeks and Slavs—whether living at home or scattered abroad—as the legitimate emperor of the Byzantines. Above all, the religious situation inside Serbia was much clearer now. Sava found himself free to give a national character to his Church, to replace the Greek bishops in the kingdom by his own Serbian nominees, and to balance the strong influence of Rome in the coastal regions by literature and liturgical practice based on the Church Slavonic tradition. There is no reason to think he opposed his brother's readiness to recognize the pope's authority: Stephen reiterated this readiness in 1220,[157] We have seen that Sava was no enemy of Rome; and, like his brother, he probably saw nothing inconsistent in recognizing the pope's spiritual authority, if not his canonical jurisdiction, while accepting consecration and ecclesiastical autonomy from the patriarch and emperor of Nicaea. To see in Stephen (as many historians have done) the champion of Latin traditions in Serbia, and in Sava the defender of the Orthodox Church, is to fly in the face of the evidence and to ignore that sense of a united Christendom, which in the first half of the thirteenth century still survived in the Balkans. The atrocities committed in Constantinople and elsewhere by the armies of the Fourth Crusade certainly caused most Greeks to harden their hearts to the West; but in many parts of the Balkans it was otherwise: there, a distinguished medievalist has written, 'people knew little and cared less about

---

[155] See Karpozilos, *The Ecclesiastical Controversy*, 51–3.

[156] For the date of Chomatianos' appointment, see Karpozilos, op. cit. 58–9; M. Petrović, *Zbornik Radova Vizantološkog Instituta*, xix (1980), 186.

[157] See above, p. 144.

differences between the two Churches and . . . cherished the naïve conviction that one should remain on speaking terms with both the great Christian centres'.[158] Sava was neither naïve nor ignorant of the crimes the Latins had committed on Athos and elsewhere. But it is possible that he did not understand the full implications of the doctrine of the Roman primacy. Even Byzantine theologians were slow to do so. Only gradually, and after the Fourth Crusade, did the Eastern Church begin to grasp its true significance.[159]

The young archbishop—Sava was then about thirty-four—stopped briefly on Mount Athos on his way home and for a longer spell in Thessalonica, where he arrived in the autumn of 1219.[160] Both his biographers inform us that he stayed in 'his own' monastery of Philokales, where, according to Domentijan, he had lived during his previous Thessalonican visit.[161] Thanks to his earlier munificence, he was reckoned to be one of the monastery's *ktitores*.[162] By 1219 Philokales was in the hands of the Knights Templar, but they may well have been absentee landlords; Greek monks were probably still living there, under Latin ecclesiastical sway. According to Teodosije, Sava paid a visit to the metropolitan on his arrival in Thessalonica, who, together with the city's prefect and leading citizens, bade him a warm farewell when he left.[163] If these statements are not merely Teodosije's fantasy, they are further evidence of Sava's friendly relations with Latins.

Sava's stay in Thessalonica, which must have lasted well into 1220, proved important for the future of Serbia's legal tradition.

---

[158] Dvornik, *The Slavs in European History*, 100.

[159] See id., *Byzantium and the Roman Primacy* (New York, 1966), 155–6; S. Hafner, *SNSS* 385–6. In the first half of the 13th c., even Greeks were not averse to a dialogue, and more, with the Church of Rome. The first two rulers of Epirus, Michael and Theodore, had placed themselves and their state under the protection of the pope, thus recognizing his spiritual authority. See A. Meliarakes, Ἱστορία τοῦ Βασιλείου τῆς Νικαίας καὶ τοῦ Δεσποτάτου τῆς Ἠπείρου (Athens, 1898), 57–9, 127. Cited in Karpozilos, op. cit. 55 n. 38. Moreover, the Nicaean Emperor Theodore Lascaris, at the very time Sava was visiting him, was planning a council of Greek and Latin churchmen to discuss a possible union of the Churches: see Karpozilos, op. cit. 54.

[160] See Živojinović, 'O boravcima svetog Save u Solunu', 68.

[161] Domentijan, 226.

[162] Teodosije, 77. The monastery of Philokales (Φιλοκάλου) was founded by a Byzantine official in the late 12 c. For its history, and connection with Sava, see Janin, *Les Églises et les monastères*, 418–19; M. Živojinović, art. cit. 63–71; A. Tsitouridou, *SNSS* 263–8.

[163] Teodosije, pp. 135–6. Domentijan, 226, states that the metropolitan was Constantine Mesopotamites, Sava's old friend. But this is an error, as Constantine was deprived of his see, and expelled by the Latins in 1204.

While he was living in the monastery of Philokales, Domentijan tells us, he 'copied many books of law, needed by his cathedral church, concerning the emendation of the true faith'.[164] This terse statement refers to the drawing up, probably in 1220, of what was to become the most authoritative Slavonic body of Byzantine canon law. 'Sava's Nomocanon', as this manual has been called, is a compilation of texts from several Byzantine collections in earlier Slavonic translations; to this he added Slavonic versions of commentaries by Aristenos and Zonaras, two leading twelfth-century Greek canonists, and a complete translation of the late ninth-century code of Byzantine civil and public law known as the *Procheiron*. Sava's 'Nomocanon' may show evidence of independent work: at least no exact Greek or Slavonic model has yet been found. The extent of Sava's share is uncertain: recent scholarship inclines to the view that he organized and supervised the work, without necessarily translating the material himself. He must have been able to assemble an expert team of canonists among Byzantine scholars still in Thessalonica.

In selecting their material, the compilers of Sava's Nomocanon (it has been claimed) deliberately omitted texts which stressed the universal authority of the emperor and the patriarch, with the purpose of safeguarding the independence of the Serbian Church and state and avoiding tension with the Church of Rome.[165] There is nothing improbable in this, but proof is lacking. Aristenos' commentary on the canons could well have been chosen by Sava for its brevity, its conciseness, and its relative simplicity.[166]

So codification of Byzantine law for the practical needs of Sava's Church became the foundation of Serbian ecclesiastical and civil legislation. Its influence spread far beyond the boundaries of medieval Serbia: St Sava's Nomocanon—known to the Slavs as *Krmčija*, or *Kormčaja Kniga*, the 'Book of the Pilot'—became the basic constitution of the Bulgarian and Russian Churches.

Sava went back to Serbia in 1220, to organize and rule his new self-governing Church. First he reported to the king on his mission to Nicaea, and then he went to Studenica, where he prayed on their

---

[164] Domentijan, 227. Teodosije, 136, confines himself to the statement that, when leaving Thessalonica, Sava 'took with him books of law'.

[165] See I. Žužek, 'Kormčaja Kniga', *Orientalia Christiana Analecta*, clxviii (1964); D. Bogdanović, *SNSS* 91–9, and *ISN* 322–3; V. Mošin, *SNSS* 120–1.

[166] For these qualities of Aristenos' commentary, see Beck, *Kirche und theologische Literatur*, 657.

father's tomb. Next he moved on to Žiča, where he set up his archdiocese. His first administrative act, according to Domentijan and Teodosije, was the selection and consecration of the bishops of the Serbian Church from among his disciples, some of whom he had recently brought from Hilandar. Unfortunately neither biographer mentions specific dioceses: they do tell us, however, that these were planned to fit the main regions of the kingdom:[167] the number, names, and location of these dioceses have been the subject of much scholarly discussion. He seems to have set up eleven bishoprics, including the centre of his archdiocese at Žiča. Some of them were based in monasteries,[168] and three—Ras, Prizren, and Lipljan— belonged to the archdiocese of Ohrid; their Greek incumbents were replaced by Serbian bishops owing allegiance to Sava. These measures seem to have been rapidly carried out, others followed, aimed at consolidating the missionary work in different parts of the kingdom: Sava picked another batch of disciples, ordained them archpriests, and sent them to the provinces as his 'exarchs', or delegates, to impose the Christian marriage laws and root out the remnants of rustic paganism.[169] It is likely that these missionaries were trained, perhaps hurriedly, to fight heresy as well: according to Domentijan and Teodosije, before sending out his 'exarchs' Sava delivered a long homily in Žiča cathedral containing condemnation of several 'heretical' beliefs. The list is specific and precise: denial of the reality of the Incarnation and of the Real Presence in the Eucharist, and refusal to venerate the cross, churches, icons, and sacred vessels.[170]

This heresy is nowhere named: but there can be little doubt that Sava and his biographers had the teachings of the Bogomils in mind. The members of this sect, first clearly attested in Bulgaria in the tenth century, held that the material world was created by the devil, and that man's only hope of salvation was as far as possible to avoid all physical contact with matter: thus the Bogomils condemned marriage, and the eating of meat and drinking of wine. Matter being intrinsically evil, they denied that Christ was born of a woman; they rejected all the sacraments of the Orthodox, especially baptism and the Eucharist, and spurned icons, crosses, church buildings and the

---

[167] Domentijan, 233; Teodosije, 140–1.
[168] See M. Janković, *SNSS* 73–84, and D. Bogdanović, *ISN* 317–20.
[169] Domentijan, 243–5; Teodosije, 151.
[170] Domentijan, 236–8; Teodosije, 149–50.

priesthood, and the whole organization of the Christian Church. By the tenth century in Bulgaria, they were preaching and practising civil disobedience and urging rebellion against all established order.[171]

The danger of this dualist sect to the Church and state authorities was enhanced by the elaborate concealment practised by its votaries: also by their courage and tenacity when discovered. They forced the Bulgarian government to persecution, and it seems to have been violent. It is virtually certain that Bogomilism was discovered in Serbia during the reign of Stephen Nemanja. Stephen Nemanjić describes his father's stern measures against the teachers of a heretical sect: some were burnt at the stake, others were exiled; their leader was condemned to have his tongue cut off.[172] The strength of this unnamed dissident movement can be measured by the fact that Nemanja was compelled to send an armed force to stamp it out. That its leaders were Bogomils can hardly be questioned. The evidence of Domentijan and Teodosije suggests that Nemanja failed to root out the heresy completely. Sava, on becoming archbishop, had to tackle a fresh outbreak.[173]

Sava's struggle against the Bogomils probably had the support of the local secular authorities, as well as that of his brother the king. There is no reason to suppose that their co-operation in state and Church matters was anything but close. Sava seems to have enjoyed a considerable reputation as a diplomatist, and he was several times employed on delicate missions of state. As abbot of Studenica, he was sent abroad about 1212, to parley with a certain Dobromir Strez. This Bulgarian chieftain had allied himself with Michael of Epirus and, from his fortress of Prosek in central Macedonia, he threatened Stephen Nemanjić, his former patron. The mission, it seems, was a failure.[174] He was more successful (*c.* 1220) when, as archbishop, he

---

[171] See D. Obolensky, *The Bogomils* (Cambridge, 1948); H.-C. Puech and A. Vaillant, *Le Traité contre les Bogomiles de Cosmas le Prêtre* (Paris, 1945).

[172] Stephen Nemanjić, 27–30.

[173] Sava's biographers describe the heretics as cowed and eventually persuaded to recant by the archbishop's eloquence and authority, but this is scarcely credible.

[174] On Strez and his relations with Stephen see D. M. Nicol. *The Despotate of Epiros* (Oxford, 1957), 33–4, 44, n. 20; R. L. Wolff, in Setton (ed.), *A History of the Crusades*, ii. 205, 208–10; B. Ferjančić, in *ISN* 298–9. According to Domentijan, 206–10, and Teodosije, 101–12, Strez died in miraculous circumstances, struck down by an angel. Wolff, p. 210, believes that he was killed on the orders of Stephen Nemanjić.

persuaded Andrew II, the king of Hungary, to break off hostilities against Serbia.[175]

By sanctioning the emergence of a self-governing Serbian Church, three of whose dioceses had hitherto belonged to the autocephalous archbishop of Ohrid, the Nicaean authorities had directly encroached on Ohrid's prerogatives; and its archbishop, Demetrios Chomatianos, whose see lay within the principality of Epirus, Nicaea's political rival, naturally took up the challenge. He did so with speed and vigour, and in May 1220, after consulting his synod, he dispatched a letter to Sava. It was delivered by one of Demetrios' suffragans, the bishop of Skoplje. The letter was full of anger and biting sarcasm. Pointedly refusing to recognize the new ecclesiastical status, it is addressed to 'the lord Sava, most honourable monk and son of the great *župan* of Serbia'; and a long list of charges follows. 'Enslaved by the love of country', Sava had abandoned Mount Athos and its ascetic life; he had steeped himself in worldly affairs, he had even acted as his sovereign's ambassador to foreign rulers. He had 'begun to take part in banquets, to ride thoroughbred horses, richly caparisoned and fair to behold, to go about with a large retinue, to give himself airs while walking in processions, and to be accompanied by a lavishly and diversely dressed bodyguard'. Sava's personal behaviour, Chomatianos admitted, was perhaps not his business; but it was plainly his duty to protest against Sava's elevation to the episcopacy; and of what Church, he inquired rhetorically, was he consecrated bishop? Serbia belonged to the Church of Bulgaria, i.e. the archdiocese of Ohrid: it was to its incumbent that Sava should have addressed himself if he wished to become a bishop. By receiving consecration elsewhere he had flouted canon law and trespassed on another bishop's domain. He had allowed himself to be made bishop, not from love of the Gospel, but impelled by 'a mad thirst for fame' (δοξομανία). To make matters worse, he had 'tyrannically' expelled the lawful bishop of Prizren and replaced him by his own nominee. Chomatianos then proceeded to cite the numerous canons which, in his view, Sava had violated; and ended his letter by threatening to excommunicate him and his followers if he persisted in his course of action.[176]

Chomatianos returned to the attack a few years later, in a letter to

[175] Ferjančić, ibid. 301–2. The accounts of this embassy by Domentijan, 251–7, and Teodosije, 152–60, ascribe miraculous powers to Sava.

[176] Chomatianos' letter to Sava was published by Pitra, *Analecta sacra et classica*, vi, cols. 381–90.

Germanos II, the patriarch of Nicaea. The patriarch had taken him roundly to task for crowning Theodore Angelos of Epirus emperor of the Romans. Chomatianos' reply follows the principle that counter-attack is the best defence. If Sava's consecration by the patriarch (Manuel I, Germanos' predecessor) is canonically valid and blameless, he argues, then so is his coronation of Theodore; and if it is not valid—the view to which Chomatianos strongly subscribed—his own action is still blameless, for he was only following the patriarch's example.[177]

For all the casuistry of this last argument, there is no doubt that, prima facie, Chomatianos had a strong case. Three of the bishoprics of the newly created church of Serbia had been subject to Ohrid since 1019. The incumbent of the one at Prizren, and perhaps of others, had been unceremoniously dismissed by Sava. Chomatianos, who was a distinguished expert in canon law, had no difficulty in citing authoritative canons which forbade a bishop to perform ordinations outside his own diocese and interfere in any way in the affairs of other territorial Churches. There is no doubt that Sava had done precisely that.

Chomatianos brought out two additional arguments against Sava and his Nicaean patrons: firstly, any suggestion that in a conflict between the Church of 'Bulgaria' (i.e. Ohrid) and the patriarchate of Nicaea (i.e. Byzantium) the former, as a relatively new-fangled institution, must yield to the claims of the latter was, he asserted, historically false. The archbishopric of Ohrid, he went on, was the legitimate successor of that of Prima Justiniana established in 535 by the Emperor Justinian. This quasi-independent archdiocese, covering most of Serbia, northern Macedonia, and western Bulgaria, was originally equal in rank to the patriarchates of Rome, Constantinople, Alexandria, and Antioch.[178] Chomatianos' second argument was more modern. He admitted that Sava could claim appointment by the emperor, and that emperors still possessed, as 'of old', the right to promote bishoprics to metropolitan or archiepiscopal rank.[179] But this argument he countered denying the right of the Nicaean ruler to call himself an emperor or to claim the heritage of Byzantium: 'Where is the Empire now?',[180] he inquired rhetorically.

---

[177] Pitra, ibid. 487–98; Karpozilos, op. cit. 81–85.

[178] See Beck, *Kirche und theologische Literatur*, 186.

[179] This right was given them by canons 12 and 17 of the Council of Chalcedon (451) and by canon 38 of the Council *in Trullo* (691–2): Pitra, ibid. col. 384.

[180] Ποῦ δὲ καὶ βασιλεία νῦν;: Pitra, ibid. col. 384.

Both these arguments of Chomatianos' are flawed. Prima Justiniana was an ephemeral creation, subjected to the bishop of Rome ten years after its birth, and extinct by the early seventh century. The theory that the archdiocese of Ohrid (which covered part of the territory) was descended from it historically is no earlier than the twelfth century, and its first vigorous champion was Chomatianos himself. No patriarch of Nicaea seems to have recognized the claim; it was patently contrived and artificial. Chomatianos' assertion in 1220 that there was no true Empire now[181] chimed in with the political stance of his secular overlords, the rulers of Epirus, but it was acceptable neither to the Slavs of Eastern Europe nor to the Orthodox Christians in the Near East. Both groups were increasingly on their way to acknowledging the Lascarid rulers of Nicaea and their patriarchs as the only true guardians of the Byzantine heritage. Chomatianos' repudiation of these Lascarid claims might have carried more conviction had it been put forward a few years later; that is, after his crowning in Thessalonica of Theodore Angelos, his secular patron, as emperor, in violation of all accepted propriety, both in Church and state.

On closer scrutiny Chomatianos' case rests mostly—perhaps entirely—on the charge that Sava, by taking possession of bishoprics belonging to Ohrid, violated his canonical duty towards his ecclesiastical superior. Before 1219, as a cleric of the Serbian Orthodox Church, Sava unquestionably owed allegiance to Chomatianos, and it is the breaking of this canonical dependence, not the creation by the Nicaean authorities of the autocephalous Serbian Church, that Chomatianos condemned. No doubt he wished to avoid a clash with Nicaea, and thought Sava was easier game. He remained cautious towards the patriarch and, despite their discord, respectful,[182] but, throughout the 1220s, was hostile to the Nicaean government. But in his letter to Sava he came dangerously near to exposing his own flank. He conceded the vital point that Sava's elevation would have been legitimate had there been an emperor to sanction it. To Chomatianos' rhetorical 'Where is the Empire now?', nearly all former Byzantine citizens (with the exception of the Epirots) would have answered: 'For the time being in Nicaea—until the Lascarids can regain their heritage, Constantinople.'

In this imbroglio of the 1220s between the patriarchate, Chomatia-

---

[181] οὐκ ἔστιν ἀληθινὴ βασιλεία: ibid.   [182] See Karpozilos, op. cit. 77–93.

nos, and Sava, the historian may find it hard to deal out praise and blame with fairness. For all its compliance with the aims of the imperial policy,[183] the patriarchate could claim that it was upholding its former 'oecumenical' traditions, that it was still, in fact, the rightful leader of the Orthodox world,[184] and that its authority over the Serbs went back to the ninth century, when Byzantine missionaries converted them. Chomatianos, also in the toils of political constraints and ambitions, felt he had canon law on his side: it was his duty to challenge the blatant territorial infringement of the integrity of his autocephalous church.[185] As for Sava, the privileges he obtained in Nicaea in 1219 had probably been already negotiated between his brother and the emperor. By accepting consecration at the hands of a patriarch whom he must have seen as the true head of the Orthodox Church, Sava recognized that the Serbian kingdom, whose sovereignty and independence had earlier been assured by his brother's coronation, now had every right to an autonomous church.

In the end this tangled situation, for which no canonical ruling seems to have given a clear precedent, was resolved by the passing of time. There is no evidence that Sava replied to Chomatianos' letter, or that the latter carried out his threat of excommunication. The conflict gradually died down; and the autocephaly of the Serbian Church was, in Sava's lifetime, recognized by the leaders of the other Orthodox Churches, as it is still recognized today.

King Stephen died in 1228. In the last years of his reign he became the friend and ally of Theodore Angelos of Epirus. Radoslav, Stephen's eldest son and the heir to the Serbian throne, had married, *c.* 1219–20,[186] Theodore's daughter Anna. The Epirot alliance continued to dominate Serbia's foreign policy during the reign (1228–33) of Sava's

---

[183] On this point, see M. Angold, *A Byzantine Government in Exile: Government and Society under the Laskarids of Nicaea (1204–1261)* (Oxford, 1975), 46–59.

[184] The attempt by B. Gardašević, *Sveti Sava* (1977), 60–1, to argue that the patriarch had the right to consecrate Sava because he was an Athonite monk, and hence a cleric of the patriarchate, is misguided. The Athonite monasteries in this period were autonomous in the strictly ecclesiastical sense, but more generally were under the emperor's direct jurisdiction. The *protos* of Athos was only placed under the patriarch's jurisdiction in 1312. See Petrović, 'Istorijsko-pravna strana', xix (1980), 197.

[185] See B. Ferjančić, *SNSS* 65–72. B. Gardašević's claim, *Sveti Sava* (1977) 48–55, that the archbishopric of Ohrid was not autocephalous is quite unjustified. Its autocephaly was explicitly recognized by the Byzantine patriarchate. See Petrović, art. cit. 183, 205.

[186] For the date of the marriage, see *ISN* 307.

nephew, Stephen Radoslav, even after the crushing defeat of Theodore Angelos at the battle of Klokotnitsa (1230) by the Bulgarian Tsar John Asen II. King Radoslav, grandson of the Emperor Alexius III through his mother Eudoxia, and husband of an Epirot princess, seems to have been an ardent Graecophile. Like his father-in-law, he liked to style himself in official acts with the high-sounding Byzantine name of Doukas.[187] His Epirot sympathies led him into a correspondence with Demetrios Chomatianos. He sent him a list of questions, most of them technical, relating to liturgical practice and discipline. They are quoted in the archbiship's long and undated reply.[188] The tone of Chomatianos' letter is warm, though, in places, condescending.[189] In an oblique though unmistakable reference to his dispute with Sava, he reminded Radoslav that no bishop may celebrate the office or perform any episcopal function in another diocese without the express permission of the ordinary of that diocese.[190]

This letter has been taken by several leading Serbian historians as evidence of Radoslav's wish to return the Serbian Church to the jurisdiction of Ohrid. Sava, they believe, now feared that the autocephaly of the Serbian Church was threatened by his nephew's change of direction; and left his country on a pilgrimage to the Holy Land in a fit of anger.[191]

The arguments in favour of this view are not wholly implausible. The king's request for a ruling on liturgical matters from Chomatianos, who had recently threatened to excommunicate the Serbian archbishop and his flock, could be construed as a deliberate slight on his uncle.[192] Furthermore, Sava left for Palestine shortly after Radoslav's accession,[193] and it is tempting to assume that he did so because of his nephew's leanings towards Ohrid.

---

[187] The name, in Greek lettering, occurs on Radoslav's engagement ring, in several Greek documents and also on a copper coin he issued with the inscription Στέφανος ῥὴξ ὁ Δούκας: ISN 307–8; D. I. Polemis, *The Doukai*, 132.

[188] Pitra, op. cit., cols. 685–710.

[189] He professes to write in 'common, simple, and prosaic style', to facilitate comprehension to one whose native 'Bulgarian' (i.e. Slavonic) language lacks 'logical skill': ibid., cols. 685–6.

[190] Ibid., col. 691. This is indeed a basic principle of ecclesiastical law.

[191] Their views are cited in Slijepčević, *Istorija*, 105–8. A recent exponent of them is B. Ferjančić, *ISN* 308–9.

[192] Unless we suppose that Radoslav's approach to Chomatianos was inspired by Sava, in an effort to make peace with Ohrid, which does not seem very plausible.

[193] Teodosije, 166.

In themselves, however, these arguments seem inconclusive. Grounds can be found for supporting the contrary view that there was no rift between king and archbishop, and that Sava's decision to go to Palestine had nothing to do with his nephew's correspondence with Chomatianos. Both Domentijan and Teodosije describe the relations between Sava and Radoslav as entirely friendly. This cannot be wholly due to the hagiographers' wish to paint an idyllic picture of love and harmony between the different members of the Nemanja family: specific facts in their narratives confirm the general picture. Radoslav was Sava's candidate for the throne, and Sava crowned him in Žiča.[194] Domentijan tells us that the king parted very unwillingly from Sava, and provided him with money and other necessities for his journey to the East.[195] As we shall see, not only personal reasons prompted Sava's journey to Palestine: he brought back with him details of several ceremonies and customs which he introduced into the public worship of the Serbian Church. Finally, on general grounds, it is difficult to believe that Sava, distressed at the king's pro-Ohrid stance, would have left his country in a fit of pique. If his whole life-work had really been in peril, he would surely have stayed behind to defend it.[196]

Sava set sail from Dalmatia for Palestine in 1229. He probably decided to go after hearing of the recent momentous events in Outremer. In September 1228 Frederick II, the Holy Roman Emperor, keeping his long-delayed promise to lead a crusade, arrived with his fleet and his army at Acre, and on 18 February 1229 the sultan peacefully surrendered Jerusalem to the Crusaders. For the first time since the city was captured by Saladin in 1187, the Holy Places were back in Christian hands. Domentijan and Teodosije are wholly silent on this event: Jerusalem, in their accounts, appears as a timeless city, inhabited only by the Orthodox Patriarch Athanasius. Topographically, however, Domentijan's account of Sava's movements (which Teodosije follows) is so detailed and precise that it warrants the suspicion that he may have had access to an itinerary written by Sava, or perhaps had even accompanied him. We follow Sava in his peregrinations through the Holy Places of Jerusalem, then to Bethlehem, the Jordan, and the monastery of St Sabas ('Mar Saba') in the Wadi en-Nar desert, near the Dead Sea. In Acre he embarked for

[194] Domentijan, 261–2; Teodosije, 165–6.   [195] Domentijan, 262.
[196] See Slijepčević, *Istorija*, 105–10, who argues that Sava and Radoslav remained on good terms.

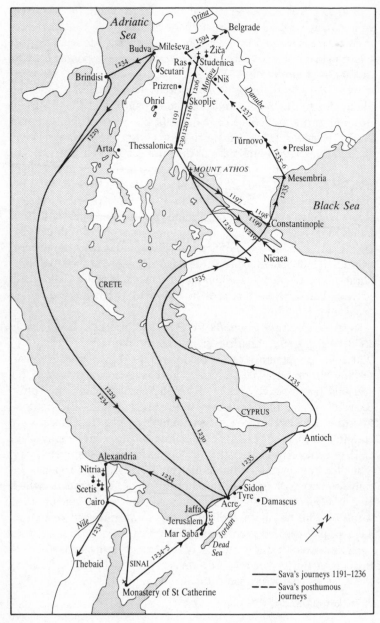

Map 4. Sava's journeys, 1191–1236

Asia Minor, intending to visit John Doukas Vatatzes, the new emperor of Nicaea. The last lap from the coast to Nicaea was covered by his party on horses provided by the emperor at Sava's request. On his way home he stopped on Mount Athos, staying in Vatopedi and Hilandar, and—probably during the winter of 1229–30—in Thessalonica, where he had talks, which Domentijan describes as very friendly, with Theodore Angelos, his relation by marriage and emperor of Thessalonica.[197] By 1230, after a journey that seems to have been rather hurried, he was back in Serbia.[198]

The religious significance of Sava's travels is stressed by his two biographers. We see him as a pilgrim, worshipping at the shrines of the Holy Land and visiting the places associated with Christ's birth, life, and passion. His visit to the *lavra* of St Sabas, his fifth-century Cappadocian patron saint, brought him in touch with some of the earliest traditions of Christian monasticism and with the Greek liturgical worship and hymnography there, for which this foundation was famous.[199] He travelled with a retinue and was clearly regarded wherever he went as an important person. We do not know the drift of his talks with the emperors of Nicaea and Thessalonica, but Domentijan tells us that some of his discussions with Athanasius, the Orthodox patriarch of Jerusalem, were concerned with liturgical matters.[200]

The liturgical tradition of the Serbian Orthodox Church, it seems, was originally modelled on that of the Constantinople monasteries, and one of them, as we know, the monastery of the Evergetis, supplied the *typicon* which, with minor changes, enabled Sava to direct the life and the liturgical practice of Hilandar and Studenica. In Hilandar the *typicon* acquired several features from Athonite usage. When Sava took it to Serbia in 1206, it must have been seen, liturgically speaking, as an Athonite constitution: both Domentijan and Teodosije believed that Sava brought the liturgical traditions of the Holy Mountain to his country.[201] However, by the twelfth century the life and organization

---

[197] Domentijan, 280.

[198] The probable chronological limits are the late spring or early summer of 1229, when the news of the recovery of Jerusalem could have been received in Serbia, and the early spring of 1230, when Theodore Angelos set out on his ill-starred war against the Bulgarians.

[199] See D. J. Chitty, *The Desert a City* (Oxford, 1966), *passim*.

[200] Domentijan, 266.   [201] Domentijan, 204–5; Teodosije, 96.

of monasteries both in Constantinople and on Athos were strongly influenced by the *typicon* of the Palestinian monastery of St Sabas.

By then this set of regulations and rubrics, known as the Jerusalem *Typicon*, had become the dominant liturgical model in the East. Monastic in character, it had by this time largely displaced the practice, and the more frequent choral offices, of the 'Great Church' of St Sophia.[202] Sava certainly studied the Jerusalem *Typicon* and the liturgical usages of the monastery of St Sabas during his Palestine visit in 1229; as a result, on his return home in 1230 he wove a number of the Jerusalem practices into the ritual of the Serbian Church. Domentijan observes that he now combined Jerusalem practice with the liturgical usages of Byzantium he had adopted earlier on.[203] This brought about, in 1230, a significant reform of the Serbian ritual.

The last four years (1230–4) of Sava's archbishopric witnessed a great political upheaval in the state. In the autumn of 1233,[204] a group of Serbian nobles deposed King Radoslav and replaced him by his younger brother Vladislav (1234–43). Teodosije claims that they were displeased by the influence exerted on Radoslav by his Greek wife.[205] But the uprising had probably another cause as well: Radoslav's father-in-law and patron, Theodore Angelos of Epirus, had lost all political influence after the battle of Klokotnitsa in 1230. The Bulgarian tsar, John Asen II, his successful rival for the hegemony of the Balkans, now claimed suzerainty over Serbia, and consequently supported Vladislav, his son-in-law.[206] Sava's attitude to this *coup d'état* is unknown. He certainly showed indulgence to both his nephews: Vladislav he crowned king;[207] and when Radoslav returned from exile, having lost both throne and wife, he befriended him in a monastery and received him 'like a father'.[208]

---

[202] See O. Strunk, 'The Byzantine Office at Hagia Sophia', *Dumbarton Oaks Papers*, ix–x (1956), 191–9. The complex relationship between different types of *typica*, most of which combine rules of monastic discipline with liturgical rubrics, is discussed by M. Skaballanovich, *Tolkovyi Tipikon* (Kiev, 1910).

[203] Domentijan, 282. On Sava's liturgical reforms, see R. Grujić, *SZ* i. 277–312; P. Simić, in *Sveti Sava* (1977), 181–205. According to Skaballanovich, op. cit. i. 323, 485; ii, 3–4, the main peculiarity of the Jerusalem *typicon* is its provision for the celebration of the Sunday all-night vigil.

[204] For the chronology, see *ISN* 309 n. 42.

[205] Teodosije, 177–8. Domentijan, more discreetly, states that the change of rulers was due to God's will.

[206] Jireček, *Geschichte der Serben*, i. 304.

[207] This is stated in the Leningrad manuscript of Domentijan's work (Serbian tr. by L. Mirković (Belgrade, 1938), 176 n. 2) and by Teodosije, 178.

[208] The former queen of Serbia had an affair with the governor of Dyrrachium. She later returned to Serbia and became a nun (Teodosije, 177–8; *ISN* 310 n. 46).

Soon after Vladislav's coronation, Sava resigned his archbishop's throne,[209] after sitting in it for some fifteen years. He announced his decision at Žiča to an assembly—*sabor*—of clergy and laity, and with their approval appointed a disciple, the monk Arsenije, as his successor. After teaching him his incumbent duties as archbishop,[210] he departed on yet another pilgrimage to the Levant.

Sava's last journey, from which he never returned, has given rise to speculation. Its motives remain uncertain. It is perhaps safer to seek them, not in any designs of far-flung diplomacy,[211] but in a personal impulse on which both Domentijan and Teodosije commented with praise: he yearned to see the holy places and the Church leaders of the Christian East once again; and, no doubt, a natural curiosity and love of travel strengthened his longing to be a pilgrim.[212]

He took ship from Budva, probably in the spring of 1234, and set sail for south Italy. News of his itinerary reached the pirates of the Adriatic, who blocked the entrance into Brindisi, but Sava's vessel managed to slip through the blockade.[213] They encountered a fierce tempest on the way to Acre, where he stayed in the monastery of St George, bought from the Latins on his previous journey and bestowed as a gift on the *lavra* of St Sabas.[214] In Jerusalem he met his old friend the Patriarch Athanasius, and from there made his way to Egypt,

---

[209] *Post hoc*, but not necessarily *propter hoc*. There is no evidence linking Sava's decision to resign with the change of ruler in Serbia. A connection between the two, however, is not impossible.

[210] See *ISN* 312.

[211] S. Stanojević has surmised that Sava's last journey was undertaken at the request of the Bulgarian Tsar John Asen II, who wished Sava to intercede with the leaders of Eastern Christendom, the patriarchs of Jerusalem, Alexandria, and Antioch, in favour of his plan to persuade the Nicaean authorities to grant the Bulgarian Church the status of an autocephalous patriarchate. This was in fact agreed between the Nicaean emperor and the Bulgarian tsar in 1235 ('Sv. Sava i proglas bugarske patrijaršije', *Glas Srpske Kraljevske Akademije*, clvi. 79 [1933], 171–88; *Sveti Sava*, 77–80). This theory, for which there is no support in the sources, has been convincingly refuted by N. Radojčić, 'Sv, Sava i avtokefalnost srpske i bugarske crkve', 239–54. Cf. Slijepčević, *Istorija*, 119–21; I. Dujčev (Duichev), 'Saint Sava à Tŭrnovo en 1235', in *Hilandarski zbornik*, iv (1978), 21–2.

[212] Unlike their Benedictine contemporaries, bound by the rule of stability, monks of the Eastern Church sometimes regarded travelling to distant lands as a form of spiritual endeavour. A contemporary biographer of a 14-c. Bulgarian saint wrote of 'wandering for the sake of the Lord': D. Obolensky, 'Late Byzantine Culture and the Slavs', 23; A. Laiou-Thomadakis, 'Saints and Society in the Late Byzantine Empire', *Charanis Studies* (New Brunswick, NJ, 1980), 97–9.

[213] Sava had many encounters with pirates in the seas round Athos when he lived there. His medieval biographers ascribe his numerous escapes to miraculous causes.

[214] Domentijan, 302.

where the Ayyubid dynasty, founded by Saladin, then ruled; but he seems to have moved about freely. In Alexandria he met the patriarch, who arranged for him to visit the monasteries of the Thebaid and of the Desert of Scetis, or Wadi en-Natrun.[215] There, in the footsteps of so many famous pilgrims of late antiquity, Sava was able, as he had done in Mar Saba, to become personally acquainted with the earliest and most venerable traditions of Christian monasticism. Wishing to visit Mount Sinai, he applied for a permit to al-Kāmil, the sultan of Egypt, who received him in person and gave him a guide to escort him to his destination.[216] The return journey from Sinai took him back to Jerusalem and then, via Antioch, to Asia Minor. According to Domentijan, the sea passage from Syria was a painful experience, for Sava suffered bitterly from seasickness, as well as physical exhaustion.

His chronicler does not tell us whether Sava visited Nicaea on his way back. He takes him on next to Latin-occupied Constantinople, where he stayed, as he had when he visited the city as a young man, in his own monastery of the Evergetis. No doubt tired and ailing still from his travels and recent illness, he wanted to get home, also to stop on Mount Athos on the way.[217] But, for unknown reasons, he accepted an invitation from the Tsar John Asen II, his relation by marriage, to visit Bulgaria. Travelling almost certainly by sea, his party landed at Mesembria—the Nesebŭr promontory in the Black Sea—and then, on horses and with an escort provided by the Bulgarian ruler, to the tsar's capital at Tŭrnovo, where he probably arrived in late December 1235 or early January 1236. And here, after a brief illness, Sava died on 14 January, aged about sixty.[218]

In a letter to the Archimandrite Spiridon, abbot of Studenica, sent from Jerusalem probably before his journey to Egypt, Sava had complained of feeling unwell. He wrote that he hoped to be back in

---

[215] On these monasteries, see Chitty, *The Desert a City*, passim.

[216] Domentijan, 311.   [217] Domentijan, 328.

[218] For a critical discussion of Domentijan's and Teodosije's accounts of Sava's death see S. Stanojević, *SZ* i. 385–92. The year of Sava's death—1235 or 1236—is still in dispute; see *ISN* 312 n. 52. The strongest argument in favour of 1236 is the chronology of Sava's travels. He could hardly have left Serbia before the spring of 1234. His extensive travels in the Near East, which included a long visit to Egypt and its monasteries, to Sinai (where he stayed the whole of Lent), two journeys to Jerusalem, a visit to Antioch, and a journey through Asia Minor to Constantinople (where he also remained for some time) and thence to Bulgaria, could scarcely have been accomplished in nine months. Cf. D. Anastasijević, 'Sveti Sava je umro 1236 g.', *Bogoslovlje*, xi (1936), 238–76.

Serbia by the following spring; but the lines contain thinly veiled intimations of approaching death. He assures Spiridon that he has prayed for him in the holy places, and begs for his prayers in return. He sends him a small cross and a belt, which he had placed on the Holy Sepulchre and which he asks Spiridon to wear in his memory; and a piece of cloth and a small stone as mementoes of the Holy Land. He condemns their common enemies (probably the Bogomil heretics) and sends to his successor on the abbot's throne of the foremost monastery in Serbia these last words of greetings:

My beloved child Spiridon . . . may the divine peace rest on you, peace on all who live and labour in the house of St Symeon, peace on all the abbots, your associates and my children, to whom through you I send my greetings. May the peace of God flow into your hearts . . . The grace of our Lord Jesus Christ, and the love of God the Father, and the communion of the Holy Spirit be with you all evermore.[219]

The letter is signed 'Sava the sinner, by the grace of God the first archbishop of the Serbian land'. It is the only letter of Sava to have survived.

Sava's legacy, even more than his earthly life, belongs to the Serbian people. The images of him which they created and cherished are too numerous and varied to be contained in a brief summary. Only a few can be mentioned here. He remains by far the most popular saint of his people; revered as their ever-present protector, at home and abroad; a familiar figure depicted in icon or fresco in every church of the land, from the grandest of royal *zadužbine* to the humblest wayside chapel; and, far transcending the bounds of religion, he is a national hero, endlessly celebrated in legend, poetry, and song.

His posthumous history begins with the story of a royal pilgrimage. On hearing of Sava's death in Tŭrnovo, his nephew, King Vladislav, journeyed to Bulgaria to beg the Tsar John Asen II to allow the body to be brought home. If we can believe Domentijan, the Serbian party, faced with strong Bulgarian opposition, resorted to trickery: Sava's body, which had been laid to rest in the church of the Forty Martyrs in Tŭrnovo, was smuggled out of the city,[220] and the coffin, escorted by

---

[219] *SSS* 187–9. The last sentence is a quotation from the text of the Orthodox Eucharist.

[220] Domentijan, 335–40.

King Vladislav, was deposited in a specially prepared tomb in the monastery church of Mileševa, which Vladislav had founded about twelve years earlier in the valley of the Lim in western Serbia. Soon afterwards Sava's body was placed in a wooden sarcophagus in the centre of the church.[221] Mileševa, third in importance among Serbian royal foundations, after Studenica and Žiča, became the focus of Sava's cult. Its architecture, like that of other thirteenth-century Serbian churches, is a blend of Byzantine and of Romanesque indirectly derived from Dalmatia. Its celebrated wall-paintings were probably executed for the most part in the early 1220s by a team of Byzantine artists, perhaps from Thessalonica.[222] They include the earliest known likeness of Sava, which may have been painted from life (Plate 6). Wholly in the tradition of late antique portraiture, it is remarkable for its spirituality and its psychological subtlety.[223]

For three and half centuries Sava's body lay in his tomb in Mileševa, drawing pilgrims to his shrine from all the Balkan lands and from every station in life. In 1377 Tvrtko I—king of Bosnia and a descendant of Stephen Nemanja—had himself crowned at the grave of St Sava; and in 1448 a semi-independent Bosnian magnate, Stephen Vukčić Kosača, obtained the title of 'Herceg' (or Duke) of St Sava from the Turks. The title was later transferred to the name of his land, which turned into Hercegovina. The miracles that Domentijan and Teodosije attribute to the saint suggest that his posthumous mercies were shared by people of every rank; they cured both a penniless paralytic[224] and his brother the king;[225] and, as though to emphasize still further the strong family character of his cult, his prayers are said to have set holy oil flowing from the relics of his father.[226] At first, Sava's cult was certainly fostered by the monarchy, the court, and the Church. In his own lifetime Serbia had been ruled successively by his father, his brother, and two nephews; their

---

[221] Domentijan, 344. According to Teodosije, 214, King Vladislav, his mission accomplished, danced with joy before Sava's coffin like David before the Ark; a detail taken over by Serbian liturgical texts on the translation of St Sava's body from Tŭrnovo to Mileševa: *Srbljak*, ed. D. Bogdanović and Dj. Trifunović, i (Belgrade, 1970), 44, 74.

[222] See V. Djurić, *ISN* 410–11.

[223] On Sava's portrait in the narthex of the Mileševa church see D. Milošević, *SNSS* 286–8.

[224] Domentijan, 211–13; Teodosije, 98–101.

[225] Domentijan, 257–8.

[226] Domentijan, 214–17.

successors, until the last quarter of the fourteenth century, were all members of the same family. Nor was the Serbian Church slow to honour its creator and first archbishop. The earliest known liturgical office in his name—which was a criterion of canonization at the time—was composed within seven years of his death.[227] The spread of Sava's cult, both at home and abroad, was fostered above all by the monasteries with which he was closely linked—with Hilandar, Studenica, Žiča, and Mileševa.

After Serbia's conquest by the Turks, which was completed by 1459, the Ottoman rulers tolerated for more than a century a cult in which even the local Turkish population had come to share.[228] Finally in 1594, by order of the grand vizier Koca Sinan Paşa, the wooden coffin with the body of St Sava was removed from Mileševa to Belgrade. There, in the suburb of Vračar, on 27 April, it was placed on a pyre and burnt.[229]

It is perhaps not wholly fanciful to suppose that the physical destruction of Sava's body was in part responsible for the volatile and timeless character of his posthumous image. In the Serbian country-side his footprints are still shown to the visitor, and many a fresh-water spring, endowed with healing properties, is named after him. Not surprisingly, signs of his supernatural presence are especially frequent in the neighbourhood of Studenica. In Serbian epic poems, folktales, legends, and songs, Sava appears in many guises: as monk, beggar, sower, boatman, traveller—especially by sea—hunter, shep-herd, physician, invincible fighter against the invading Turks, and—in a truly timeless incarnation—as lord of the wolves.[230]

---

[227] Published by Lj. Stojanović, *Spomenik Srpske Kraljevske Akademije*, iii (1890), 165–75. St Sava's cult soon spread beyond the confines of Serbia to the Slav Orthodox countries. Among the Greeks it is attested by the 16th c.: see J. Tarnanidis, 'Kult svetog Simeona kod Grka', *Hilandarski zbornik*, v (1983), 101–78.

[228] Stanojević, *Sveti Sava*, 106; I. Božić, *SNSS* 390.

[229] The evidence on the burning of Sava's body comes from two 17th-c. sources: the Latin Life of St Sava by Marnavitius, *SZ* ii. 135 (see the critical study of his work by N. Radojčić, ibid. i, 319–82), and the Life of Tsar Uroš by Pajsije, the Serbian patriarch of Peć, ed. I. Ruvarac, in *Glasnik Srpskog Učenog Društva*, v (1867), 231.

[230] L. Pavlović, *Kultovi lica kod Srba i Makedonaca* (Smederevo, 1965), 68–71; I. Božić, in *SNSS* 389–95. In pre-Christian times the Serbs venerated the wolf as their totem. Vasko Popa, the modern Yugoslav poet, has written a cycle of poems entitled 'St Sava's Spring', in which the patron saint of Serbia is portrayed as a wolf-shepherd, the healer and protector of the wolves, which represent the Serbian people: *Earth Erect*, tr. Anne Pennington (London, 1973), 21–30, 61; *Collected Poems*, tr. A. Pennington (Manchester, 1978), 104–8. On the treatment of Sava in Serbian heroic poetry, see S. Koljević, *The Epic in the Making* (Oxford, 1980), 107, 118, 142, 229–30, 307.

The image of St Sava cherished by his Church naturally differs greatly from these folk avatars; though few would deny points of contact between them. The Serbian Orthodox Church continues to regard him as the greatest of her sons. His compatriots have sometimes extolled him as the creator of all that is valuable in the national tradition of the Serbs: an attitude that has not always been free of romantic nationalism.[231] Yet the historian seeking to encompass the extraordinary variety of his life-work—as prince, monk, bishop, pilgrim, diplomat, administrator, patron of the arts, writer, and teacher of his people[232]—can hardly fail to conclude that in the Greek and Slav world of the East European Middle Ages, it was not given to many, in a life-span of sixty years, to achieve so much.

[231] A modern example of such idealization is the concept of 'Svetosavlje', an untranslatable word, named after Sava, which appears to have originated in recent times among the teachers and students in the Belgrade theological faculty. Bishop Nikolai Velimirović has described it as 'Orthodox Christianity of the Serbian style and tradition' (*Pravoslavno Hrišćanstvo srpskog stila i iskustva*) in his preface to Fr. Justin Popović's book, *Svetosavlje kao filosofija života* (Munich, 1953). Cf. M. Matejić, *Biography of Saint Sava*, 85–8. In so far as *Svetosavlje* is not synonymous with Orthodox Christianity (in which case it is redundant), the term is open to the charge of being excessively nebulous.

[232] See J. Matl, 'Der heilige Sawa als Begründer der serbischen Nationalkirche: seine Leistung und Bedeutung für den Kulturaufbau Europas', *Südslawische Studien* (Munich, 1965), 33–5.

5

Metropolitan Cyprian
of Kiev and Moscow

It has become a commonplace of late Byzantine studies to comment
on the striking contrast during the last century of the Empire's
existence between its growing impotence as a political body and the
astonishing vitality of its culture, exemplified in the achievements of
Byzantium in art, scholarship, and theology. The 'last Byzantine
Renaissance' was indeed, in the words of a modern scholar, a time
when 'the State was collapsing but learning never shone more
brightly'.[1] This light was visible far beyond the political boundaries of
the now greatly shrunken Empire. Indeed, except for Constantinople,
Mount Athos, Mistra, and, during the periods when the Empire held it,
Thessalonica, the fairest flowers of this late Palaeologan blossoming
were to be found in the non-Greek-speaking lands of Orthodox Eastern
Europe—in Serbia, Bulgaria, Rumania, and Russia. Except for the two
centuries between 850 and 1050, the spread of Byzantine culture
throughout Eastern Europe was never so marked, nor so successful, as
during the last hundred years of the Empire's history.

This cultural expansion was, of course, part of a wider network of
multiple relations—political, diplomatic, economic, and ecclesiastical—established for centuries past between Byzantium and the
peoples of Eastern Europe. These relations owed their origin to two
convergent impulses: the needs, usually defensive, of the Empire's
foreign policy; and the desire of those East European peoples who were
drawn into the Empire's orbit to 'reach out' for the fruits of its
civilization, and to tap the sources of its technological expertise.

This chapter is concerned with the life of a man who played a
crucial role in this encounter, a role which, I believe, has not yet been
sufficiently appreciated. During the last quarter of the fourteenth
century and the opening years of the fifteenth, when the Byzantine

[1] S. Runciman, *The Last Byzantine Renaissance* (Cambridge, 1970), p. vii.

Empire was on the verge of collapse, when only its ecclesiastical arm—the oecumenical patriarchate—remained to champion its interests abroad, and when it seemed that it might lose the allegiance even of its East European satellites, he strove to withstand the local forces of separatism and nationalism, to gain friends for the Empire in its hour of need, and to unite the Slav Orthodox peoples through a newly found loyalty to their mother church of Constantinople. Successively a Bulgarian monk trained on Mount Athos, a confidential agent of the Byzantine patriarch, the latter's representative as metropolitan in Kiev, a victim of the political rivalry between Muscovy and Lithuania, and, in the end, the unchallenged incumbent of the see Moscow which had eluded him for so long, Kyprianos, or Kiprian, or Cyprian, epitomizes in his far-flung journeys, in the breadth of his mental horizon, and in his multiple loyalties the rich cosmopolitan culture which flourished in Eastern Europe during the late Middle Ages. It is strange that relatively little has yet been published on the career of this remarkable man.[2] The present study cannot, of course, fill this gap; it is no more than a very preliminary sketch.

THE FORMATIVE YEARS (*c.* 1330–1370)

The first forty years or so of Cyprian's life are poorly documented. In text books, unfortunately, the early phase of his biography is often recounted with quite spurious precision. In fact, very little is known for certain. We can probably accept the general view that he was born about 1330.[3] He was certainly a Bulgarian, for his distinguished contemporary Gregory Tsamblak, a reliable source, says so explicitly.[4] It was once commonly believed that Cyprian was Gregory's

---

[2] See, however, the brief but perceptive study by A.-E. Tachiaos, "Ὁ μητροπολίτης Ῥωσίας Κυπριανὸς Τσάμπλακ", Ἀριστοτέλειον Πανεπιστήμιον Θεσσαλονίκης, Ἐπιστημονικὴ Ἐπετηρὶς τῆς Θεολογικῆς Σχολῆς, vi (1961). Except for the first paragraph, it is reprinted in id., Ἐπιδράσεις τοῦ ἡσυχασμοῦ εἰς τὴν ἐκκλησιαστικὴν πολιτικὴν ἐν Ῥωσίᾳ (Thessaloniki, 1962) (hereafter Tachiaos, Ἐπιδράσεις). See also the extensive and in places repetitive monograph by N. Doncheva-Panaiotova, *Kiprian, starobŭlgarski i staroruski knizhovnik* (Sofia, 1981).

[3] E. Golubinsky, *Istoriya russkoy tserkvi*, ii/1 (Moscow, 1900), 298–9 n. 2; P. A. Syrku, *K istorii ispravleniya knig v Bolgarii v XIV veke*, i (St Petersburg, 1898; repr. London, 1972), 254; Tachiaos, Ἐπιδράσεις, 62.

[4] *Pokhvalno slovo za Kipriyan*, in B. St. Angelov, *Iz starata bŭlgarska literatura*, 181: 'ego zhe ubo nasha otechestvo iznese'; ET in M. Heppell, *The Ecclesiastical Career of Gregory Camblak* (London, 1979), 110. Cyprian is described as a Serb in 16th-c. Russian

uncle, on the sole evidence of a passing remark in Gregory's Church Slavonic encomium on Cyprian that 'he [i.e., Cyprian] was the brother of our father.'[5] The Tsamblaks were a distinguished family with branches in Bulgaria and Byzantium,[6] and historians have supposed that the young Cyprian's career was advanced by his highly placed family connections. These agreeable possibilities, however, have little basis in fact. In 1968, in a paper presented to the International Congress of Slavists in Prague, the German scholar Johannes Holthusen argued cogently that the words 'the brother of our father' should be understood in a spiritual, not a physical, sense: the 'brotherly' relationship was that between two episcopal colleagues, Cyprian, head of the Church of Russia, and his contemporary, the Patriarch Euthymius, primate of Bulgaria. To a Bulgarian churchman such as Gregory, Euthymius would indeed have been 'our father'.[7] There can be little doubt that Holthusen is right and that Cyprian must therefore be stripped of the surname Tsamblak, so confidently given him by most historians (myself included). We must be prepared to admit that we know nothing about his family background. We do not even know his baptismal name, for Cyprian was his name in religion.

The same uncertainty surrounds the time and place of his monastic profession. We know from a Byzantine document that in 1373 Cyprian was the οἰκεῖος καλόγηρος of the Patriarch Philotheos of

chronicles: *Patriarshaya ili Nikonovskaya Letopis'*, s.a. 1407, in *Polnoe sobranie russkikh letopisey* xi (St. Petersburg, 1897), 194 (hereafter PSRL); and *Kniga Stepennaya Tsarskogo Rodosloviya*, in PSRL xxi/2 (1913), 440. Attempts have been made to explain this mistake: see Tachiaos, '*Ἐπιδράσεις*, 62 n. 1; and, for the most detailed discussion of the problem, I. Ivanov, 'Bŭlgarskoto knizhovno vliyanie v Rusiya pri Mitropolit Kiprian', *Izvestiya na Instituta za bŭlgarska literatura*, vi (1958) (hereafter Ivanov, 'Bŭlgarskoto knizhovno vliyanie'), 29–37.

[5] Ibid. 185: 'brat beashe nashemu otsu'.

[6] G. I. Theocharides, "Οἱ Τζαμπλάκωνες", *Μακεδονικά*, v (1961–3), 125–83.

[7] J. Holthusen, 'Neues zur Erklärung des Nadgrobnoe Slovo von Grigorij Camblak auf den Moskauer Metropoliten Kiprian', in E. Koschmieder and M. Braun (eds.) *Slavistische Studien zum VI. Internationalen Slavistenkongress in Prag 1968* (Munich, 1968), 372–82. Holthusen's view is accepted in *Prosopographisches Lexikon der Palaiologenzeit*, vi, ed. E. Trapp (Vienna, 1983), 85, s.v. Κυπριανός; and may find further support in the fact that on two occasions Cyprian, then metropolitan of Kiev and Lithuania, referred to the recently deceased primate of Muscovy Alexius as 'my brother': see Cyprian's letter to St Sergius of Radonezh and Theodore, abbot of the Simonov monastery (*Russkaya Istoricheskaya Biblioteka*, vi (St Petersburg, 1880), cols. 173–86). Ivanov, 'Bŭlgarskoto knizhovno vliyanie', 36, doubted whether Cyprian belonged to the Tsamblak family, but his view that the fathers of Cyprian and Gregory were half-brothers is not supported by the sources.

Constantinople, that is a monk who enjoyed his close confidence.[8]
Presumably, to have gained such a position of trust, he must have
been in Philotheos' immediate entourage for at least a few years,
which pushes the date of his arrival in Constantinople, and probably
of his monastic profession as well, at least as far back as *c.* 1370.[9] We
may, though with less certainty, go back even further. We possess a
letter, written by the Patriarch Euthymius of Bulgaria and addressed,
in the words of its superscription, 'to the monk Cyprian, who lives on
the Holy Mountain of Athos'.[10] It contains Euthymius' replies to
various questions of a disciplinary and liturgical nature which this
monk had addressed to him. The identification made by the letter's
editor and by modern scholars of the addressee as our Cyprian seems
to me to raise chronological difficulties. Euthymius was patriarch of
Bulgaria from 1375 to 1393. During those years Cyprian was
commuting between Constantinople, Lithuania, and Muscovy, and
could not conceivably have 'lived on the Holy Mountain of Athos'. So
we must conclude that if Euthymius wrote the letter during his
patriarchate (as the superscription in the manuscript says that he did)
it must have been addressed to another Cyprian. It is possible,
however, that the words 'Patriarch of Tŭrnovo' were appended to
Euthymius' name by the fifteenth-century scribe,[11] and that Euthymius, in fact, wrote the letter before he became patriarch. If so, we
must look for a time when he could have written the letter and when
Cyprian could have been on Mount Athos. Between about 1365 and
1371 Euthymius was himself on Mount Athos,[12] and would
obviously have had no need to write this letter; and by 1371 Cyprian

---

[8] *Acta et diplomata Graeca medii aevi sacra et profana. Acta Patriarchatus Constantinopolitani,* ed. F. Miklosich and J. Müller (hereafter *APC*), ii (Vienna, 1862), 118.

[9] A number of scholars believe that Cyprian had spent some time in Constantinople
before going to Mount Athos, and that he worked for Philotheos during his second stay
in the city. See Syrku, op. cit. 254; E. Turdeanu, *La Littérature bulgare du XIVe siècle et sa
diffusion dans les pays roumains* (Paris, 1947) (hereafter Turdeanu, *La Littérature
bulgare*), 115; Tachiaos, Ἐπιδράσεις, 71; L. A. Dmitriev, 'Rol' i znachenie mitropolita
Kipriana v istorii drevnerusskoy literatury', *TODRL* xix (1963) (hereafter Dmitriev,
'Rol' i znachenie'), 216; I. Dujčev, 'Tsentry vizantiisko-slavyanskogo obshcheniya i
sotrudnichestva', ibid. 113. There is no evidence to support the view that Cyprian
visited Constantinople so early.

[10] *Werke des Patriarchen von Bulgarien Euthymius (1375–1393),* ed. E. Kałużniacki
(Vienna, 1901; repr. London, 1971), 225–39.

[11] Vladislav the Grammarian: see ibid. ciii; Turdeanu, *La Littérature bulgare,* 115–
19.

[12] See Turdeanu, ibid. 68; P. Dinekov *et al.* (eds.), *Istoriya na bŭlgarskata literatura,* i
(Sofia, 1962), 286.

was presumably already in Constantinople. If we assume that the letter was indeed addressed to our Cyprian, we may conclude that it was probably written before 1363 (the date of Euthymius' departure from Bulgaria to Constantinople), at a time when its writer was a monk in the famous monastery of Kilifarevo in northern Bulgaria.[13] This seems a perfectly acceptable solution: the letter's tone and contents show that there was a strong spiritual bond between writer and recipient; Cyprian and Euthymius were compatriots; and we know from Gregory Tsamblak's encomium that the relationship between them was indeed a close one.[14] We have the best possible evidence that Cyprian did go to Athos: in a letter he wrote much later to the Russian monk Afanasy Vysotsky, Cyprian mentions 'the Holy Mountain, which I have seen myself'.[15]

We may thus conclude with a fair degree of certainty that by the time Cyprian entered the inner ranks of the patriarch's civil service he had been a monk for some years, and that he received his monastic training on Mount Athos.[16] Both conclusions will help us understand his subsequent outlook and career. In the fourteenth century Mount Athos underwent a great spiritual and cultural renaissance. The revival of contemplative prayer, the cultivation of Christian learning, and the newly acquired prestige of the theology of Gregory Palamas attracted men in search of the spiritual life from all parts of the Orthodox world. Many were Slavs; and through them the theory and practice of Byzantine hesychasm spread between 1350 and 1450 to the farthest confines of Eastern Europe.[17] Another feature of this Athonite world of the late Middle Ages was its cosmopolitanism: in the

[13] Different dates for Euthymius' letter have been proposed: between 1360 and 1369: Archimandrite Leonid, 'Kipriyan do vosshestviya na moskovskuyu mitropoliyu', *Chteniya v Imperatorskom Obshchestve Istorii i Drevnostey Rossiiskikh pri Moskovskom Universitete*, 1867, pt. 2, p. 19; between 1372 and 1375: Syrku, op. cit. 575, n. 2; between 1371 and 1373: Turdeanu, *La Littérature bulgare*, 115. The last two of these datings are obviously too late. Tachiaos, Ἐπιδράσεις, 75 n. 50, is unwilling to commit himself.

[14] Gregory uses the possessive pronoun to describe the relationship between Cyprian and Euthymius: ;'svoego zhe i velikago Eufimia' (*Pokhvalno slovo za Kipriyan*, 184; ET 113).

[15] *Russkaya istoricheskaya biblioteka*, vi, col. 263.

[16] It is widely believed that Cyprian had earlier been a monk in the Bulgarian hesychast monastery of Kilifarevo; see V. Kiselkov, *Sv. Teodosy Tŭrnovski* (Sofia, 1926), 34; Turdeanu, *La Littérature bulgare*, 115; Tachiaos, Ἐπιδράσεις, 68. Others accept this view as probable: Syrku, op. cit. 253; Dmitriev, 'Rol' i znachenie', 216. In the absence of any direct evidence, this cannot be regarded as more than a possibility.

[17] See Dujčev, 'Tsentry vizantiisko-slavyanskogo obshcheniya', 121–6; id., 'Le Mont Athos et les Slaves au Moyen Âge', in id., *Medioevo bizantino-slavo*, i (Rome, 1965), 487–510.

coenobitic houses of Athos Slavs and Rumanians lived and worked alongside their Greek companions, studying, copying, and translating Greek spiritual (and sometimes secular) writings and relaying the new Slav versions back to their native countries. It proved of great importance to Cyprian's future development that these two features of fourteenth-century Athos, allegiance to the hesychast tradition of contemplative prayer and a broad cosmopolitan outlook, were imprinted upon him so early in life. Both were soon reinforced by his move to Constantinople and by his association with the Patriarch Philotheos.

THE YEARS OF STRUGGLE (*c.* 1370–90)

If Cyprian's biographer suffers from a dearth of information regarding the first period of his life (i.e. until 1370), he may justly complain of a superabundance regarding the second (the next twenty years). It is hard not to feel overwhelmed by the plethora of contemporary evidence, often highly tendentious, derived from the acts of Church councils, chronicles, pamphlets, biographies, and letters. Sometimes the sources give diametrically opposite versions of the same event, and modern historians, taking up these medieval cudgels, have tended to divide into rival parties, often defined on national lines, in accordance with their own ethnic prejudices. No wonder that, faced with this welter of passion and bias, the prospective biographer of Cyprian must at times have felt discouraged.

It would need more than one chapter to explore this forest of conflicting testimony. My aim here is simply to look at some of the evidence with a critical eye and, as far as possible, to consider Cyprian's career against the background of the ecclesiastical, political, and cultural history of his time.

In the early 1370s, it will be recalled, Cyprian was residing in Constantinople as an οἰκεῖος καλόγηρος of the Patriarch Philotheos. The epithet οἰκεῖος, applied to him in an official Byzantine document, seems significant. In late Byzantine society it had become something of a technical term. The οἰκεῖοι were trusted and influential officials who served the emperor or sometimes other highly placed persons, and who were bound to their employers by a particularly close professional relationship.[18] There can be no doubt that in his capacity

---

[18] On the οἰκεῖοι, see J. Verpeaux, 'Les Oikeioi: Notes d'histoire institutionnelle et sociale', *REB* xxiii (1965), 89–99; G. Weiss, *Joannes Kantakuzenos—Aristokrat,*

of patriarchal οἰκεῖος Cyprian would have been entrusted with confidential and important missions. Though, for lack of evidence, we must resist the temptation, to which several historians have succumbed,[19] to suppose that he took part in the negotiations which led in 1375 to the restoration of full communion between the Byzantine patriarchate and the Churches of Serbia and Bulgaria, we can certainly accept that by 1375, when he was appointed envoy to Kiev, Cyprian enjoyed the reputation of an able and experienced diplomat. Both his hesychast training on Mount Athos and the experience he had gained as Philotheos' *homme de confiance* were a good preparation for this mission. In the fourteenth century, as the imperial government proved increasingly impotent in its foreign policy, the Byzantine patriarchate assumed the role of chief spokesman and agent of the imperial traditions of East Rome. The hesychast patriarchs of the second half of the fourteenth century were particularly determined and successful champions of these traditions; and among them Philotheos was pre-eminent.[20] In this period the patriarchate's oecumenical claims were often defined in documents issued by its chancellery as κηδεμονία πάντων (literally 'solicitude for all' or 'guardianship of all'). Save for a larger dose of rhetoric and the patriarchate's manifest inability to enforce this doctrine for more than brief spells, there was little to distinguish it, *mutatis mutandis*, from the more forceful declarations of papal supremacy which emanated from the Roman Curia. Here is a sample, among many: 'God', wrote the Patriarch Philotheos to the princes of Russia in 1370, 'has appointed our Humility (τὴν ἡμῶν μετριότητα) as the leader (προστάτην) of the

---

Staatsmann, Kaiser und Mönch (Wiesbaden, 1969), 143–5 and *passim*; Lj. Maksimović, *Vizantijska provincijska uprava u doba Paleologa* (Belgrade, 1972), 14–15, 18–19, 33, 35, 117.

[19] See, in particular, P. Sokolov, *Russky arkhierey iz Vizantii* (Kiev, 1913), 434–5, who advances the fanciful suggestion that in 1366 Cyprian was the abbot of the monastery of Brontocheion at Mistra. It is by no means impossible that he took part in the negotiations which led to the healing of the schism between the Serbian Church and the Byzantine patriarchate; during part of the time when these negotiations were proceeding he was an οἰκεῖος of the Patriarch Philotheos; and a key figure in these diplomatic exchanges, Metropolitan Theophanes of Nicaea, seems to have been a close friend of Cyprian. See Tachiaos, Ἐπιδράσεις, 100, 115; and below, p. 189. But here again direct evidence simply does not exist.

[20] See O. Halecki, *Un empereur de Byzance à Rome: Vingt ans de travail pour l'union des Églises et pour la défense de l'Empire d'Orient 1355–1375* (Warsaw, 1930; repr. London, 1972), 235–42; J. Meyendorff, *Byzantium and the Rise of Russia* (Cambridge, 1981), *passim* (hereafter Meyendorff).

Christians in the whole world and the guardian ($\kappa\eta\delta\epsilon\mu\acute{o}\nu\alpha$) and curator ($\phi\rho o\nu\tau\iota\sigma\tau\acute{\eta}\nu$) of their souls; all are dependent on me, as the father and teacher of all. Since, however, it is not possible for me to go myself the round of the cities and countries of the earth and to teach the word of God therein . . . our Humility chooses the best men most distinguished in virtue, and appoints and consecrates them pastors and teachers and bishops, and sends them to the different parts of the world.'[21]

Naturally enough it was to the Slav Churches of Eastern Europe that the efforts of the patriarchate to maintain and strengthen its authority were primarily directed in the fourteenth century. For centuries these Churches had maintained a wavering yet real loyalty to their mother Church; and it was hoped in Constantinople that the rulers of these lands could be persuaded to provide money or troops to the embattled Empire. The patriarchate's chosen instruments in this imperial and pan-Orthodox policy were mostly monks, not a few of them Slavs, who by conviction and training could be counted upon to propagate throughout Eastern Europe the belief that Orthodox Christendom was a single body whose spiritual head was the oecumenical patriarch. One of their tasks was to resist the growth of local forms of ecclesiastical nationalism. It is not surprising to find that the leaders of the pro-Byzantine 'pan-Orthodox' parties in the different Slav countries in the second half of the fourteenth century all belonged to the hesychast movement. Of this movement I will attempt no comprehensive definition beyond suggesting that it drew its spiritual force from the Athonite tradition of contemplative prayer, was sustained on the administrative level by the 'oecumenical' policy of the Byzantine patriarchate, had a wide impact upon the cultural life of Eastern Europe in the late Middle Ages, and was fostered by an international brotherhood of men with close personal links with each other and a strong loyalty to Byzantium.[22] It was the hesychasts who healed the schism which in the third quarter of the fourteenth century had separated the Churches of Bulgaria and Serbia from the Byzantine patriarchate. Their most promising opportunities, however, seemed

---

[21] *APC* i. 521; cf. Meyendorff, 'O vizantiiskom isikhazme i ego roli v kul'turnom i istoricheskom razvitii Vostochnoy Evropy v XIV v.', *TODRL* xxix (1974), 302–3; and id., *Byzantium and the Rise of Russia*, 283–4, for an English translation of Philotheos' letter.

[22] See A.-E. Tachiaos, 'Le mouvement hésychaste pendant les dernières décennies du xive siècle', *Κληρονομία*, vi/1 (1974), 113–30; Obolensky, 'Late Byzantine culture and the Slavs'.

at that time to lie further north, in Russia. Of all the ecclesiastical satellites of Byzantium, the Russians had been consistently the most loyal since the early Middle Ages. And now that the Empire was facing financial ruin, and, with the Ottoman invasions, beginning to fight for its very life, aid, whether in money or in kind, from the populous and rich Russian lands was becoming almost a necessity. However, the political situation in that sector presented the patriarchate and the imperial government with an awkward dilemma.

In the second half of the fourteenth century, in the area between the Carpathians and the upper Volga, two states had emerged competing for the allegiance of the Eastern Slavs: the grand duchy of Lithuania and the principality of Moscow. The former had gradually absorbed the greater part of western Russia: by 1375 the grand dukes of Lithuania had replaced the Tatars as overlords of the middle Dnieper valley and had advanced their eastern frontier to within a hundred miles of Moscow. Muscovy, still the lesser of the two states, was emerging as the leader of the principalities of central Russia and was claiming to embody the political and cultural traditions of early medieval Kievan Rus'. The most potent symbol of this continuity was the metropolitan-primate of Russia. Though his residence had been moved from Kiev to Vladimir in 1300 and thence to Moscow in 1328, he still retained his traditional title of 'metropolitan of Kiev and All Russia'. In practice, most of the fourteenth-century metropolitans, whether they were native Russians or Byzantine citizens, tended to identify themselves with the policies and aspirations of the princes of Moscow. This was scarcely to the liking of the grand dukes of Lithuania, Moscow's rivals for political hegemony in Eastern Europe, who naturally sought to deprive their opponents of the considerable advantages derived from the presence within their city of the chief bishop of the Russian Church. Their best hope lay in persuading the Byzantine authorities either to transfer the seat of the metropolitan to Lithuania, or at least to set up a separate metropolitanate in their country.

The dilemma which faced the Byzantines was the following: could the authority of the patriarchate best be maintained by the traditional policy of keeping the Russian Church under the jurisdiction of a single prelate appointed from Constantinople? And if so, should he reside in the historic see of Kiev, which from the early 1360s was in Lithuanian territory, or in Moscow? Or alternatively, on a realistic assessment of

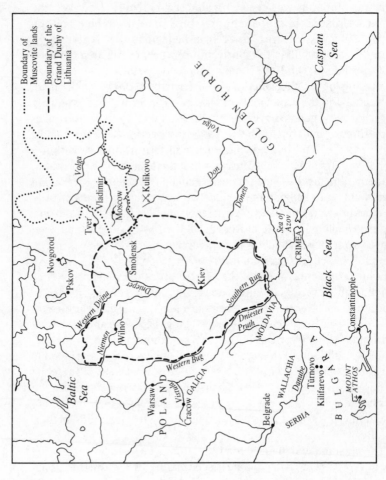

Map 5. Eastern Europe, c. 1390

the power structure in Eastern Europe, should there now be two separate metropolitanates, one in Moscow and the other in Kiev?[23]

Most of the hesychast patriarchs of Constantinople in the second half of the fourteenth century favoured a unified pro-Muscovite solution, none more so than Philotheos, who in June 1370 wrote a spate of letters to Moscow fulsomely praising its primate, Metropolitan Alexius of Kiev and All Russia. He went as far as solemnly to excommunicate several princes of Russia who, breaking their agreements with the prince of Moscow, allied themselves against him with Olgerd, the pagan grand duke of Lithuania,[24] and in so doing acted against 'the holy commonwealth of Christians' ($\tau\hat{\eta}s$ $\hat{\iota}\epsilon\rho\hat{\alpha}s$ $\pi o\lambda\iota\tau\epsilon\hat{\iota}as$ $\tau\hat{\omega}\nu$ $\chi\rho\iota\sigma\tau\iota\alpha\nu\hat{\omega}\nu$).[25]

By 1371, however, Philotheos began to have second thoughts about the wisdom of supporting Alexius. Serious complaints about the metropolitan's behaviour had begun to reach the patriarchate. Michael of Tver', a Russian prince at loggerheads with Muscovy, had been treacherously arrested in Moscow, undoubtedly with the metropolitan's connivance, after being promised safe conduct; he now wished to cite Alexius before the patriarch's tribunal in Constantinople.[26] More ominous still was a letter received by Philotheos from the grand duke of Lithuania, in which he bitterly accused Alexius of showing no interest in his western Russian dioceses and of inciting the Muscovites to attack his subjects. In peremptory tones Olgerd demanded a separate metropolitan for the Orthodox of the Grand Duchy.[27]

Philotheos was caught on the horns of a dilemma: to accede to Olgerd's request was to divide the Russian Church in two and to risk the displeasure of the prince of Moscow. To ignore the request might result in the patriarchate losing control over the Church of Lithuania. So he decided to play for time. He wrote to Alexius, rebuking him for

[23] See J. Meyendorff, 'Alexis and Roman: A Study in Byzantino-Russian Relations', *Byzantinoslavica*, xxviii (1967), 278–88; id., *Byzantium and the Rise of Russia*, 145–172; Obolensky, *The Byzantine Commonwealth*, 262–3.

[24] APC i. 516–25; ET in Meyendorff, 285–6.   [25] APC i. 524.

[26] Ibid. 582–6. As A. S. Pavlov rightly noted, the letter addressed to the Metropolitan Alexius (ibid. 320–1) was wrongly ascribed to the Patriarch Kallistos I (1350–3, 1355–63) by the editors of the Acta Patriarchatus; in fact it was written by Philotheos and belongs to the collection of letters which he sent to Russia in 1371: *Russkaya istoricheskaya biblioteka*, vi, Appendix, cols. 155–6; ET in Meyendorff, 290–1. For two other letters wrongly ascribed to the Patriarch Kallistos, see J. Darrouzès, *Le Registre synodal du Patriarcat byzantin au XIVe siècle* (Paris, 1971), 105.

[27] APC i. 580–1.

never visiting his Lithuanian dioceses and reminding him that 'when we consecrated you, we consecrated you metropolitan of Kiev and All Russia, not of one part, but of all Russia.'[28] However, since his repeated injunctions were having no effect, Philotheos decided in 1373 to send to Russia a confidential envoy charged with restoring peace between Muscovy and Lithuania and with persuading Alexius to visit the western Russian part of his metropolitanate. This envoy was Cyprian.[29]

Probably during the winter of 1373–4 Cyprian arrived in Kiev and established contact with the Lithuanian authorities. These then sent an embassy to Constantinople, reiterating their former request for a separate metropolitan, independent of Moscow. Philotheos could no longer sit on the fence; he hit on an ingenious solution which, though of dubious canonical propriety, at least satisfied Olgerd's immediate demands without sacrificing the principle of the unity of the Russian metropolitanate. He appointed Cyprian metropolitan of Kiev and Lithuania, with the proviso that after Alexius' death he would reunite under his authority the whole Russian Church.[30] Cyprian's consecration took place in Constantinople on 2 December 1375.[31]

This much regarding Cyprian's first mission to Russia is uncontro-

---

[28] *APC* i. 321.   [29] *APC* ii. 118.

[30] Ibid. 14. 120. The sources disagree over the title granted to Cyprian in 1375. According to the Acts of the patriarchal synod of 1380 it was μητροπολίτης Κυέβου καὶ Λιτβῶν (*APC* ii. 14). On the other hand, the Acts of the synod of 1389 give it as μητροπολίτης Κυέβου, Ῥωσίας καὶ Λιτβῶν (*APC* ii. 120). F. Tinnefeld ('Byzantinisch-russische Kirchenpolitik im 14. Jahrhundert', *BZ* lxvii (1974), 375) believes the evidence of the synod of 1380; I put more trust in that of the 1389 synod.

[31] There can be little doubt that Cyprian's appointment as prospective successor of Alexius was uncanonical. The Acts of the patriarchal synod of 1380, so frequently at variance with the truth, rightly point this out: τὴν αὐτοῦ [Κυπριανοῦ] δὲ χειροτονίαν, ὡς ζῶντος ἔτι τοῦ μητροπολίτου Ἀλεξίου γεγενημένην ἀκανόνιστον ἡγουμένη (*APC* ii. 15). Even the signatories of the synodal Act of 1389, who were entirely favourable to Cyprian, sounded uncomfortable when referring to his appointment in 1375 as Alexius' successor: he was appointed, they state, as metropolitan of All Russia 'as though beginning afresh' (ὡς ἐξ ἄλλης ἀρχῆς: ibid. 128). This prospective appointment was certainly a far-reaching example of the exercise of ecclesiastical *oikonomia* (see Meyendorff, 200–1). However, it was not wholly unprecedented: Philotheos' predecessor, the patriarch Kallistos, soon after Alexius' appointment as metropolitan of Kiev and All Russia, seems in 1354 to have consecrated a Lithuanian candidate in terms sufficiently vague to enable him to claim jurisdiction over at least some of Alexius' dioceses: see Meyendorff, 'Alexis and Roman', 284–7. Only a small fragment of the synodal Act of 1375 by which Cyprian was appointed has survived; it is cited in the Act of 1389 (*APC* ii. 120). For a modern view on the uncanonical nature of Cyprian's appointment in 1375, see N. Glubokovsky, 'Kiprian', in *Pravoslavnaya bogoslovskaya entsiklopediya*, x (St Petersburg, 1909), col. 42.

versial. The rest, and notably his own role in these events, provides the student of medieval documents with an interesting exercise in textual criticism. Our knowledge of these events is derived mainly from two Byzantine sources, the Acts of the patriarchal synods held in Constantinople in 1380 and 1389. They are in total disagreement on every point of substance. The synod of 1380, presided over by the Patriarch Neilos, painted Cyprian as a villainous intriguer who wormed his way into Olgerd's confidence, grossly deceived Alexius, and himself wrote and delivered to Constantinople the letter in which the Lithuanian authorities requested his appointment as their primate.[32] In the Acts of the synod of 1389, convened by the Patriarch Antony, the blame is laid squarely on the shoulders of Alexius, who as acting-regent of the Muscovite realm forsook the government of the Church for politics, provoked Olgerd by his aggressive behaviour, and wholly neglected his Lithuanian dioceses. Cyprian, on the other hand, is said to have done his best to reconcile Olgerd and Alexius, and is described as 'a man distinguished in virtue and piety.'[33]

It stands to reason that at least one of these synodal Acts is blatantly lying. Most Russian Church historians, apparently unwilling to admit any blemish in the character of Metropolitan Alexius, a national hero and a popular saint, prefer to believe the synod of 1380. Hence, even if they occasionally tone down the harshness of the synod's strictures on Cyprian (who, incidentally, was also canonized by the Russian Church), their description of his behaviour is less than edifying.[34] This is not the place for detailed *Quellenkritik*; I will say, however, that a careful study of these two documents has convinced me that the synodal Act of 1380 contains far too many evasive statements, inconsistencies, and factual distortions to merit serious credence.[35]

---

[32] *APC* ii. 12–18; abridged ET in Meyendorff, 303–6.

[33] Ibid. 116–29; abridged ET in Meyendorff, 307–10.

[34] Metropolitan Makary, *Istoriya russkoy tserkvi*, iv/1 (St Petersburg, 1886), 59–63; Glubokovsky, loc. cit.; Golubinsky, *Istoriya russkoy tserkvi*, ii/1, 211–15; and A. V. Kartashev, *Ocherki po istorii russkoy tserkvi* (Paris, 1959), i. 321–3. A fairer and more convincing picture of Cyprian's actions in 1375–8 is given by I. N. Shabatin, 'Iz istorii Russkoy Tserkvi', *Vestnik Russkogo zapadno-evropeyskogo Patriarshego Ekzarkhata* (hereafter Shabatin, *Vestnik*), xiii/49 (1965), 42–4. Another, earlier exception to this chauvinistic bias against Cyprian is the judgement of Archimandrite Leonid, 'Kipriyan do vosshestviya', 28 n. 28.

[35] Here are a few samples: (1) The Act of 1380 alleges that on one occasion when Alexius was visiting his Lithuanian dioceses he was arrested on Olgerd's orders and almost killed (*APC* ii. 12). This is contradicted not only by the Act of 1389, which states

There is reason to believe that in several respects the synod echoed the view of official Muscovite circles, which the government of John V and Manuel II, having regained power in Constantinople the previous year, was concerned to placate.[36] By contrast the synodal Act of 1389, though not wholly free of disingenuousness and special pleading,[37] gives an account that is coherent and convincing, and in several particulars agrees with the evidence of other sources. I believe there are no valid grounds for imputing any dishonourable action to Cyprian during the events of 1373–5.

The first three years of his tenure of the see of Kiev seem to have been uneventful.[38] In a letter he later wrote to St Sergius of Radonezh

that by 1373 Alexius had not set foot in his Lithuanian dioceses for nineteen years, i.e. since his appointment as metropolitan of Kiev and All Russia in 1354 (ibid. 118), but also by Philotheos' letter of 1371, in which he rebukes Alexius for refusing to visit Kiev and Lithuania (*APC* i. 321; see above, n. 26). (2) The statement that in 1379 the Russian envoys asked the patriarchate to appoint Pimen as metropolitan (*APC* ii. 15) is outrageously disingenuous. For the facts, see below, pp. 188–9. (3) The Act of 1380 claims that the Orthodox Church of Lithuania had so many bishops that there was no need for Alexius to come to Kiev, and simultaneously states that Alexius considered it unnecessary to make this journey for 'the small remnant (μικρὸν λείψανον) of his Kievan flock' (ibid. 13)—a remarkable example of the wish to have one's cake and eat it! (4) Cyprian is accused of establishing close relations with Olgerd upon his arrival in Kiev (ibid. 13–14), as though it were not his plain duty to do so.

[36] See Meyendorff, op. cit. 218–19.

[37] Thus the synod seems unduly concerned with whitewashing the Patriarchs Makarios and Neilos by minimizing the extent to which Makarios acted under pressure from Moscow over the acceptance of Michael-Mityai's candidature (*APC* ii. 120–1), and by alleging that Neilos acted innocently in consecrating Pimen (ibid. 121, and below, pp. 188–9).

[38] In a passage of the 16th-c. *Nikonovskaya Letopis'* (s.a. 1376: PSRL xi. 25), it is alleged that soon after his arrival in Kiev Cyprian went to Moscow in an attempt, thwarted by Prince Dimitri, to seize Alexius' metropolitan see. This would have been an act as senseless as it was uncanonical. A later passage in the same chronicle (s.a. 1380: ibid. 49) makes it clear that until Alexius' death in 1378 Cyprian resided in Kiev and made no attempt to go to Moscow. See also *Voskresenskaya Letopis'*, s.a. 1376 (PSRL viii (1859), 25). There can be no doubt that Cyprian did not go to Moscow before 1378: see Golubinsky, *Istoriya russkoy tserkvi*, ii/1. 214 n. 2; A. E. Presnyakov, *Obrazovanie velikorusskogo gosudarstva* (Petrograd, 1918), 316 n. 1; ET, *The Formation of the Great Russian State* (Chicago, 1970), 260–1. Nevertheless, somewhat inconsequentially, both Golubinsky, op. cit. 212–15, and Kartashev, *Ocherki*, i. 322, accuse Cyprian of unlawfully attempting to seize Alexius' see. The most Cyprian can be accused of is an attempt, soon after his arrival in Kiev, to detach the Novgorod archdiocese from Moscow and to subject it to his own jurisdiction. The Novgorodians, who were then on good terms with Moscow, stated that they would accept his jurisdiction if he was first acknowledged as primate of Russia by the grand prince of Moscow: see *Voskresenskaya Letopis'*, loc. cit. Shabatin, *Vestnik*, nos. 49, pp. 43–4; 50, p. 110, has convincingly rebutted the charge that Cyprian plotted against Alexius. Cf. Dmitriev, 'Rol' i znachenie', 226–7.

he listed some of his achievements, which were no more than one
would expect of a competent and conscientious administrator.[39]
However, Cyprian's life soon entered a new phase filled with variety
and drama, beginning with the death of the Metropolitan Alexius on
12 February 1378 and lasting for twelve years.

It will be recalled that in 1375, when Cyprian was appointed
metropolitan of Kiev and Lithuania, it was stipulated that, on Alexius'
death, he should reunite under his authority the Lithuanian and the
Muscovite parts of the metropolitanate and become primate of All
Russia. Trusting in this promise, Cyprian set out for Moscow as soon
as the news of Alexius' death reached him. He seems to have had some
intimation of trouble ahead, for on the way he wrote to two
distinguished Muscovite abbots on whose support he clearly counted.
One of them was St Sergius of Radonezh, and the other was Sergius'
nephew Theodore, abbot of the Simonov monastery. When he
reached Muscovite territory he realized that he was, in the eyes of the
government, an undesirable alien. Prince Dimitri of Moscow had
placed armed guards on the road to the capital, with orders not to let
him through. By a roundabout route Cyprian managed to reach
Moscow. He was promptly arrested, subjected to gross indignities, and
expelled from Muscovy. We learn these facts from Cyprian's own vivid
account in a letter he wrote to Sergius and Theodore on his way back
from Moscow in June 1378, while still under the emotional shock of
his experience. He sternly rebukes the Russian abbots for failing to
stand up before the Muscovite authorities for their lawful metropolitan, and announces his intention of going to Constantinople to 'seek
protection from God, the holy patriarch, and the great synod'. The
Byzantine authorities, he adds, with a note of bitterness however,
'place their hope in money and the Franks [i.e., the Genoese]. I place
mine in God and in the justice of my cause.'[40]

The reason for Prince Dimitri's hostility to Cyprian can be inferred

[39] *Russkaya istoricheskaya biblioteka*, vi, cols. 181–3; ET in Meyendorff, 296–7.

[40] Ibid., cols. 173–86; G. M. Prokhorov, *Povest' o Mityae: Rus' i Vizantiya v epokhu
Kulikovskoy bitvy* (Leningrad, 1978), 195–201; ET in Meyendorff, 293–9. Cyprian
states that after his arrest he was insulted, mocked, robbed of his possessions, locked up
hungry and naked for a whole night, and on the evening of the next day led out of
prison, not knowing whether he was being led to his execution. He complains of still
suffering from the effects of that freezing night. It is interesting that several passages of
this letter, no doubt for security reasons, are written in cipher: see *Russkaya
istoricheskaya biblioteka*, vi, cols. 173 n. 3, 175 n. 1, 183 n. 4, 185 n. 3. Cf. N. S. Borisov,
'Sotsial'no-politicheskoe soderzhanie literaturnoy deyatel'nosti mitropolita Kipriana',
Vestnik Moskovskogo Universiteta, ser. 9 (1975), no. 6, pp. 60–2; Prokhorov, 56–9.

from the latter's letter to Sergius and Theodore. 'He imputes it to me as a crime', he complained, 'that I went first to Lithuania'.[41] Since Cyprian had resided in Kiev for the past two years the Muscovite government no doubt chose to regard him as little more than a Lithuanian agent. Although the hated Olgerd had died in the previous year, the political relations between Muscovy and Lithuania were still tense. And Dimitri had little use for the idea of a single metropolitanate of All Russia unless he could control it himself. In his eyes the patriarchate's decision of 1375 to sever western Russia from Alexius' jurisdiction and to place it under Cyprian's authority was a breach of faith and an act of gross pro-Lithuanian favouritism. This explains the complaint in Cyprian's letter that the Muscovites 'were abusing the patriarch, the emperor and the great synod: they called the patriarch a Lithuanian, and the emperor too, and the most honourable oecumenical synod.'[42]

Cyprian travelled to Byzantium across the Rumanian lands and his native Bulgaria. His reception in the Bulgarian capital of Tŭrnovo, probably early in 1379, is described in conventionally rhetorical terms in Gregory Tsamblak's encomium of him.[43] In Constantinople a fresh disappointment awaited him. The new Patriarch Makarios, under pressure from the Muscovite authorities and no doubt from his patron, the Emperor Andronikos IV, declined to honour his predecessor's pledge to Cyprian and declared his intention of appointing the Russian cleric Michael (Mityai), the candidate of the grand prince of Moscow, to succeed Alexius.[44] The outcome of this deal was one of the most sordid and disreputable episodes in the history of Russo-Byzantine relations. Michael, the Muscovite candidate, died on board ship within sight of Constantinople. His Russian escort, thoughtfully provided by the prince of Moscow with blank charters adorned with his seal and signature and with a considerable sum of money, used the charters to substitute the name of one of their party, the Archimandrite Pimen (Ποιμήν), for that of the deceased Michael and probably distributed the money as bribes to officials in Constantinople.[45] With the help of these forged documents they persuaded Makarios'

---

[41] Russkaya istoricheskaya biblioteka, vi, col. 182.   [42] Ibid., col. 185.

[43] _Pokhvalno slovo za Kipriyan_, 183–5; ET in Heppell, _The Ecclesiastical Career of Gregory Camblak_, 112–14.

[44] _APC_ ii. 120–1.

[45] Ibid. 121. Cf. Golubinsky, _Istoriya russkoy tserkvi_, ii/1. 242–7; Kartashev, _Ocherki_, i. 328–9; Tachiaos, 'Ἐπιδράσεις, 113–15; Prokhorov, _Povest' o Mityae_, 82–101.

successor, the Patriarch Neilos, to appoint Pimen as 'metropolitan of Kiev and Great Russia,[46] while Cyprian, by the synod's special 'condescension' (συγκαταβάσει),[47] was allowed to retain jurisdiction over the Orthodox Church of Lithuania. This was the very decree which, as I suggested earlier, so blatantly tampered with the truth and dishonestly slandered Cyprian.

When the synod issued the decree in June 1380, Cyprian had already left Constantinople for Kiev. We can imagine his anger and frustration: to judge from his letter to St Sergius, written after his expulsion from Moscow, he was a man easily roused to anger. Slowly, however, things began to move in his favour. He had influential friends in Constantinople; one of them was Theophanes, metropolitan of Nicaea, who did not hesitate to express to the synod his view that Cyprian was fully entitled to the see of Kiev and All Russia which he was promised in 1375. It is significant that Theophanes was a noted hesychast who had been used by Philotheos to restore communion with the Serbian Church.[48] Cyprian's chances were improving in Muscovy, too. His former enemy, the Grand Prince Dimitri, was falling increasingly under the influence of the group of Russian hesychast monks who were strong supporters of Cyprian.[49] Their leaders were his former correspondents, St Sergius of Radonezh and his nephew the Abbot Theodore, who was now the grand prince's confessor. Their influence probably became greater still after Dimitri's victory over the Tatars at the battle of Kulikovo in September 1380, which finally established Moscow's hegemony among the central Russian principalities. In the spring of 1381 Theodore was sent to Kiev to invite Cyprian to take over the leadership of the Muscovite Church (Plate 7).[50]

When Cyprian entered Moscow on 23 May 1381 there was much popular rejoicing, if the Russian chronicles are to be believed;[51] it seemed that justice had finally prevailed and the policy of his late mentor and protector, the Patriarch Philotheos, had at last been vindicated. Except for Galicia on the north-eastern slopes of the Carpathians, which in deference to the wishes of its new sovereign,

---

[46] *APC* ii. 12–18.

[47] Ibid. 17.

[48] Ibid. 16–17. On Theophanes of Nicaea, see Beck, *Kirche und theologische Literatur*, 746; Prokhorov, *Povest' o Mityae*, 97–8; Meyendorff, 220–1.

[49] See Presnyakov, *Obrazovanie velikorusskogo gosudarstva*, 360; ET 266–7; Shabatin, *Vestnik*, no. 50, p. 110; Prokhorov, *Povest' o Mityae*, 101–5.

[50] M. D. Priselkov, *Troitskaya Letopis'* (Moscow–Leningrad, 1950), 421.

[51] Ibid. *Nikonovskaya Letopis'*, 41, misdates the event to 1378.

the Polish king, had been given a metropolitan of its own in 1371,[52] the entire Russian Church was now united under Cyprian's authority. Yet his relations with Prince Dimitri remained uneasy. The Muscovite sovereign may have tempered the rigour of his views under the influence of the Russian hesychast monks; but he remained at heart an unrepentant nationalist, interested in the aggrandizement of his domains and in freeing his country from Tatar rule. He could not be expected to entertain much sympathy for the opinions of his primate, who believed that the Church should be independent of secular control and that the metropolitanate of Kiev and All Russia was not a national institution, let alone an instrument of Muscovite state policy, but a constituent part of the oecumenical patriarchate. No doubt feeling the need to strengthen his position in Moscow, Cyprian took to the pen. It was probably in 1381 that he wrote his *magnum opus* in Church Slavonic, the life of his predecessor but two, the Metropolitan Peter (1308–26).[53] It is a work of considerable sophistication, both literary and ideological. Although it is based on an earlier, anonymous biography of Peter, like Cyprian's letter to the abbots Sergius and Theodore it affords us more than a glimpse of its author's personality, motives, and outlook. It was noticed long ago that Cyprian's Life of St Peter of Moscow has strong autobiographical overtones.[54] In order to detect them it is scarcely necessary to read between the lines. The careers of the two prelates had indeed a number of striking similarities: both had close connections with western Russia; each had a rival who tried to supplant him unlawfully; both were slandered by their Russian enemies before the authorities in Constantinople; both eventually overcame these obstacles and were enthroned as metropolitans in Moscow. Cyprian, without naming himself, pointedly highlights these similarities. He repeatedly eulogizes the city of Moscow and what he calls 'the high throne of the glorious metropolitanate of Russia'; and, the better to drive home his message to Prince Dimitri and his government, he paints an idyllic picture of the relations between the Metropolitan Peter and the Muscovite ruler of the time, and condemns attempts by

---

[52] *APC* i. 577–80.

[53] Published in B. St. Angelov, *Iz starata bŭlgarska literatura*, 159–76, and in Prokhorov, *Povest' o Mityae*, 204–15. For the dating, see Dmitriev, 'Rol' i znachenie', 251–2. See also Doncheva-Panaiotova, *Kiprian*, 165–78.

[54] See V. O. Klyuchevsky, *Drevnerusskie zhitiya svyatykh, kak istorichesky istochnik* (Moscow, 1871), 82–8, and Dmitriev, 'Rol' i znachenie', 236–50, who provides a detailed literary analysis of the work.

laymen to divide the Russian metropolitanate and to interfere in ecclesiastical appointments.

If the autobiographical element is latent in Cyprian's Life of Peter of Moscow, it is quite explicit in his encomium to the same saint, probably also written in 1381.[55] He writes of his own initial appointment as metropolitan of Russia in 1375; of his ill-fated attempt to come to Moscow in 1378 when he was so brutally treated on the prince's orders—an event over which he slides, with tactful euphemism, by merely saying 'something adverse happened, on account of my sins'; of his failure to obtain justice in Constantinople at the patriarchal court of 'the wickedly appointed senseless Makarios'; and of his stay in Constantinople in 1379–80, which lasted for thirteen months because, he says, 'it was not possible to leave the imperial city: for the sea was held by the Latins'—an allusion to the Chioggia War between Venice and Genoa, fought mainly in Byzantine waters from 1377–81—'and the land by the godless Turks.' This autobiography, which ends with an account of his second, triumphant arrival in Moscow in 1381, includes a lengthy eulogy of the Patriarch Philotheos. The encomium and also the Life of St Peter of Moscow are indeed precious documents for Cyprian's biographer. Mgr. Louis Petit once wrote: 'A Byzance, un hagiographe qui se respecte ne manque jamais de parler un peu de lui.'[56] One can only add that Cyprian went a good deal further in this direction than was normally considered proper in that age.

These tactful literary exercises, however, availed him little in the short run. Another severe trial lay in store for him. In August 1382 the army of Tokhtamysh, a Mongol vassal of Tamerlane, approached Moscow; before the Tatars captured and looted the city Cyprian slipped out and made his way to the town of Tver'. The circumstances of his departure from Moscow remain obscure, since the Russian chronicles give discordant versions.[57] It is possible, though not certain, that he displayed a certain failure of nerve and leadership. Whether because Cyprian had behaved pusillanimously or, more probably, because he had sought refuge in Tver', Moscow's traditional enemy, Prince Dimitri was furious. Cyprian was again

[55] *Velikiya Minei Chetii*, 21 Dec. (Moscow, 1907); ET in Meyendorff, 300–2.

[56] *Vie et office de Michel Maléinos, suivis du Traité Ascétique de Basile le Maléinote*, ed. L. Petit, in L. Clugnet, *Bibliothèque hagiographique orientale*, iv (Paris, 1903), 3. I owe this reference to Professor Ihor Ševčenko.

[57] See L. V. Cherepnin, *Obrazovanie russkogo tsentralizovannogo gosudarstva v XIV–XV vekakh* (Moscow, 1960), 636–7.

expelled from Muscovy, and returned to Kiev. The egregious Pimen, fraudulently appointed metropolitan in Constantinople and then imprisoned by Dimitri on his return to Russia, was hauled out of jail and solemnly deposited on the primate's throne in October 1382. There is reason to believe that this was done under pressure from Constantinople, where the Patriarch Neilos had been whiping up a campaign in favour of Pimen and consistently maligning Cyprian in his letters to the Muscovite government.[58]

These discreditable manœuvres were almost at an end. In 1385, after Pimen had been abandoned by Moscow and excommunicated by the patriarch,[59] Cyprian was summoned to Constantinople for a final decision on his future. While awaiting the outcome, he lived in the monastery of Stoudios, which, along with Mount Athos, was then a prominent centre of scholarly collaboration between Byzantine and Slav monks. A note in a manuscript of St John of the Ladder in Cyprian's own hand states: 'On 24 April 1387 this book was completed [i.e., copied] in the Studite monastery by Cyprian, the humble metropolitan of Kiev and All Russia'.[60] It is worth noting that, despite all his misfortunes, he still regarded himself as the lawful incumbent of that see. The same year he was sent to Lithuania by the Emperor John V on a political mission ($\delta\iota\grave{\alpha}$ $\delta o\upsilon\lambda\epsilon\acute{\iota}\alpha\varsigma$ $\beta\alpha\sigma\iota\lambda\iota\kappa\acute{\alpha}\varsigma$).[61] We do not know its purpose, but it is hard to resist the impression that it was connected with the personal union concluded between the Grand Duchy of Lithuania and the Kingdom of Poland in the previous year (1386), which threatened to jeopardize the entire future of the

---

[58] *APC* ii. 121–2.

[59] In 1384 Prince Dimitri of Moscow, having withdrawn his support from Pimen, sent the Russian Archbishop Dionysius of Suzdal' to Constantinople, apparently with the intention of persuading the patriarch to consecrate him metropolitan. Neilos declined to be forced into hasty action, and sent a commission of inquiry to Moscow with power to appoint Dionysius if it thought fit: *APC* ii. 122–4. Before any decision was reached Dionysius was arrested in Kiev by Olgerd's son, Prince Vladimir, and on 15 Oct. 1385 died in prison: Priselkov, *Troitskaya Letopis'*, 427–9; *Nikonovskaya Letopis'*, 86. Dionysius was a notable scholar, and acted as a cultural mediator between Byzantium and Russia: Prokhorov, *Povest' o Mityae*, 176; Meyendorff, 230–3. The two Russian Church historians distinguished by their bias against Cyprian, Golubinsky, *Istoriya russkoy tserkvi*, ii/1. 253, and Kartashev, *Ocherki*, i. 332, have no scruples in charging him with the responsibility for Dionysius' death, though there is not the slightest evidence that he was involved in it. Shabatin, *Vestnik*, no. 50, p. 115, comes somewhat hesitantly to Cyprian's defence. Meyendorff, 233 n. 25, rightly exonerates him.

[60] Ivanov, 'Bŭlgarskoto knizhovno vliyanie', 48; C. Mango, 'A Russian Graffito in St. Sophia, Constantinople', *Slavic Word*, x/4 (1954), 437.

[61] *APC* ii. 124.

Orthodox Church in the Grand Duchy. Whatever its purpose, Cyprian's imperial mission is evidence of the esteem in which he was then held by the Byzantine government. In February 1389, under the new Patriarch Antony IV, the synod met to decide the future of the Russian Church and to put an end to the disgraceful anarchy of the past ten years. The Acts of the synod admit that the Russians were pouring on the Byzantines a flood of 'insults . . . and reproaches and accusations and grumblings' (ὕβρεις πολλὰς . . . καὶ μώμους καὶ κατη-γορίας καὶ γογγυσμούς).[62] This was no doubt an understatement. After the villainy perpetrated by their envoys in Constantinople and the brutalities and vacillations of Prince Dimitri, the Russians for their part had scarcely a better press in Byzantium. The synod wisely opted for reconciliation. It appointed Cyprian metropolitan of Kiev and All Russia, and decreed that the unity of the Russian metropolitanate be maintained for all times (εἰς τὸ ἑξῆς εἰς αἰῶνα τὸν ἄπαντα).[63]

THE YEARS OF ACHIEVEMENT (1390–1406)

Early in 1390, after a stormy passage on the Black Sea in which he nearly lost his life, Cyprian, escorted by a retinue of Byzantine and Russian prelates, made his solemn entry into Moscow via Kiev.[64] Prince Dimitri had died the previous year and his son and successor, Basil I, seems to have accepted his new primate readily. For fifteen years Cyprian had reached out for the metropolitanate of All Russia, that glittering prize promised him by his patron Philotheos and so rudely denied him by Dimitri of Moscow and by Philotheos' two successors on the patriarchal throne. Now, with the final obstacles removed, he could at last put into practice the programme for Eastern Europe he and Philotheos had devised together in the early 1370s: its aim was to attach the South Slav and Russian Orthodox Churches more firmly to the oecumenical patriarchate by the concerted action of a group of men bound to each other by ties of friendship or discipleship, and owing a common loyalty to the hesychast tradition and to the mother-Church of Constantinople. The linchpin of this programme of ecclesiastical diplomacy was the undivided metropoli-tanate of Kiev and All Russia, with its effective centre in Moscow.

---

[62] Ibid. 123.   [63] Ibid. 128.
[64] Priselkov, *Troitskaya Letopis'*, 435–6; *Nikonovskaya Letopis'*, 101, 122.

Though we lack detailed information about these last sixteen years of Cyprian's life, there is reason to think that they were not unproductive.

Much of his administrative work during those years is of little interest to anyone save the historian of the Russian Church.[65] Two areas of his activity, however, impinged on the wider field of European history. The first was Lithuania. In 1386 one of the most fateful marriages in the history of Eastern Europe took place when Olgerd's son Jagiełło, grand duke of Lithuania, married Queen Jadwiga of Poland. Jagiełło, who had earlier undertaken to marry the daughter of Prince Dimitri of Moscow and to become a member of the Orthodox Church,[66] had to promise to convert his subjects to the Roman faith and to unite his Grand Duchy with the kingdom of Poland. Fortunately for the Orthodox, who formed the majority of the population of the Grand Duchy, Jagiełło was unable to enforce this conversion to Rome. His cousin Witold, who become grand duke of Lithuania under Jagiełło's suzerainty in 1392, was an Orthodox and the father-in-law of the grand prince of Moscow. A period of peaceful relations thus began between Muscovy and the Polish–Lithuanian federation, which lasted until 1406.

There can be no doubt that Cyprian played a major role in fostering this *rapprochement*. According to the Russian chronicles, he paid two further visits to Lithuania—in 1396[67] and in 1404[68]—and each time stayed there for some eighteen months. On both occasions he met Witold, and in 1405 he had a long and very friendly encounter with King Jagiełło.[69] He must have got to know him on an earlier occasion,

---

[65] For Cyprian's ecclesiastical activity between 1390 and 1406, see Golubinsky, op. cit. ii/1. 302–56; Presnyakov, *Obrazovanie*, 363–73; ET 297–310; Kartashev, *Ocherki*, i. 333–8; Shabatin, *Vestnik*, no. 51, pp. 192–4, no. 52, pp. 237–57.

[66] See Dvornik, *The Slavs in European History*, 221–2.

[67] The date of Cyprian's first visit varies in the different chronicles: 1396: *Voskresenskaya Letopis'*, 69; 1397: *Nikonovskaya Letopis'*, 166; 1398: Priselkov, *Troitskaya Letopis'*, 449. The correct date is presumably 1396, since in Jan. 1397 the Patriarch Antony wrote both to Cyprian and to King Jagiełło in reply to their joint proposal for a Church council, no doubt made after a personal meeting between them (see below). It was doubtless in 1396 that Cyprian wrote to the patriarch from Lithuania, complaining of overwork. In his reply, dated January 1397, the patriarch referred to Cyprian's 'many exertions and travels' (τῶν πολλῶν κόπων καὶ περιόδων) and attempted to console him by pointing out that they are but the professional duty of every true bishop (*APC* ii. 282).

[68] Priselkov, *Troitskaya Letopis'*, 458; Voskresenskaya Letopis', 77; *Nikonovskaya Letopis'*, 191.

[69] This summit meeting took place in the Lithuanian town of Milolyub, lasted for a

for in a letter written to Cyprian in January 1397 the Patriarch Antony IV remarks: 'as you have written yourself, the king [of Poland] is a great friend of yours' (φίλος σου πολὺς ἔνι ὁ κράλης).[70] It was doubtless in 1396 that Cyprian and Jagiełło thought up their remarkable scheme for the reunion of the Byzantine and Latin Churches, to be effected at a council, presumably on Lithuanian soil. Both sent their written proposals to the patriarch, who showed a cautious interest in the project but pointed out in his replies, dated January 1397, that 'Russia' (presumably Lithuania) was an unsuitable venue for such a council, and that in any case the blockade of Constantinople by the Turkish armies of Bayezit made its summoning inexpedient. Let the kings of Hungary and Poland organize another crusade against the Turks; then, said the patriarch, a council could be held, for the roads would be open. As for Cyprian, it was his bounden duty to use his influence with the Polish king to secure this desirable end.[71] It is with justice that John Barker, commenting on Antony's letter to Jagiełło, remarks: 'This passage makes clear that the Byzantines regarded union as the cart and aid as the horse, and that they had very strong opinions as to which should come first.'[72]

The second aspect of Cyprian's activity which is of general interest is the role he played as a representative of the Byzantine authorities in Russia. There has been much speculation about the degree of his involvement in the famous conflict which broke out in the 1390s between the grand prince of Moscow, Basil I, and the oecumenical patriarch Antony IV. In 1393 the patriarch wrote a letter to the Muscovite ruler in which he rebuked him for forbidding his metropolitan to commemorate the emperor's name in the liturgy of the Russian church. He took a particularly grave view of the statement he ascribed to the Russian ruler: 'We have the Church, but not the emperor.' In rebutting this grievous error, and mindful of his duty as 'universal teacher of all Christians', the patriarch reiterated the basic principle of

---

week, and was also attended by the Grand Duke Witold: *Troitskaya Letopis'*, 459; *Voskresenskaya Letopis'*, 77. *Nikonovskaya Letopis'*, 192, claims that the meeting lasted for two weeks.

[70] APC ii. 283.　　　　　　　　　　　　　　　　　　　　[71] Ibid. 280–5.

[72] J. W. Barker, *Manuel II Palaeologus (1391–1425): A Study in Late Byzantine Statemanship* (New Brunswick, NJ, 1969), 150–4. On this project of union, see also Golubinsky, op. cit. 337–9; Presnyakov, *Obrazovanie*, 370; ET 308; O. Halecki, 'La Pologne et l'Empire byzantin', *Byzantion*, vii (1932), 49; Kartashev, *Ocherki*, i. 336–7; Tachiaos, 'Επιδράσεις, 127–30; Shabatin, *Vestnik*, no. 52, pp. 250–2; Meyendorff, 252–4.

Byzantine political philosophy: 'The holy emperor', he writes, 'is not as other rulers and governors of other regions are ... He is anointed with the great chrism, and is elected *basileus* and *autokrator* of the Romans, that is, of all Christians'. His universal sovereignty is made manifest by the liturgical commemoration of his name in the churches of Christendom; and by prohibiting this practice within his realm the grand prince of Moscow has flouted the very foundations of Christian law and government.[73]

Historians have often pointed out that the Patriarch Antony's letter is a classic exposition of the Byzantine doctrine of the universal East Roman Empire, ruled by the *basileus*, earthly vicegerent of God, supreme lawgiver of Christendom, whose authority was held to extend, at least in an ideal and 'metapolitical' sense, over all Christian rulers and peoples. The fact that this uncompromising profession of faith was made from the capital of a state that was facing military and political collapse only highlights the astonishing strength and continuity of this political vision, which pervades the entire history of the Byzantine body politic.[74]

Antony's words have usually been taken at their face value, and Basil I's refusal to allow the emperor's name to be inscribed in the commemorative diptychs of the Russian Church regarded as a nationalistic revolt against Byzantine claims to hegemony, and a revolutionary break with tradition. In recent years, however, John Meyendorff has suggested that it was Cyprian, not Basil I, who was innovating; and that, in the teeth of conservative opposition led by the grand prince, he was trying to introduce into Muscovy the novel practice of commemorating the emperor's name in the churches of the land.[75] No sure conclusion on this matter seems possible until the Slavonic liturgical books used in Russia during the Middle Ages are published and studied; and in default of new evidence, the question remains an open one. We can, however, be certain of two things: firstly, in this conflict between Moscow and Constantinople, Cyprian

---

[73] *APC* ii. 188–92; abridged ET in E. Barker, *Social and Political Thought in Byzantium*, 194–6 and in J. W. Barker, op. cit. 105–10. For the correct dating of the letter—1393 and not 1394–7 (as Ostrogorsky, *History*, 554 n. 1, argued)—see J. W. Barker, op. cit. 109–10 n. 31; and Darrouzès, *Le Registre synodal*, 125 n. 34.

[74] 'The doctrine of one oecumenical Emperor had never been laid down more forcibly or with more fiery eloquence than in this letter which the Patriarch of Constantinople sent to Moscow from a city blockaded by the Turks': Ostrogorsky, *History*, 554.

[75] *Byzantium and the Rise of Russia*, 254–6.

took the Byzantine side; secondly, he won in the end, for in a letter he wrote about 1397 to the clergy of Pskov he stated explicitly that the emperor is commemorated liturgically in the churches of Moscow.[76]

As a Byzantine agent in Russia, Cyprian was also useful as a fund raiser. His good offices were repeatedly sought by the Byzantine government and Church during the Turkish siege of Constantinople, which lasted from 1394 to 1402.[77] According to Russian sources, in 1398 he helped collect a considerable sum of money which, perhaps surprisingly, reached Constantinople safely.[78] The patriarchal archives preserved the draft of a letter addressed to Cyprian and dated to 1400, in which the Patriarch Matthew urged him, 'as a Byzantine-loving man' ($\dot{\omega}\varsigma$ $\phi\iota\lambda o\rho\rho\dot{\omega}\mu\alpha\iota o\varsigma$ $\ddot{\alpha}\nu\theta\rho\omega\pi o\varsigma$), to start another fund-raising campaign; he was to assure his Russian flock that it was more meritorious to contribute money for the defence of Constantinople than to build churches, to give alms to the poor, or to redeem prisoners. 'For this holy city', wrote the patriarch, 'is the pride, the support, the sanctification, and the glory of Christians in the whole world.'[79]

Cyprian's efforts as a $\phi\iota\lambda o\rho\rho\dot{\omega}\mu\alpha\iota o\varsigma$ $\ddot{\alpha}\nu\theta\rho\omega\pi o\varsigma$ should not obscure his services to his country of adoption during this last and more serene period of his life. They can be enumerated only briefly. In 1375, when the armies of Tamerlane were approaching Moscow, Cyprian had the famous icon of Our Lady of Vladimir, Russia's palladium, transferred to Moscow in order to instil courage in the inhabitants of the threatened city. On that very day, according to a Russian chronicle, Tamerlane ordered a general retreat.[80]

Cyprian has also a secure and not undistinguished position in the history of Russian letters. I have already referred to some of his writings. Russian archival collections have preserved manuscripts

---

[76] *Russkaya istoricheskaya biblioteka*, vi, col. 239. This commemoration appears to have been the imperial *polychronia*, which formed part of the Synodicon for the Sunday of Orthodoxy. See J. Gouillard, 'Le Synodikon de l'Orthodoxie: Édition et commentaire', *TM* ii (1967), 93–5, 253–6. Cf. F. Uspensky, *Ocherki po istorii vizantiiskoy obrazovannosti* (St Petersburg, 1891), 109–45.

[77] On the siege of Constantinople, see J. W. Barker, op. cit. 123–99.

[78] *Troitskaya Letopis'*, 448; *Nikonovskaya Letopis'*, 168; *Sofiiskaya vtoraya Letopis'*, PSRL vi (1853), 130; *Voskresenskaya Letopis'*, 71. Cf. Dölger, *Regesten*, v 85 (no. 3267). Neither the Byzantine appeal for help nor the Russian response justifies the epithet 'supposed' (J. W. Barker, op. cit. 153 n. 45).

[79] *APC* ii. 361.

[80] See G. Vernadsky, *The Mongols and Russia* (New Haven, 1953), 275–6; Cherepnin, *Obrazovanie*, 673–8.

copied by him, mostly Church Slavonic translations from the Greek. Among them are the Psalter, St John Climacus' *Ladder*, and works of pseudo-Dionysius.[81] He inserted into the Russian version of the Synodicon for the Sunday of Orthodoxy the new articles of the Byzantine Synodicon which endorsed the theological teaching of the hesychasts, thus contributing to the subsequent spread of hesychasm in Russia.[82] He also played an important role in the development of Russian liturgical practice,[83] making new translations into Church Slavonic of Greek liturgical texts, introducing into Russia the *ordo* of the liturgy of St John Chrysostom in current use in late medieval Byzantium,[84] issuing detailed instructions on liturgical problems,[85] and generally attempting to bring the ritual of the Russian Church fully into line with Constantinopolitan practice of the late fourteenth century.[86] Finally, he is believed to have played an active part in the compilation of the first comprehensive Muscovite chronicle, which included material collected from different parts of the country and which was completed in 1409, three years after his death.[87]

[81] For general studies of Cyprian's literary work, see Ivanov, 'Bŭlgarskoto knizhovno vliyanie', 25–79; Dmitriev, 'Rol' i znachenie', 215–54; Doncheva-Panaiotova, *Kiprian*, 113–207. Cyprian's liturgical and historical works fall outside the scope of this chapter, and merit a separate study.

[82] *Russkya istoricheskaya biblioteka*, vi, cols. 239, 241. See Meyendorff, 259–60.

[83] The standard work on Cyprian's liturgical activity is still the thorough study by I. Mansvetov, 'O trudakh Mitropolita Kipriana po chasti bogusluzheniya', *Pribavleniya k izdaniyu tvoreniy svyatykh otsev v russkom perevode*, xix (1882), 152–205, 413–95; ibid. xxx (1882), 71–161. Cf. Ivanov, 'Bŭlgarskoto knizhovno vliyanie', 37–47, 52–67.

[84] This was the Διάταξις τῆς θείας λειτουργίας, attributed to the Patriarch Philotheos. See P. N. Trembelas, Αἱ τρεῖς λειτουργίαι κατὰ τοὺς ἐν 'Αθήναις κώδικας (Athens, 1935), 1–16; Beck, *Kirche und theologische Literatur*, 726. Cyprian made available in Russia the Church Slavonic translation of this διάταξις, made by the Patriarch Euthymius of Bulgaria (ed. Kałužniacki, 283–306).

[85] *Russkaya istoricheskaya biblioteka*, vi, cols. 235–70.

[86] The contrast is worth noting between the high praise meted out to Cyprian in a Russian document dated 1403 for his 'correction of the [Church] books' (see A. I. Sobolevsky, *Perevodnaya literatura Moskovskoy Rusi XIV–XVII vekov* (St Petersburg, 1903), 12–13 n. 3) and the storm that broke over a similar issue in Russia three centuries later, when the decision of the Patriarch Nikon to enforce upon his Russian Church the liturgical texts and practices of the contemporary Greek Church caused millions of 'Old Believers' to go into schism. In this area too it is remarkable how the hesychast, pro-Byzantine party was able in the late Middle Ages to offer a viable alternative to the growth of religious nationalism.

[87] See M. D. Priselkov, *Istoriya russkogo letopisaniya XI–XV vv.* (Leningrad, 1940; repr. The Hague, 1966), 128–40; id., *Troitskaya Letopis'*, 3–49; D. S. Likhachev, *Russkie letopisi i ikh kul'turno-istoricheskoe znachenie* (Moscow–Leningrad, 1947), 296–7; Dmitriev, 'Rol' i znachenie', 226–8.

A modern scholar has attributed to Cyprian the following statement: 'I seek peace and ecclesiastical unity between north and
south.'[88] I have not been able to find these exact words in any of
Cyprian's published works, though I believe them to be a none too
faithful rendering of something he did, in fact, write in one of his
letters to St Sergius and his nephew Theodore.[89] Genuine or not, this
quotation seems an appropriate epitaph for a man who, drawing his
spiritual and intellectual inspiration from the hermitages of Athos and
the example of his mentor, the Patriarch Philotheos, devoted the
greater part of his active life to the task of keeping together the
disparate fragments of the Byzantine commonwealth. He fought hard,
and in the end achieved a large measure of success.

A Russian chronicle, in its account of Cyprian's death, tells us that
his favourite place of residence was his country estate near Moscow.
'The place', we are told, 'was quiet, silent and free from noise, between
two rivers . . . beside a pond, and there was much forest all round.'[90]
There he would retire to pray, read, and indulge in his favourite
pastime, the copying of manuscripts. One is reminded of Peter the
Venerable's account, written to Héloïse, of the last years of Abelard's
life: *libris semper incumbebat*.[91] There he died, probably in his late
seventies, on 16 September 1406. Four days before his death,
seriously ill, he dictated a farewell letter to his friends and his enemies,
begging forgiveness and sending to all his 'peace and blessing and last
embrace'. He asked that it be read at his funeral, while his body was
being lowered into the coffin. The Russian chronicler, who cites in full
the text of the letter, tells us that many were in tears as they heard it
read.[92]

We may perhaps best take leave of Cyprian in the quiet surround-

---

[88] Archimandrite Leonid, 'Kipriyan do vosshestviya', 29.

[89] 'I seek neither glory, nor riches, but my metropolitanate, which the holy Great
Church of God [i.e. the Patriarchate of Constantinople] entrusted to me': Prokhorov,
Povest' o Mityae, 202. The letter was written on 18 Oct. 1378 in Kiev.

[90] *Nikonovskaya Letopis'*, 194–5.

[91] *The Letters of Peter the Venerable*, ed. G. Constable, i (Cambridge, Mass., 1967), 307
(Letter 115).

[92] *Troitskaya Letopis'*, 462–4; *Nikonovskaya Letopis'*, 194–7. Two 16th-c. chronicles
state that some of Cyprian's successors on the metropolitan throne had the text of his
letter read at their funeral and placed in their coffins: *Nikonovskaya Letopis'*, 197; *Kniga
Stepennaya Tsarskogo Rodosloviya*, PSRL xxi/2 (1913), 443–4. On Cyprian's 'testament'
see A.-E. Tachiaos, 'The Testament of Photius Monembasiotes, Metropolitan of Russia
(1408–1431): Byzantine Ideology in XVth-century Muscovy', *Cyrillomethodianum*,
viii–ix (1984–5), 77–109.

ings of his Russian country home which he loved so much. A southerner by birth, he must have found the scenery very unlike the rolling hills of his native Bulgaria and the dark blue sea, the sun-baked cliffs, and the chestnut groves of Mount Athos. It is pleasant to think that in his adopted northern home, where in the autumn and on long summer days the translucent sky falls gently on the silent waters, he may have found peace at last.

6

Maximos the Greek

IN the spring of 1553 the Tsar Ivan IV (later known as the Terrible) left his capital, Moscow, on a pilgrimage. The journey, to a monastery in the far north, was intended as an act of thanksgiving for his recovery from a recent, and nearly fatal, illness. The royal party, including the tsaritsa and Ivan's newly born child, stopped on the way in St Sergius' monastery of the Holy Trinity, Russia's most hallowed monastic house. Within its walls lived a man of almost legendary fame. A Greek monk from Mount Athos, over eighty years of age, he had spent the past thirty-five years in Russia, more than half of them in monastic gaols. To educated Russians he was known as a scholar of great learning, a prolific writer in their language, and a man of great constancy and courage. His name was Maximos—Maxim to the Russians. The aged monk and the young sovereign met and talked. Maxim urged the tsar to abandon his pilgrimage and return to Moscow. Far better, he argued, to comfort the families of the Russian soldiers killed in the recent war against the Tatars than to persist on what was clearly a long and dangerous journey; and he warned Ivan that, if he did so persist, his infant son would die. The tsar declined to alter his plans; and the child died on the way.

The story of this brief encounter between arguably the two most remarkable men in sixteenth-century Russia was told, some twenty year later, by a fervent admirer of Maxim, Prince Andrey Kurbsky.[1] This distinguished general, a former favourite of Ivan, disgusted at the tsar's growing absolutism, had deserted to Lithuania in 1564. He certainly knew much about his teacher's life: including the fact that as a young man Maxim had lived in Italy. Exactly how much of his biography Maxim revealed to Kurbsky we do not know: there were several episodes in it which, as we shall see, he would have been wise to conceal.

---

[1] *Prince A. M. Kurbsky's History of Ivan IV*, ed. with translation and notes by J. L. I. Fennell (Cambridge, 1965), pp. 76–81, 90–1.

Some of these episodes have come to light only recently. In 1942 the Russian scholar Élie Denissoff published in Louvain a book entitled *Maxime le Grec et l'Occident*.[2] In it he proved conclusively that Maxim was none other than Michael Trivolis, a Greek expatriate who frequented the humanistic schools of Italy in the late fifteenth century. It is not often that the biography of a major historical figure is so unexpectedly enlarged by a scholarly discovery; and Denissoff could justifiably claim that, thanks to his book, the life of Maximos the Greek assumed the shape of a diptych, of which Mount Athos is the hinge, and Italy and Muscovite Russia are the two leaves.

There is no need to rehearse here Denissoff's arguments. They are based on compelling historical, literary, and graphological evidence, and are generally accepted today. Thus, in any account of the life and work of Maximos the Greek, we must start with Michael Trivolis.

The Trivolai were a Byzantine family of moderate distinction. They supplied a patriarch of Constantinople in the mid fourteenth century[3] and, a little later, a correspondent of the Emperor Manuel II.[4] One branch settled in Mistra in the Peloponnese. Michael was born in Arta, the capital of the Greek province of Epirus, about 1470. Some twenty years earlier the city had fallen to the Turks, and before long the family decided to emigrate. The nearest refuge was the island of Corfu, then under Venetian sovereignty. Greek families from the mainland had been gathering there for some time, drawn not only by the prospect of security, but also by the presence on the island of a group of distinguished Greek scholars.

Michael was probably about ten years old when his family moved from Arta to Corfu. When he was about twenty he stood for election to the island's Governing Council. The results were not calculated to guide him towards a public career: 20 votes were cast for him, 73 against.[5] It was probably in 1492 that he moved to Florence, then the leading centre of Greek studies in Europe. In Florence, where he remained for three years, his vocation as a scholar was shaped by the teaching of the Greek philologist John Lascaris and by the influence of the great Platonist Marsilio Ficino. Many years later, writing in

---

[2] E. Denissoff, *Maxime le Grec et l'Occident: Contribution à l'histoire de la pensée religieuse et philosophique de Michel Trivolis* (Paris–Louvain, 1942).

[3] Kallistos I. See Denissoff, op. cit. 119 n. 5.

[4] Denissoff, op. cit. 119; *The Letters of Manuel II Palaeologus*, ed. G. T. Dennis (Washington DC, 1977), 24–7; J. W. Barker, *Manuel II Palaeologus*, 36 n. 93.

[5] Denissoff, op. cit. 84–6, 143–5, and pls. I and II.

Moscow, Maximos remembered Florence as the fairest of all the Italian cities he had known.[6] The influence of Plato and of the Florentine 'Platonic Academy' was to remain with him, for better or for worse, all his life.

Another, very different influence was felt by Michael during his years in Florence: that of the Dominican friar Savonarola. He probably never met him personally; but he certainly heard him preach. The full impact of this influence was to come later, after Savonarola's execution in 1498. Later still, in Moscow, he wrote for the Russians a detailed account of Savonarola's life, describing his famous Lenten sermons, his conflict with the pope, and his grisly execution in Florence. He extolled him as a man 'filled with every kind of wisdom', and added, perhaps with a touch of tactful self-censorship, that, had Savonarola not belonged to the Latin faith, he would surely have been numbered among the Church's holy confessors.[7] Attempts have been made—not wholly convincing, in my view—to trace in Maxim's Russian writings the influence of several works of Savonarola, in particular of his *canzone De ruina ecclesiae*, and his meditation on the Psalm *Miserere mei Deus*, written in a Florentine prison, while he was awaiting his last trial and execution.[8] More easily identifiable, and more important, is the influence of the Italian friar on Maxim's later concern with moral problems, on his love of poverty, and perhaps too on his outspokenness and courage in adversity.

In one of his later writings Maxim described in some detail the University of Paris. He dwelt on its curriculum of studies, the high quality of the teaching, given free of charge thanks to a royal endowment, and its role as an international institution: its students, he wrote, who come from all over western and northern Europe, return home, to become ornaments and useful members of their societies.[9] It has sometimes been assumed that Michael visited Paris. This is unlikely; though he did announce to the Russians—quite

[6] *Sochineniya prepodobnogo Maksima Greka*, iii (Kazan', 1862), 194; Denissoff, op. cit. 156–7, 423.

[7] *Sochineniya*, iii. 194–202; Denissoff, op. cit. 423–8; V. S. Ikonnikov, *Maksim Grek i ego vremya*, 2nd edn. (Kiev, 1915), 118–23; A. I. Ivanov, *Literaturnoe nasledie Maksima Greka* (Leningrad, 1969), 156–7.

[8] K. Viskovaty, 'K voprosu o literaturnom vliyanii Savonaroly na Maksima Greka', *Slavia*, xvii (1939–40), 128–33; A. I. Ivanov, 'Maksim Grek i Savonarola', *TODRL* xxiii (1968), 217–26.

[9] *Sochineniya*, iii. 179–80; Denissoff, op. cit. 430–1.

possibly for the first time—the discovery of America, more precisely of a large land called Cuba.[10]

The next stage in Michael's life in Italy, after brief visits to Bologna, Padua, and Milan, took him in 1496 to Venice where he remained for the next two years. There he became associated with Aldus Manutius, who was then producing his celebrated editions of the Greek classics. He later told a Russian correspondent that he often visited Aldus for reasons which had to do with books.[11] It may be that Michael was actually employed in the Aldine press, and that he worked on the edition of Aristotle which Aldus was then preparing in Venice; but we cannot be certain of this. His later work as a translator from Greek into Slavonic suggests that he had been trained to edit texts; an expertise which, we shall see, was not without its dangers in Muscovite Russia.

By this time Michael must have acquired some reputation as a scholar. In a letter dated 1498 he mentions several offers of gainful employment he has recently received.[12] In the same year we find him in the service of another Italian, the distinguished Hellenist Gianfrancesco Pico della Mirandola, nephew of the celebrated Platonist Giovanni Pico. The four years which he spent at Mirandola were an important landmark in his life. Gianfrancesco Pico was not only a classical scholar, a true ἑλληνομανής, as Michael wrote to a friend in March 1500.[13] He was also a convinced Christian, a student of patristic writings, and a great admirer of Savonarola. The news of Savonarola's execution was received at Mirandola while Michael was there.

It is hardly possible to gain a clear impression of the state of Michael's mind around the year 1500. Three distinct influences undoubtedly worked on him at the time, and they must have been hard to reconcile: Platonic philosophy and classical scholarship; the Christian patristic tradition, no doubt familiar from his early youth, but now apprehended more deeply after his stay at Mirandola; and the impact of the life and teaching of Savonarola. Of the three the last, for the moment, proved the strongest. A note in an unpublished chronicle of the monastery of San Marco in Florence states that in 1502 Michael ('Frater Michael Emmanuelis de civitate Arta') was

[10] *Sochineniya*, iii. 44; Denissoff, op. cit. 423. Cf. I. Ševčenko, 'Byzantium and the Eastern Slavs after 1453', *Harvard Ukrainian Studies*, ii (1978), 13.

[11] Denissoff, op. cit. 190–7, 429–30; Ikonnikov, op. cit. 134–5; Ivanov, op. cit. 207–9.

[12] Denissoff, op. cit. 398–401.   [13] Ibid. 402.

professed as a monk of that monastery.[14] It is worth noting that this was the very house of which Savonarola had been the prior. Many years later Michael described to the Russians in considerable detail the life and organization of the Dominican order, while carefully concealing the fact that he had belonged to it himself.[15] His secret was to remain undiscovered for more than four centuries.

Michael Trivolis's career as a Dominican was brief. On 21 April 1504 he wrote from Florence to an Italian friend, to announce that he had abandoned the monastic life. In evident distress, he compared himself to a ship tossed by the waves in the midst of the sea, and begged for help in his present affliction ($\tau\hat{\eta}s$ $\pi\alpha\rho o\acute{v}\sigma\eta s$ $\theta\lambda\acute{\iota}\psi\epsilon\omega s$).[16] Denissoff, who published this letter, concluded, no doubt rightly, that Michael was deliberately vague as to the reasons for the apparent collapse of his religious vocation.[17]

In 1505 or 1506, after yet another change whose causes remain mysterious, we find Michael, now as the monk Maximos, in the monastery of Vatopedi on Mount Athos, back in the Church of his fathers. It is perhaps unwise to imagine a formal conversion. The hostility between Greeks and Latins had certainly hardened during the past centuries, and the ill-starred Council of Florence in 1439 had, on the whole, not helped matters. Yet in a number of Greek communities, not least in Venice and Corfu, a more tolerant attitude towards the Latin Church prevailed, and a surprising degree of liturgical concelebration and intercommunion was permitted; the rift in the body of Christendom was not yet complete. The same, in the first half of the sixteenth century, seems to have been true of one of the leading Athonite houses, the Great Lavra; though not of Maximos's own monastery of Vatopedi, where a harsher attitude towards the Latins prevailed.[18] In his Russian writings Maximos severely criticized several Latin beliefs and practices, which he roundly denounced as heretical. Foremost among them was the doctrine of the *Filioque*, the major bone of theological contention between the Greek and the Latin Churches since the ninth century. The other major issue, the claims of the papacy to exercise direct and universal jurisdiction throughout the Christian Church, is touched upon more lightly by Maximos. Most of his strictures are directed at what he considered to be the popes' arrogant desire to extend their own power. On the

[14] Ibid. 95, 458; Ivanov, op. cit. 163.
[15] *Sochineniya*, iii. 182–94; Denissoff, op. cit. 249–52.
[16] Denissoff, op. cit. 404–6.   [17] Ibid. 95–6, 261–2.   [18] Ibid. 436–45.

whole, Maximos's criticism of the Latin Church was measured and courteous, and lacked the emotional overtones of the anti-Latin pronouncements of many of his contemporaries, Greek and Russian.[19]

The ten years or so which Maximos spent on Mount Athos were a crucial period in his life. Unfortunately, it is also the least well documented. A few writings by him have survived from this period, mostly Greek epitaphs in verse.[20] They are distinguished by elegance of form and a liking for classical imagery. On a deeper level, there is no doubt that on Mount Athos Maximos immersed himself in Byzantine literature, both religious and secular. The libraries of Mount Athos, well stocked in the Middle Ages, had become richer still after the fall of Constantinople. Thus Maximos's former teacher John Lascaris had purchased from the Athonite monks a large number of manuscripts for the Library of Lorenzo de' Medici. It was almost certainly in Vatopedi that Maximos studied in depth the works of John of Damascus, the Byzantine theologian who seems to have been the most congenial to him, and whom he later described as having reached 'the summit of philosophy and theology'.[21] Among the early Fathers Gregory of Nazianzus appears to have been his favourite.[22] Of the secular Byzantine works, the one he used, and translated most frequently in Russia, was the encyclopaedia known today as *Suda* and formerly believed to have been written by a certain Suidas.[23]

Another feature of Mount Athos which bears directly upon Maximos's subsequent life and outlook was its cosmopolitanism. Since the early Middle Ages the Holy Mountain had been a place of meeting and co-operation between men from different countries of eastern Europe. In the late Middle Ages, partly owing to a considerable increase in the number of Slav monks, it played a particularly important role as a pan-Orthodox monastic centre. The revival of the contemplative tradition of Byzantine hesychasm attracted men from Serbia, Bulgaria, Rumania, and Russia, as well as Greeks from Byzantium, to this famed nursery of the spiritual life. In the Greek and

[19] On Maximos's views of the *Filioque*, see B. Schultze, 'Maksim Grek als Theologe', *Orientalia Christiana Analecta*, clxvii (1963), 245–55; on his attitude to the papal claims, see ibid. 283–90.

[20] See Denissoff, op. cit. 97–9, 412–20.

[21] *Sochineniya*, iii. 66. Cf. ibid. 210, 227, 232–3. Cf. Ikonnikov, op. cit. 144–5.

[22] See D. M. Bulanin, *Perevody i poslaniya Maksima Greka* (Leningrad, 1984), 30–52.

[23] Ivanov, op. cit. 68–79; N. V. Sinitsyna, *Maksim Grek v Rossii* (Moscow, 1977), 58–60, 67–9; Bulanin, op. cit. 53–81, 128–81.

Slav monasteries of Athos, manuscripts were copied and collated, literary works were exchanged, and Byzantine texts translated into Slavonic.[24] In the early sixteenth century, despite the Ottoman conquests, this spiritual and cultural co-operation continued, and it is hard to believe that Maximos remained unaffected by this cosmopolitan Graeco-Slav environment. It must have prepared him in some degree for his future work in Muscovy.

It has been suggested that Maximos, as a product of the humanist schools of Renaissance Italy, and with the burden of his recent Dominican past, may have felt isolated, if not ostracized, in the contemporary climate of Mount Athos.[25] His superiors at Vatopedi were certainly not ignorant of his life in Italy. And it is true that his attachment to Plato, which went back to his early days in Florence, was a potential hazard in an Orthodox monastic society whose thinking, recently moulded by the teachings of the hesychast theologian Gregory Palamas, was profoundly hostile to all forms of Platonism. Yet there is no evidence that Maximos encountered on Mount Athos any difficulties on this score. To judge from his later Russian writings, he was fully aware, from a strictly orthodox standpoint, of the pitfalls of Platonism; and he explicitly rejected some of Plato's teachings, such as the belief he ascribed to him in the coeternity of God and the world.[26] Maximos's views on the relationship of faith to knowledge were unimpeachably orthodox. 'Do not think', he wrote in Russia, 'that I condemn all external [i.e. secular] learning that is useful . . . I am not so ungrateful a student of this learning. Although I did not long remain on its threshold, yet I condemn those who pursue it through excessive rational inquiry.'[27] It seems that Maximos adapted quickly to his Athonite environment: certainly for the rest of his life he regarded the Holy Mountain as his true spiritual home.

It was in 1516 that the last period of Maximos's life began. In that year an embassy from the Muscovite ruler, Basil III, arrived on Mount Athos. Its purpose was to invite to Moscow a competent Greek translator. The Russian Church, from its birth in the tenth century

---

[24] See I. Duichev, 'Tsentry vizantiysko-slavyanskogo obshcheniya i sotrudnichestva', *TODRL* xix (1963), 107–29.

[25] Denissoff, op. cit. 293–301.

[26] J. V. Haney, *From Italy to Muscovy. The Life and Works of Maxim the Greek* (Munich, 1973), 138–52.

[27] *Sochineniya*, i (Kazan', 1859–60), 462.

and until the mid fifteenth, had been subordinated to the patriarch of Constantinople. During this period, and especially between 1350 and 1450, the royal library had been enriched by a large number of Greek manuscripts brought from Byzantium.[28] By the early sixteenth century few Russians were capable of reading them. There was need of an expert to decipher them and translate them into Slavonic.

The choice of the Muscovites had fallen on the Greek monk Savvas of the Vatopedi monastery, who seems to have been a translator of repute. Savvas, however, was too old and infirm to travel and, as the next best, the Athonite authorities chose Maximos. In his letter to the metropolitan of Moscow, the abbot recommended Maximos in terms which show that the latter was respected on Mount Athos not only for his spiritual qualities: he described him as 'our most honourable brother Maximos . . . , proficient in divine Scripture and adept in interpreting all kinds of books, both ecclesiastical and those called Hellenic [i.e. secular], because from his early youth he has grown up in them and learned [to understand] them through the practice of virtue, and not simply by reading them often, as others do'.[29]

On his journey north Maximos and his companions stopped for a while in Constantinople. There can be little doubt that the patriarchate took this opportunity to brief him on the two vital issues which then dominated its relations with Russia: the wish to restore its authority over the Russian Church, which had lapsed in the mid-fifteenth century; and the hope of obtaining from Muscovy aid, material or political, for the Greek Orthodox subjects of the sultan.

Maxim (as we may now call him, using the Russian form of his name) arrived in Moscow in March 1518; he would there become a versatile writer (Plate 8a). His first task was to prepare a translation of patristic commentaries on the Psalter. On purely linguistic grounds, his qualifications were meagre. His abbot, in a letter to the Muscovite sovereign, stated that Maximos knew no Russian. He may well, however, have had at least a smattering of one of the other Slavonic languages spoken on Mount Athos. He seems, in any case, to have acquired some knowledge of Russian fairly soon after his arrival in Moscow. And in his old age, one of his disciples tells us, he knew

---

[28] Doubts have been cast on the existence of this library: S. Belokurov, *O biblioteke moskovskikh gosudarey v XVI stoletii* (Moscow, 1898). See, however, Ikonnikov, op. cit. 157–66.

[29] *Akty istoricheskie, sobrannye i izdannye Arkheograficheskoyu Kommissieyu*, i (St Petersburg, 1841), no. 122, p. 176.

Russian, Serbian, Bulgarian, and Church Slavonic, in addition to Greek and Latin.[30] For the present, however, faced with translating the commentaries on the Psalter, it must be admitted that his equipment was poor. According to a reliable contemporary source, Maxim translated from Greek into Latin, which his Russian collaborators then rendered into Slavonic.[31] This astonishingly cumbersome procedure could hardly fail to result in errors of translation: for these Maxim was later to pay dearly.

The request to translate a collection of patristic commentaries on the Psalter was not due to a passing interest of Russian churchmen in biblical exegesis. It was prompted by hard and urgent necessities. In his introduction to the completed translation, Maxim assured the grand prince that the work would be useful in fighting heretics.[32] At that time, the Muscovite state and the Russian Church were struggling to eradicate the remains of the heresy of the 'Judaizers', which at the turn of the fifteenth century had posed a serious threat to the Orthodox Church in their domains. The tenets of the Russian 'Judaizers' are imperfectly known: they appear to have included a disbelief in the Trinity, the rejection of the cult of icons, and a strong attack on the hierarchy of the Church. It is possible, though not certain, that the 'Judaizers' had links with early 'Protestant' movements in central Europe. The heresy was first attested in Novgorod in 1470, and ten years later spread to Moscow, where it is said to have gained powerful support in government and church circles.[33] Russian society divided sharply over the right manner of treating the heretics, one party demanding their physical extermination, the other urging milder measures, particularly when they repented of their errors. The militants were led by two formidable churchmen, Gennady, archbishop of Novgorod, and Joseph, abbot of the monastery of Volokolamsk. Gennady was a great admirer of the Spanish

[30] Ivanov, op. cit. 43.

[31] This was stated, at the time the work was carried out, by Dimitri Gerasimov, a leading diplomat who was Maxim's principal Russian assistant: *Pribavleniya k izdaniyu tvoreniy svyatykh ottsev*, xviii (Moscow, 1859), 190. Cf. Ivanov, op. cit. 41; Haney, op. cit. 46.

[32] *Sochineniya*, ii (Kazan', 1860), 303 ; Ikonnikov, op. cit. 168–9.

[33] On the 'Judaizers', see N. A. Kazakova and Ya. S. Lur'e, *Antifeodal'nye ereticheskie dvizheniya na Rusi XIV—nachala XVI veka* (Moscow–Leningrad, 1955); A. I. Klibanov, *Reformatsionnye dvizheniya v Rossii v XIV—pervoy polovine XVI vv.* (Moscow, 1960); Ya. S. Lur'e, *Ideologicheskaya bor'ba v russkoy publitsistike kontsa XV—nachala XVI veka* (Moscow—Leningrad, 1960).

Inquisition. He and Joseph finally won over the grand prince to their view, and in 1504 the leaders of the 'Judaizers' were publicly burnt. The 'Josephians', as the militants were now called after their leader, were opposed by a group of laymen and ecclesiastics whose leaders came from remote hermitages in the north of the country, and were known as 'Elders from beyond the Volga'. They had no truck with heresy, but did not believe that the heretics should be executed. By the early sixteenth century their influence was on the wane. The militants were on the war-path, pointing to the fact that the heresy had not been eliminated by the blood-bath of 1504.

One of the texts which the 'Judaizers' used to support their teaching was the Book of Psalms. According to Archbishop Gennady, they doctored some of its passages for their own exegetical purposes.[34] It is hence not surprising that Maxim was put to work so soon on a translation of authoritative commentaries on the Psalms. It may indeed have been the main purpose of his invitation to Moscow.

Maxim took seventeen months to complete his task. This was the first of the many literary works he produced in Russia. The Soviet scholar Aleksey Ivanov, in a valuable study published in 1969, listed and briefly described 365 works attributable to Maxim, nearly half of them still unpublished at the time of writing.[35] The great majority are undated. They range over a wide variety of topics. Jack Haney, the author of the only book in English on Maxim, has divided them into four general categories: theology, secular philosophy, statecraft, and social problems.[36] The classification is useful, though it leaves out two important kinds of work: translations from the Greek (over 100 of them, mostly unpublished, are listed by Ivanov), and works on grammar and lexicography, fields in which Maxim was a pioneer in Russia. We badly need a critical edition of Maxim's writings.[37] The only existing edition, published in Kazan' in 1859–62, falls far short of this requirement.

Maxim seems to have had every reason to believe that, on completing his translation of the commentaries on the Psalter, he would be allowed to return to Mount Athos. Whether or not he was

[34] Kazakova-Lur'e, op. cit. 310, 316, 319.

[35] Ivanov, op. cit. 39–215. Cf. Sinitsyna, op. cit. 221–79.

[36] Haney, op. cit. 114.

[37] Some of the problems facing scholars in this task are discussed briefly by Bulanin, op. cit. 124–7.

given a formal assurance to this effect,[38] the Muscovite authorities were clearly in no hurry to let him go home. They had other plans for Maxim. He was quickly put to work on further translations, and on the revision of the existing Slavonic texts of the Scriptures and liturgical books. These he found to be less than satisfactory: the earlier Russian translators had shown themselves deficient in their knowledge of Greek. This, Maxim observed with a touch of condescension, was hardly surprising. For the Greek language, he stressed, is difficult and complex, and requires many years of study to be mastered, especially if the student is not a Greek by birth, sharp-witted, and highly motivated.[39] It became obvious to him that the howlers committed by early translators, compounded by scribal errors, had led to mistranslations which at best were absurd, and at worst heretical. Some of the most glaring he corrected himself, unaware of the trouble he was storing up for the future.

It was not only by his correction of textual errors that Maxim sailed rather close to the wind. Through his contacts with local personalities he was becoming dangerously involved in public controversy. The first half of the sixteenth century was a period of great ferment in Muscovy: educated Russians seemed to be locked in endless and passionate debate. The momentous changes that were taking place in their society meant that they had indeed much to argue about: whether the sovereign was omnipotent, or should share his power with the aristocracy; whether heretics should be burnt at the stake; what was the role of monasteries in the contemporary world; and what was the right relationship between Church and state. The treatment of heretics, we have seen, was an issue over which the 'Josephians' and the 'Elders from beyond the Volga' clashed violently.

---

[38] The monk Savvas of Vatopedi, the Muscovites' original choice (see above, p. 208), was given just such an assurance: Basil III of Moscow, in a letter to the *prōtos* of Athos (the head of the Athonite community) dated 15 Mar. 1515, stated that Savvas' services as a translator would be required only for a time, and that he would be sent back to Mount Athos on completion of his task: 'Akty, kasayushchiesya do priezda Maksima Greka v Rossiyu', ed. M. A. Obolensky, *Vremennik Imperatorskogo Moskovskogo Obshchestva Istorii i Drevnostey Rossiyskikh*, v 3 (Moscow, 1850), 31–2. While there is no direct evidence that Maxim was given a similar promise, he doubtless regarded the Russians as morally bound by the undertaking they had given to Savvas. It is worth noting, furthermore, that the abbot of Vatopedi, in his letter recommending Maxim to the metropolitan of Moscow (see above, p. 208), requested that he and two other monks of his monastery, who were to travel to Moscow together, be eventually sent back to Athos 'in good health': *Akty istoricheskie*, i. 176.

[39] *Sochineniya*, iii. 80; cf. ibid. 62; ii. 312; cf. Ikonnikov, op. cit. 178.

We must now briefly examine another, closely related, issue, for it was to have a lasting effect on Maxim's fate.

During the late Middle Ages two different types of monasticism were prevalent in Russia. On the one hand, we find, mainly in the central areas, the large coenobitic house, owning land, often on a large scale, exploiting peasant labour, practising works of charity, and immersed in administrative and economic activity. This type of monastery came to be known as 'Josephian', after the name of Joseph, abbot of Volokolamsk, the leader of the hard-liners who wished to see the heretics physically destroyed. On the other hand, in the far north of the country, groups of small hermitages, known as *lavrai* in Greek and *skity* in Russian, clustered round clearings in the forest. Their monks came increasingly to believe that landowning was incompatible with the monastic estate. It was in these remote *skity* that the contemplative tradition burnt with a brighter flame; and the leaders of this movement, the very same 'Elders from beyond the Volga' who urged that heretics be treated leniently, became the spokesmen in late medieval Russia of the mystical teachings of Byzantine hesychasm.[40]

The 'Josephian' party gained a notable victory in 1503, when Ivan III was compelled to abandon his plan for the secularization of Church lands. Yet the 'Non-Possessors', as the opponents of monastic estates were also called, retained some influence in government circles, and when Maxim came to Moscow in 1518, they were still far from beaten. Their leader, Vassian Patrikeev, was a resourceful and vigorous campaigner. This former general and diplomat, who belonged to a princely family, was disgraced in 1499 and compelled to become a monk. A few years later he was back in Moscow, with a powerful influence over the new grand prince, Basil III.[41] Vassian and Maxim were to become close friends and associates.

When Maxim arrived in Moscow Vassian had just completed, with the approval of the Church, his main life-work, a new edition of the *Nomocanon*, the Orthodox manual of canon law. Arranged by subjects and no longer, as in previous editions, chronologically, Vassian's *Nomocanon* was intended to demonstrate that monasteries which owned landed estates were violating canon law. Maxim not surprisingly sided with the 'Non-Possessors', and placed his knowledge of

[40] See J. Meyendorff, *Une controverse sur le rôle social de l'Église: La querelle des biens ecclésiastiques au XVIᵉ siècle en Russie* (Chevetogne, 1956).

[41] See N. A. Kazakova, *Vassian Patrikeev i ego sochineniya* (Moscow–Leningrad, 1960).

Greek and experience of Mount Athos at the disposal of his new Russian friend. He was asked to arbitrate on a contentious problem of philology. The Greek *Nomocanon* permitted monasteries to own προάστεια, a word which in classical Greek means either 'suburbs' or 'houses or estates in suburbs'. Previous Russian translators had taken the word to mean 'villages with resident peasants', a translation which was vigorously endorsed by the 'Possessors'. Maxim, on the other hand, assured Vassian that the true meaning of προάστεια was 'ploughed fields and vineyards', which, by restricting the scope of the word, seemed to provide ammunition to the 'Non-Possessors'. This explanation was incorporated by Vassian into his edition of the *Nomocanon*.[42]

At the same time, during his first years in Moscow, Maxim, at the request of Vassian, wrote several descriptions of the monasteries of Mount Athos.[43] He was careful to write in a non-polemical tone, and avoided any explicit reference to monastic landowning. Yet he made it clear that of the different types of Athonite monasteries he much preferred the kind of coenobitic house where all property was held in common and the monks supported themselves by their own labour. His accounts of Mount Athos were hardly calculated to please the 'Josephians'. As for his friendship with Vassian, it was soon to become a serious liability.

Their enemies doubtless carefully noted these words of Vassian's, who, unlike Maxim, was prone to overstatement: 'All our books are false ones, and were written by the devil and not by the Holy Spirit. Until Maxim we used these books to blaspheme God, and not to glorify or pray to him. Now, through Maxim, we have come to know God.'[44]

However cautious Maxim may have been in his public utterances, he seems to have behaved at times with a certain lack of elementary prudence. He allowed his cell in the Simonov monastery to become a kind of dissident *salon*, where critics of Muscovite society, mostly members of the nobility, gathered to air their grievances.[45] This, in sixteenth-century Russia, was asking for trouble. Meanwhile, in the higher councils of Church and state his luck was running out. In 1522 the leader of the 'Possessors', Daniel, abbot of Volokolamsk and

---

[42] See Ivanov, op. cit. 51; Kazakova, *Vassian Patrikeev*, 62, 236; Haney, op. cit. 47–8.

[43] *Sochineniya*, iii. 243–5; Ivanov, op. cit. 192–8; Sinitsyna, op. cit. 110.

[44] Ikonnikov, op. cit. 409.

[45] See V. O. Klyuchevsky, *Kurs russkoy istorii*, *Sochineniya*, ii (Moscow, 1957), 161–4.

a disciple of Joseph, was appointed primate of the Russian Church; almost at once Vassian's influence at court began to wane.

Some time during the winter of 1524/5 Maxim was arrested. His arrest was followed in February 1525 by the trial of two of his regular visitors. Both these Russian associates of Maxim were charged with high treason, and found guilty. One was beheaded, the other sentenced to have his tongue cut out. In May 1525 Maxim himself was tried by a court presided over by the Grand Prince Basil III and by Metropolitan Daniel of Moscow, who also acted as chief prosecutor.

After a manifestly biased trial Maxim was sentenced to solitary confinement in the Volokolamsk monastery (the stronghold of the 'Possessors'), put in chains, excommunicated and allowed neither to read nor to write. His imprisonment was to last for twenty-three years. In 1531 he was tried again, at least partly because of his refusal to confess to the earlier charges, and was sentenced to imprisonment in a monastery in Tver'.[46]

The charges brought against him are known primarily from a near-contemporary document which Russian scholars have called the Trial Record (*Sudnyi spisok*) of Maxim the Greek.[47] In fact it is not a copy of the proceedings but a literary pamphlet based on an official transcript of his trials. Until recently this document was known only in late and incomplete manuscripts. In 1968 a fuller version came to light, in a late sixteenth-century manuscript discovered in Siberia.[48] It has added much to our knowledge of Maxim's two trials. In one respect, however, this version is as deficient as the later ones. It combines materials relating to the two trials, and thus fails to distinguish between the charges brought against Maxim in 1525 and 1531. So for the present we too must be content with this unfortunate conflation.

The list of the charges is long and impressive. It included holding heretical views, practising sorcery, criticizing the grand prince, having treasonable relations with the Turkish government, claiming that the Russian Church's independence from the patriarchate of Constantinople was illegal, and denouncing the monasteries and the Church for owning land and peasants.

[46] Ikonnikov, op. cit. 455–97; Sinitsyna, op. cit. 130–49; Haney, op. cit. 64–85.

[47] See the discussion of this document, and other relevant sources, by N. A. Kazakova, *Ocherki po istorii russkoy obshchestvennoy mysli: Pervaya tret' XVI veka* (Leningrad, 1970), 177–87.

[48] *Sudnye spiski Maksima Greka i Isaka Sobaki*, ed. N. N. Pokrovsky and S. O. Shmidt (Moscow, 1971); cf. Kazakova, op. cit. 187–93.

The allegation of sorcery was patently absurd, and merely shows the lack of scruples displayed by the prosecution, and particularly by the Metropolitan Daniel.[49] The accusation of heresy, equally unjust, was based on evidence no more substantial than some grammatical errors in Maxim's translations and occasional infelicities in his emendation of liturgical texts. These mistakes were due to his inadequate knowledge of the Russian language, a fault he readily acknowledged himself.[50] Criticism of the grand prince was a charge that Maxim denied: and it seems at the very least to have been unproven.[51]

The charge that Maxim entertained relations with the Ottoman government prejudicial to the Muscovite state raises more complex issues. At one or both of his trials he was accused of writing to the Turkish pasha of Athens, urging him to persuade the sultan to declare war on Russia; and it was further alleged that he held secret meetings for the same purpose with the Turkish envoy in Moscow. Maxim vigorously denied these charges; and the recently discovered Siberian manuscript of the Trial Record makes it clear that no letters from him to the Ottoman authorities were available to the prosecution. The charges of treason and espionage could not be made to stick.[52] Yet a lingering suspicion remains that Maxim may have been less than discreet in his political table-talk. He admitted saying that one day the sultan was bound to invade Russia, since he detested all members of the imperial house of Byzantium, from which Basil III of Moscow, through his mother, was descended.[53] As a Greek, Maxim hoped that one day the Muscovite sovereign, the most powerful Orthodox ruler on earth, would come to the help of his enslaved people and liberate them from the infidel yoke. A war between Russia and the Ottoman Empire was a necessary prelude to the liberation of the Christians of the Balkans. Maxim could hardly have concealed his irritation at the foreign policy of the Muscovite government, which, faced with the hostility of the Polish–Lithuanian state and the constant military threat from the Tatar Khanates of the Crimea and Kazan', pinned its hopes on an alliance with the Ottoman Turks.

The last two charges against Maxim were straightforward, and mostly true. He never concealed his belief that the situation of the Russian Church, which had been electing its primates without

---

[49] Kazakova, 230–1. [50] Kazakova, *Ocherki* 231–3; Haney, op. cit. 70–1.

[51] Kazakova, 221–6. [52] *Sudnye spiski*, 44; Kazakova, *Ocherki* 203–21.

[53] *Sudnye spiski*, 70; Kazakova, 219–20.

reference to the patriarch of Constantinople for almost a century, was uncanonical, and that it should return to the obedience of its mother-Church.[54] Equally outspoken was his opposition to ownership of land by monasteries. He wrote repeatedly on this topic, denouncing Russian monks for accumulating lands and riches, exploiting their peasants, and practising usury.[55] He compared them unfavourably with the Carthusians, Franciscans, and Dominicans he had known in Italy, who led a life of dedicated poverty.[56] It was in this sensitive area of monastic ethics and economy that the Metropolitan Daniel and his minions must have felt the most threatened. In 1525, the year of Maxim's first trial, the 'Non-Possessors' were still a force to be reckoned with. It seems quite possible that Maxim's condemnation of monastic landownership was the main reason for the harshness of his sentence. And it is highly probable that one of the aims of his prosecutors in 1531 was to break Vassian Patrikeev. Almost at once Vassian was tried and sentenced to imprisonment in the Volokolamsk monastery.[57] The condemnation in the same year of Maxim and his once powerful friend marked in a real sense the defeat of the 'Non-Possessors' party in Russia.

The harshness of Maxim's treatment slowly diminished in the 1530s, thanks to the humanity of the local bishop Akakiy, and especially after his chief tormentor, the Metropolitan Daniel, was removed from office in 1539. Though still at first deprived of communion, he was given his books back and allowed to write. In the mid 1540s the patriarchs of Constantinople and Alexandria wrote to Ivan IV, requesting his release.[58] Maxim repeatedly begged his gaolers to let him return to Mount Athos. The stony-hearted Russian authorities refused all his requests to be allowed to go home, at least once on the grounds that he knew too much about their country.[59]

In the last few years of Maxim's life his torments at last came to an end. He was released from imprisonment, probably about 1548, when the excommunication was lifted, and he was allowed to reside

---

[54] Kazakova, Ocherki, 196–203; Haney, op. cit. 75–7, 82.

[55] Sochineniya, ii. 5–52, 89–118, 119–47, 260–76, iii. 178–205; Ivanov, op. cit. 156–60.

[56] V. F. Ržiga, 'Neizdannye sochineniya Maksima Greka', Byzantinoslavica, vi (1935–6), 85–109.

[57] N. A. Kazakova, Vassian Patrikeev, 75–7.

[58] Ikonnikov, op. cit. 507–8.

[59] Akty, sobrannye Arkheograficheskoyu Ekspeditsieyu, i (St Petersburg, 1836), 143; cf. Golubinsky, Istoriya russkoy tserkvi, ii/1. 816.

in St Sergius' monastery of the Holy Trinity near Moscow (in what today is Zagorsk). He spent his time reading, writing and teaching. Despite his fading eyesight, he taught Greek to a fellow monk, and wrote (a little earlier) to his chief persecutor, the Metropolitan Daniel, comforting him on his fall from power and offering him the hand of reconciliation.[60] He died in the Trinity monastery, at the age of almost ninety.

The posthumous fate of Maxim the Greek in Russia was a curious one. His opinions on many matters of great concern to Russian society were too much at variance with official policy to make him fully acceptable, at least in the next few generations. It is true that the wonderful patience with which he endured twenty-three years of cruel torments caused him to be revered as a saint (Plate 8*b*) and a martyr, especially by those Russians who were at variance with the official church.[61] He had, moreover, in his lifetime a small circle of Russian admirers, some of whom were outstanding men. It is perhaps surprising to find among them the Tsar Ivan the Terrible. It was on Ivan's orders that he was released from prison.[62] But it remains true that Maxim's influence in Russia was always very limited. It is remarkable that this Byzantine scholar was long revered in Russia for his statements on the correct way of making the sign of the cross, while his references to Greek classical literature were largely ignored.[63]

There may indeed be something symbolic in Maxim's Russian destiny. The rejection of a man who, in the depth of his spirituality and scholarship, typified what was best in the culture of post-Byzantine Greece marked in one sense Russia's turning away from her ancient heritage of Byzantium.[64] It is true that, at the very time he was in Muscovy, the Russian churchmen were developing their egregious theory of Moscow the Third Rome, which ascribed to their capital city the role of focus of universal power and central repository for the true Orthodox faith. But Maxim's attitude to this theory seems to have been ambiguous. As a patriotic Greek, he welcomed the sixteenth-century version of the 'Great Idea'—the prospect of a

[60] *Sochineniya*, ii. 367–76; cf. Ikonnikov, op. cit. 535; Haney, op. cit. 85–6.

[61] The nationwide cult of Maxim as a saint dates from the second half of the 17th c.: Denissoff, op. cit. 391 n. 1.

[62] Sinitsyna, op. cit. 151.

[63] I. Ševčenko, art. cit., *Harvard Ukrainian Studies*, ii (1978), 14.

[64] See G. Florovsky, *Puti russkogo bogosloviya* (Paris, 1937), 22–4; ET in his *Collected Works*, v (Belmont, Mass., 1979), 25.

victorious Russian entry into Constantinople, leading to the liberation of his people and their resurgence under the sceptre of an Orthodox tsar. In the introduction to his translation of commentaries on the Psalter, the very first work he carried out in Russia, Maxim addressed the grand prince of Moscow, Basil III, in these terms:

> Let the poor Christians living there [in Greece] learn from us that they still have a tsar, who not only rules over innumerable peoples and abounds in all else that is royal and is worthy of amazement, but who has been glorified above all others by reason of his justice and his orthodoxy, so that he may be likened unto Constantine and Theodosius the Great, whom your majesty succeeds. Oh, if only we could one day be liberated through you from subjection to the infidels and receive our own tsardom . . . So even now, may [God] be pleased to free the New Rome [Constantinople], cruelly tormented by the godless Muslims, through the pious majesty of your tsardom, and to bring forth from your paternal throne an heir, and may we, the unfortunate ones, receive through you the light of freedom . . . [65]

Perhaps Maxim genuinely hoped that this rhetoric would advance the cause of his people's liberation. He wrote these words during his early days in Russia. His belief that Moscow, as the successor of Constantinople, was the third and last Rome, if it ever was sincere, soon foundered on the reality he saw around him. He was too much of a Byzantine at heart to be taken in for long by this meretricious substitute for the East Roman oecumenical idea, propounded in Russia by his sworn adversaries, the 'Josephian' monks. And he was probably too much of a realist not to observe how, in sixteenth-century Russia, through the narrowing of cultural horizons and in the wake of the *Realpolitik* of its rulers, the Christian universalism of Byzantium was being transformed and distorted within the more narrow framework of Muscovite nationalism. Perhaps this is why Maxim's vision of the Christian commonwealth was, in the last resort, pessimistic. In a passage of pointed allegory, written in the early 1540s, he tells us that, toiling one day down a hard and wearisome road, he encountered a woman dressed in black, sitting by the roadside and weeping disconsolately. Around her were wild animals, lions and bears, wolves and foxes. 'The road', she said to Maxim, 'is desolate and prefigures this last and accursed age.' Her name, she told him, was Vasileia (which in Greek means 'empire' or 'kingdom').[66]

---

[65] *Sochineniya*, ii. 318–19. I have, in the main, followed the translation of this passage by Haney, op. cit. 163.

[66] *Sochineniya*, ii. 319–37; cf. Haney, op. cit. 164–7.

It is not easy to assess precisely the place which should be allotted to Michael-Maximos-Maxim in the cultural history of each of the three worlds to which he belonged. Before this can be done satisfactorily we need, I think, a fuller answer to three questions: what was the nature of his Platonism, and how did he square it with his Christian beliefs? What led him to leave the Dominican order and retire to Mount Athos? And what impact did his writings have upon later Russian literature? In the meantime we can perhaps agree to accept the following conclusions: Maximos, though not a creative thinker, was at least a sound and wide-ranging scholar, with an excellent training in ancient philosophy and textual criticism; though he played an important role in the controversies that shook sixteenth-century Muscovite society, his learning was, with a few notable exceptions, above its head; and he lived in a cosmopolitan world where the Byzantine heritage, the late medieval Italo-Greek connections, and the traditional links between Russia, Mount Athos, and Constantinople were still to some extent living realities. He was one of the last of his kind.

Index